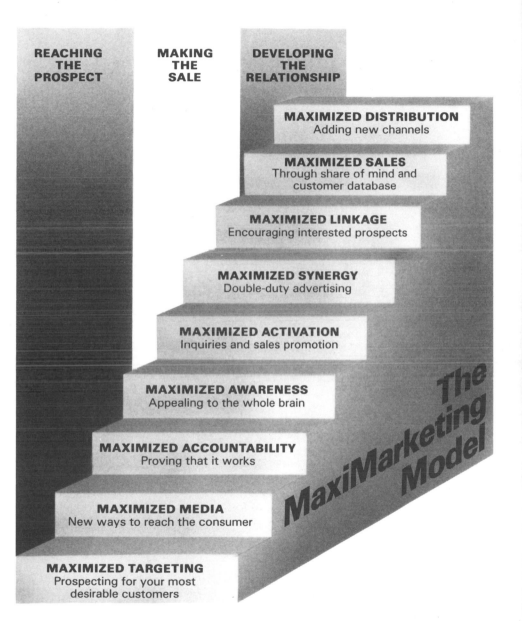

REACHING
THE
PROSPECT

MAKING
THE
SALE

DEVELOPING
THE
RELATIONSHIP

MAXIMIZED DISTRIBUTION
Adding new channels

MAXIMIZED SALES
Through share of mind and
customer database

MAXIMIZED LINKAGE
Encouraging interested prospects

MAXIMIZED SYNERGY
Double-duty advertising

MAXIMIZED ACTIVATION
Inquiries and sales promotion

MAXIMIZED AWARENESS
Appealing to the whole brain

MAXIMIZED ACCOUNTABILITY
Proving that it works

MAXIMIZED MEDIA
New ways to reach the consumer

MAXIMIZED TARGETING
Prospecting for your most
desirable customers

MaxiMarketing The Model

MaxiMarketing

The new direction in advertising, promotion, and marketing strategy

Stan Rapp and Thomas L. Collins

Cofounders, Rapp & Collins, Inc.

*"Those who are going to be in
business tomorrow are those who
understand that the future, as always,
belongs to the brave."*
WILLIAM BERNBACH
Doyle Dane Bernbach

McGraw-Hill Book Company

New York   St. Louis   San Francisco   Auckland   Bogotá
Hamburg   London   Madrid   Mexico   Milan   Montreal
New Delhi   Panama   Paris   São Paulo   Singapore
Sydney   Tokyo   Toronto

Library of Congress Cataloging-in-Publication Data

Rapp, Stan.
  MaxiMarketing: the new direction in advertising,
promotion, and marketing strategy.
  Includes index.
  1. Marketing.   2. Advertising.   3. Sales promotion.
I. Collins, Thomas L.   II. Title.
HF5415.R325   1987   658.8   86-15345
ISBN 0-07-051191-8

  34567890   DOC/DOC   893210987

ISBN 0-07-051191-8

The editors for this book were William A. Sabin and Barbara B. Toniolo,
the designer was Naomi Auerbach, and the production supervisor
was Thomas G. Kowalczyk. It was set in Baskerville by T.C. Systems.

Printed and bound by R. R. Donnelley & Sons Company.

For Isabel,
who, rightly or wrongly,
would have been so proud
of both of us

Contents

Contents

Preface

In the summer of 1985, over lunch at the Helmsley Palace in New York, we had an eye-opening conversation with a top marketing executive. It made us feel more strongly than ever that this book, which we were then writing, was urgently needed.

Our luncheon companion was Clay Timon, the newly appointed director of worldwide advertising for Colgate-Palmolive Company, the nation's twenty-fourth largest advertiser, with sales close to $5 billion. Clay had just moved to Colgate from Doyle Dane Bernbach (DDB), the parent company of our direct-marketing advertising agency. We had met Clay a few years earlier, when DDB had commissioned us to acquire or establish a network of ad agencies throughout Europe and the Pacific in response to the growing interest in a more personalized kind of marketing. As Pan-Asia coordinator for DDB, Clay had worked with us on our start-up of the first specialized direct-marketing agency to hang out its shingle in Tokyo. Now he had moved back to the client's side and was excited about being in a position to do something about the sweeping changes taking place in the world of marketing.

"Do you remember," asked Clay, "in the movie *The Graduate,* when the family friend takes young Dustin Hoffman aside and murmurs that famous one word of advice—'Plastics!'? Well, when I was coming up through the ranks in the sixties, the magic word we would whisper to one another in the corridors was *marketing!* And do you know what they are whispering in the halls at Colgate these days? It's *direct marketing!*"

Yes, a new generation is talking about a powerful new force at work in the marketplace. But it is not classic direct marketing that fascinates them, if by that we mean mail-order selling which eliminates the middleman.

It is something quite different—a whole new direction in marketing strategy, a new way of advertising, selling, and thinking—which is affecting and will increasingly affect not just direct marketers, but *all* providers of advertised goods and services.

The computer revolution that has profoundly changed production and communication is destined to change marketing just as profoundly. The common wastefulness of the mass advertising of the past is giving way to the newly affordable ability to locate and communicate directly with a company's best prospects and customers. And this new-found ability can be equally rewarding to a manufacturer, a retailer, a service company, or a catalog merchant. Product sales in stores can now be supported with the same precise accountability once reserved for mail-order advertising.

This new kind of marketing goes under many names. Database marketing, relationship marketing, integrated marketing—these are just a few. But we have observed that none of these labels fully described or captured what is happening or, more important, what we believe is coming.

For in addition to the computer, other changes—technological, social, political, and economic—are sweeping through the marketplace and demanding a review of every component of the traditional advertising, promotion, and marketing process.

"An entirely new set of dynamics is emerging that will dictate success and failure in the marketplace of the late 1980s and beyond," points out Jeffrey Hallet, president of Trend Response and Analysis Company, one of the many voices warning of change. "The protocols, techniques, methods, and assumptions that have formed the foundation of sound marketing may no longer be relied on."

The eighties will be remembered in marketing history as the decade of transition. Every established norm in advertising and promotion is being transformed by the new economy and the new technology. We are living through the shift from selling virtually everyone the same thing a generation ago to fulfilling the individual needs and tastes of better-educated consumers by supplying them with customized products and services. The shift from "get a sale *now* at any cost" to building and managing customer databases that track the lifetime value of your relationship with each customer. The shift from crudely accountable "creativity" in advertising to the scientific accountability of each advertising expenditure. The shift from reliance on a company's familiar single channel of distribution to a multichannel mode which breaks rules as it breaks down walls.

Of all these changes, surely the most revolutionary is the ability to store in the computer information about your prime prospects and customers and, in effect, create a database that becomes your private marketplace. As the cost of accumulating and accessing the data drops, the ability to talk directly to your prospects and customers—and to build one-to-one relationships with them—will continue to grow. A rising tide of technological change has brought this golden moment of opportunity.

The fifties and sixties were the heyday of mass marketing. There was one kind of Coca-Cola soft drink for the thirsty. One kind of Clairol hair dye for hair coloring. One kind of Holiday Inn motel for the traveler.

The seventies became a decade of segmentation and line extension. It was followed in the early eighties by intensified niche marketing that sliced markets into smaller and smaller groups of consumers—each group with particular needs and wants to satisfy.

By the mid-eighties, Robitussin was offering four kinds of medicine for four kinds of coughs. If you wanted to color your hair, Bristol-Myers offered eight kinds of Clairol in a choice of lotion, mousse, gel, foam, or shampoo. Even travel establishments like Holiday Inn and Hilton offered a choice of deluxe or budget accommodations.

The trend is as clear as the name on your checkbook. From mass marketing to segmented marketing to niche marketing to tomorrow's world of one-to-one marketing—the transformation will be complete by the end of the eighties.

When the bright sun of a new day breaks on the marketing scene on January 1, 1990, the once-familiar terrain of 1980 will be as foreign to the new marketers as the 1960 scene seems to us today.

In this new land, you will know the name and address of the end-user of your product—regardless of where or how the purchase is made. Your advertising will be linked directly to measurable sales. You will hunt down individual users of competing brands and lure them away with a dazzling array of value-added services.

We believe the time has come for every company that advertises its products or services (or should) to review its advertising and promotion strategic planning in light of these new developments.

Just as John Naisbitt and Patricia Aburdene have urged "re-inventing the corporation," we are urging you to reinvent your approach to advertising, promotion, and marketing.

This book can help you prepare for the new marketplace of the nineties—and get your big guns in place before your competition fully realizes that the rules of the game have changed.

And the name we have given to this new direction in strategic thinking is MaxiMarketing. We hope that when the present generation of Young Turks in companies large and small meets in hallways, they will use the *new* password to corporate and individual success: "MaxiMarketing!"

More than that, we hope that what this book describes and advocates will not just be whispered in the hallways but openly discussed in the conference rooms and boardrooms, whether under the name we have chosen or another. We believe that is what will happen—indeed, *is* happening already—in the smart companies.

Of course, what this new way of thinking is called is not important. What *is* important is that almost every business, whatever its size and whatever product or service it sells, can benefit from the principles of MaxiMarketing. Not all these principles are new. Some are as much as 100 years old but call for a new look and a new application. Others are emerging from the conditions and capabilities of the new era we are entering.

MaxiMarketing is not a textbook or a how-to book. It is a "think" book that aims not to solve your advertising and marketing problems but to stimulate you to think about them in a new way so that you can solve them yourself.

This book will *not* give you a magic formula for marketing success. It *will* tell you how other marketers are building new structures as they observe the old order crumbling. In it we point out ways to make your advertising, promotion, and distribution more effective every step of the way.

We hope you will find many of the specific case histories and ideas relevant to your own strategic thinking, but we designed the book to be broad enough to be useful and stimulating to *all* companies engaged in marketing to consumers—large and small companies; manufacturers and retailers of hard goods, soft goods, and packaged goods; companies selling services and products; single-product companies and diversified companies; direct and indirect marketers; and promoters of both high-ticket and low-ticket sales.

The case histories and references are provided to illustrate the themes of the book, and often they will not come from your own industry situation. Some of the case histories include marketing results, and some do not. As you know, many companies jealously guard their trade secrets, including marketing results. Where the results were public knowledge or where we were able to ascertain the facts, we included this information. Even though we could not obtain the results for all cases, we have included a number of fascinating and soundly conceived advertising and promotion experiments which are noteworthy for being on the cutting edge of change.

If you find that some part of the book does not apply directly to your current problems, we hope you will go through it with us anyway in order to comprehend the entire process. Besides, you may surprise yourself with sudden insights and innovative lateral thinking while reading material you had considered irrelevant to your situation.

We have, by and large, confined ourselves to examples of the marketing of consumer goods and services, although much of the thinking certainly applies to business-to-business selling. The recent surge of breakthrough developments in business-to-business marketing is a very large subject that could take an entire book to cover adequately.

We are also acutely aware that because of the extraordinarily accelerating rate of change, some details of this book may already be out of date by the time the book comes off the press. And some of the promising marketing experiments we describe will already have been abandoned, for a variety of reasons. (Sometimes it is simply because a brilliant marketing director has moved on to another job!) Nonetheless, these details and these experiments will still serve the purpose of the book—namely, to stimulate a way of thinking.

Our book is part description, part advocacy. In it we point out both efficient and wasteful current practices, and we offer a number of specific antidotes to the ills of current obsolete practice.

Finally, we want to emphasize that MaxiMarketing is not just another buzzword. Whatever you choose to call it, for many companies the new strategic thinking we present will be literally a matter of life or death.

The hurricane winds of change have already toppled some corporate giants that seemed as indestructible as California redwoods. And more are threatened. MaxiMarketing is a fundamental shift in viewpoint that can help provide the strength and flexibility that today's marketing giants need to survive. MaxiMarketing can also help the smallest of companies survive and thrive and perhaps become giants themselves.

The book grew out of our experiences and observations over a number of years as founders and operators of a successful advertising agency specializing in direct marketing—both the classic variety and the new database-driven variety. We work with clients ranging from *Fortune* 500 corporations to struggling young entrepreneurs on their way up.

We began our advertising careers in the field that a generation ago was called "mail-order advertising." But as the computer, the credit card, and the telephone transformed mail order—and as an increasing number of large companies of all kinds began to communicate and deal directly with their prospects, even though they did not necessarily complete the transaction by mail or direct delivery—the term *direct marketing* was born to describe this broader kind of activity.

In 1976 our agency, Rapp & Collins, joined the billion-dollar Doyle Dane Bernbach family of agencies and began a new life as the direct-marketing arm of one of the world's largest and best-known groups of agencies. This gave us a chance to observe and participate in meeting the challenges faced by a broad spectrum of leading U.S. businesses and multinational corporations.

To meet the emerging need for responsive advertising, DDB asked us to establish Rapp & Collins direct-marketing agencies in London, Paris, Zurich, Hamburg, Amsterdam, Sydney, Tokyo, and Mexico City. Working with this international network has given us priceless new insights into the common nature of advertising and marketing challenges found throughout the industrialized world.

We have frequently observed that a customary way of thinking—whether it is the thinking of a manufacturer, a service company, a department store chain, or a cataloger—can limit growth in today's consumer marketplace.

Now we believe the time has come for all companies to break out of the box of past assumptions. Time to push ahead into a brave new world of virtually unlimited options. Time to master the new computer capabilities and take direct control of your future. Time to move in a new strategic direction and reap the rich rewards of MaxiMarketing.

1

Problems and Challenges in Today's Marketplace

The Big Picture

Remember what Gertrude Stein said about California? "There is no there there."

Veteran marketing executives must feel like muttering Stein's line as they search in vain for the familiar, understandable marketing scene of the early 1970s.

The mass market has splintered into the "demassified" market. Norman Rockwell's American family of husband, wife, and 2.4 children has almost disappeared: Mom's not home watching the soap operas—she's working at the soap factory. Banks, airlines, and telephone companies are no longer monolithic institutions—

deregulation has them slugging it out toe-to-toe in a most undignified manner.

Companies are now spewing out each year enough cents-off coupons to circle the globe 50 times.

Network television, which seemed as eternal and indestructible as the great pyramids, is beginning to lose much of its audience. And the television commercials are losing even more of their audience than are the programs, because viewers are "zapping" commercials during playback on their videocassette recorders (VCRs).

The movie industry is making more money from movies watched at home—without commercials—than from those played in theaters.

Most astonishing, advertisers are finding out who their end-users are—by name, address, telephone number, family income, lifestyle, brand preferences, and personal tastes and enthusiasms. And they are gaining the rewards and satisfaction of serving these people according to their individual needs and interests.

There is a new there there.

If it can be said that a fire bell in the night warned U.S. business of a changed marketplace and the need to respond, then the November 21, 1983, cover story in *Business Week,* "Marketing: The New Priority," was that bell.

"Vast economic and social changes have made better marketing an imperative," the article declared. It went on to quote James R. McManus, chairman of Marketing Corporation of America: "Today, companies realize that their raw material, labor, and physical resource costs are all screwed down and that the only portion for dramatic improvement will come from doing a better marketing job."

The article then sketched the dimensions of a radically altered marketplace, beginning with a useful definition of marketing:

> As companies define marketing more clearly, they no longer confuse it with advertising, which uses media to let consumers know that a certain product or service is available. In essence, marketing means moving goods from the producer to the consumer. It starts with finding out what consumers want or need, and then assessing whether the product can be made or sold at a profit. Such decisions require conducting preliminary research, market identification, and product development; testing consumer reaction to both product and price; working out production capacities and costs; determining distribution; and then deciding on advertising promotion and strategies.

Simple as these steps may sound, many of them were all but forgotten in the 1970s, when inflation kept sales pacing upward and marketing was of secondary importance. Corporate strategies emphasized acquisitions, cash management, or the pursuit of overseas markets. Then came the recession, with its stranglehold on consumer spending, and companies were forced into trying to understand what made the domestic marketplace tick. *They soon discovered that demographic and lifestyle changes had delivered a death blow to mass marketing and brand loyalty. A nation that once shared homogenous buying tastes had splintered into many different consumer groups— each with special needs and interests.* [Italics added.][1]

McManus describes some of the marketing tasks that have established the need for the new approach of MaxiMarketing. Let's take a closer look at these and other tasks that challenge so many businesses today.

No doubt you will have read about most of the following phenomena and dealt with many of the numbers in your own planning. However, you will find that when these phenomena are viewed in the aggregate, the cumulative impact is overwhelming. So no matter how much you may already have heard about many of these changes, stay with us on this guided tour of the new marketplace. Only when the marketplace is viewed as a whole can you appreciate the full impact of change and the urgent need for new marketing strategies for everyone from the product manager to the chief executive.

"Demassification" of the Market

Alvin Toffler coined the wonderful new word "demassification" in his book *The Third Wave*. Toffler describes brilliantly how and why the mass society created by the industrial revolution is splintering more and more into the "demassified" society:

"The mass market has split," he warned us at the beginning of the eighties, "into ever-multiplying, ever-changing sets of mini-markets that demand a continually expanding range of options, models, types, sizes, colors, and customizations."[2]

John Naisbitt developed this theme a few years later in his book *Megatrends:*

The social upheavals of the late 1960's, and the quieter changes of the 1970's, which spread 1960's values throughout much of traditional society, paved the way for the 1980's—a decade of unprecedented diversity. Remember when bathtubs were white, telephones were black, and checks green?

This is the analog for what is going on in society. Advertisers are forced to direct products to perhaps a million clusters of people who are themselves far more individualistic and who have a wide range of choices in today's world. The multiple-option society is a new ballgame, and advertisers know that they must win consumers market by market. . . .[3]

As we move through the second half of the eighties, this trend is intensifying. Nine Lives now offers 23 kinds of cat food. Revlon makes 157 shades of lipstick, 41 of them pink.

Perhaps the most dramatic example is General Motors's announced plans for its new Saturn automobile plant, in which each car will virtually be designed by its owner and manufactured to order by computer-driven robots.

When Coca-Cola bowed to public protest and brought back the old Coke as Coca-Cola Classic while keeping the new Coke, it added still another segment to the already finely segmented soft drink market. Now the company had new Coke, Coca-Cola Classic, Diet Coke, Tab, Caffeine-Free Coke, Fresca, Cherry Coke—and who knows what comes next?

And why not? "The more products you can go to market with, the more constituencies you can attract," said Jesse Meyers, publisher of *Beverage Digest*.[4]

But, in a reversal of the old Chinese proverb, opportunities are problems in disguise. After a different product has been created for each of the many constituencies in the marketplace, is it possible to sell them all, and keep them sold, with the same old shotgun approach of mass marketing that worked so well in the past? Experts say it takes a minimum of $5 million of brand advertising in mass media to effect any change in share of mind and share of market. Obviously niche marketers must develop new, more targeted, more efficient ways to reach and convert their special markets.

The Changing American Household

Remember the good old days when the marketing target was the typical American family of husband, wife, and 2.4 children? The 1980 census shattered that image. It revealed that only 7 percent of the 82 million households surveyed fit that description. Other interesting statistics were included:

- Today 53 percent of all households have only one or two members.
- Singles now head 24 percent of all households.

- The number of singles living alone increased from 13 percent of all households in 1960 to 23 percent in the mid-eighties.

- The number of unmarried couples living together tripled in the 1970s, increasing from 523,000 to 1.6 million.

One of the biggest census bombshells was the number of working mothers. In the families with children under 17, approximately 54 percent of the mothers reported working full- or part-time outside the home. Avon representatives who formerly sold door-to-door are increasingly selling at offices, schools, and nurseries—because that's where their customers are.

Over 70 percent of the new households are two-income households. These households tend to have more money to spend but less time to spend it. The before-tax income of working couples averaged $37,360 in 1984 dollars.

Toffler has pointed out that there is even a new kind of family growing by leaps and bounds, the "aggregate family." Two divorced people with children remarry, bringing the children of both marriages into the new, expanded family form. It is estimated that 25 percent of American children are now or soon will be members of such family units.

The "new old" are emerging—healthy, vigorous, and solvent. The 26 percent of the population over age 50 controls three-fourths of the nation's financial assets and half the spending power—an $800 billion-a-year market with $130 billion in discretionary income.

Because the birthrate is dropping and longevity is rising, there are only half as many grandchildren per grandparent as there were a generation ago.

Guess where the majority of Americans now live? In the South and West. In the 1970s, California, Florida, and Texas had 42 percent of the nation's total growth. The movement of population from big cities to nonmetropolitan areas in the 1970s reversed in 1980 and is now flowing back to the cities. But many people are still moving to smaller, less-crowded communities.

Approximately 10 million adults aged 25 or over are going to school! Nearly two-thirds of them are women.

And so on. We won't know to what extent these demographic changes are continuing until the next census. But periodically we are hit by startling new numbers that dramatize the accelerating rate of change in our society.

Communicating with and selling to these moving, changing households demands radically new marketing strategies and models.

The Decline of Brand Loyalty

Though it may seem hard to believe, not so long ago consumers swore by, and were doggedly loyal to, their Pepsodent toothpaste, Arrow shirts, Listerine mouthwash, Florsheim shoes, Texaco gasoline, Camel cigarettes, 7 Crown whiskey, and Chevrolet automobiles.

As recently as 1975, in a survey of 4000 male and female heads of household, 74 percent of the women and 80 percent of the men agreed with the statement: "I try to stick to well-known brand names." It seems likely that they meant their favorite brands. But by 1984, after a decade of product proliferation, increased imports, inflation, recession, and couponing, agreement with the statement had dropped to 58 percent among women and 52 percent among men.

In packaged-goods promotion, as cents-off coupons have proliferated like the progeny of sex-starved rabbits, the temptation to jump from brand to brand has been too great, and the price of consistent loyalty has been too high.

People may still respect brands (although generic canned and packaged goods in many supermarkets seem to be holding their own), but they have become accustomed to—and comfortable with—switching back and forth among several well-known brands.

And as we will see, frantic promotion efforts just to maintain share of market can actually end up producing the opposite effect.

Deregulation

Who could have imagined it in 1970 . . .

- Formerly monopolisitc old Ma Bell scrambling for customers like the rest of us—AT&T Opportunity Calling program reaching out with a grab bag full of merchandise just to reward you for making your usual long-distance calls, and spending $100 million to tell you about it

- Airlines spending millions on direct-response ads . . . to recruit new members for their frequent flyer clubs

- "Local" banks seeking national customers, and "bankless" banks competing with them; companies like Sears and Merrill Lynch slugging it out with the banks for the same consumer dollars

These are just a few ramifications of the trend in national government to deregulate certain industries. Fierce competition has resulted.

"As a result of deregulation, the theme of the 80's is choice," points out Barbara Berges Opatowsky, president of the Better Business Bureau of Metropolitan New York. "Never before have consumers had as many choices in areas like financial services, travel, and telephone service."[5]

To win the free-for-all to become the consumer's choice, the service companies in these fields jumped feet first into the new world of catering to the individual consumer. They discovered that it pays to know your customers by name and address and to track each transaction. Before long, they found out, you know who your frequent users were and discover the benefits of concentrating advertising and sales promotion dollars on the 20 percent of the market that produces 80 percent of your revenue.

New Ways to Shop and Pay

By the end of the eighties, the world will have 1 billion telephones, all interconnected and almost all accessible by direct dial.

Of course, in the United States a phone in almost every home is not news. What is news is the coupling of the telephone with a new method of payment, the credit card.

From its modest beginnings in the 1950s by holders of Diners Club, American Express, and BankAmericard (now Visa), the credit card is now used in 29 million transactions a day, adding up to $331 billion in annual sales. An estimated 830 million cards are in use in the United States today.

This has made possible the establishment of a broad base of credit-worthy customers—its segmentation into special interests and tastes based on proven purchasing patterns and other marketing data—and extraordinary ease of ordering via the toll-free telephone numbers and credit cards.

These developments have been combined with computerization of customer purchase records and product development for changing life-styles to make mail-order catalogs a substantial marketing force. By 1982, some 6500 catalog titles and a total of 5 billion copies a year were being mailed.

Meanwhile, the computer is also changing the way people shop in stores. It is estimated that by 1990 we will see 50,000 "transactional terminals"—video kiosks that can display a more complete line of merchandise than a store can stock, write up the order, and accept payment.

"Superstores," supermarkets so vast that they distribute maps to guide shoppers, are springing up. One chain, Cub Foods, stocks as many as 25,000 items in each store, twice as many as the average supermarket.

Because more women are working outside the home, they are buying more and shopping less—they go to a store to buy purposefully in their limited time rather than merely to browse, or shop by catalog.

New ways to shop mean new distribution opportunities for companies willing to look beyond their traditional outlets or method of selling. Sylvania recently began marketing their extensive line of bulbs and lighting accessories by catalog employed at the retail level. They made the catalog part of a self-standing in-store display unit complete with a hot line connected directly to their telemarketing center. Calvin Klein's Obsession is taking phone and mail orders for its fragrance products from the very same ads that build consumer awareness and store sales.

The Development of Database Marketing

Not all the profound changes in the marketplace are creating problems. Some provide extraordinary new opportunities.

One such development is database marketing. Thanks to the computer, detailed profiles of millions of prospects and customers can be developed using geographic, demographic, and psychographic characteristics and buying history. Special products, services, and offers can be tailored to selected segments of the database to increase both return on investment and customer satisfaction. Writes Michael Shrage in *Adweek*:

> If a company has a database replete with the phone numbers and addresses of key customers, it can target potential customers with a higher level of confidence than it could in merely spraying a few spot-television ads in key markets around the country. Thus, a blend of computer and telecommunications networks can become a strategic asset for service companies seeking to position themselves in their markets. And, by extension, the absence of such a capability can cripple an otherwise strong marketing effort. . . .
>
> In order to survive beyond the immediate future, advertising agencies will need to accommodate themselves to the fact that their clients rely increasingly on computers to store, index, and analyze more and more information about their customers. The agencies are going to find themselves deluged with information and analyses about target markets, and they will have to integrate this material into their advertising plans. "Know thy client" will mean "Know thy client's database."[6]

Because the cost of accessing data has fallen so swiftly, many people in marketing don't fully comprehend what database marketing can mean and what it can do. In 1973 it cost $7.14 to access 1000 bits of information; 1000 bits equals about 20 words of data—about enough to record a customer's name, address, and purchase. Today it costs about a nickel to do the same thing. By 1988 it will cost about a penny.

Thus keeping track of an individual consumer's preferences and purchases—and responding to them—is becoming increasingly affordable. This includes preferences not only in substantial purchases such as air travel and car rental transactions but even those involved in a modest purchase like a bottle of headache tablets or a box of corn flakes.

The Rise of the Service Economy

In the lawn-care field, in a single decade, 40 percent of retail product sales were wiped out by the rise of lawn-care services. Services now generate 67 percent of the gross national product and employ 7 out of 10 Americans who have jobs. Manufacturing employment has remained around 25 million for a number of years, but services have gone from 47 million to 65 million jobs, and the trend is certain to continue.

For shallow thinkers, such statistics can create a chill of anxiety. They make it sound too much like surviving by doing each other's laundry. But, as a perceptive article in *Forbes* pointed out, this is not the case:

> The services are no longer merely the passive instruments of the manufacturing economy. They are not only productive in their own right, but the source of much of the strength of the manufacturing economy.
>
> Far from filling the parasitic role economists from Adam Smith to Karl Marx have assigned to them, the services stimulate the demand for goods and draw the economy firstward like Dr. Doolittle's Pushmi-Pullyu. You buy an auto because GMAC or Beneficial will extent the credit on favorable terms. You buy a Chrysler instead of a Volkswagen, or a Toyota rather than either, because you can count on the local repair and maintenance services.[7]

However, a service, whether it offers to invest your money, insure your life, tow your car, or keep your washing machine going, cannot be packaged and shelved. A service requires a different kind of marketing, one that combines the oldest techniques of persuasion with the newest refinements of database management.

Great opportunities exist for a threatened product manufacturer to find innovative ways to wrap a service around the product—and to let the target prospect know about it.

The Flowering of the Information Society

Closely related to the development of the service economy is the rise of the "information society." As Naisbitt pointed out:

> The overwhelming majority of service workers are actually engaged in the creation, processing, and distribution of information. . . . In 1950, only about 17% of us were working in information jobs. Now more than 60% of

us work with information as programmers, teachers, clerks, secretaries, accountants, stock brokers, managers, insurance people, bureaucrats, lawyers, bankers, and technicians, processing, or distributing information.[8]

This phenomenon involves marketing because a great deal of information needs to be sold and information is needed to sell information—whether it is a magazine subscription, a newsletter, an encyclopedia, a library of books, a financial advice, or a public-access database service for computer owners.

And remember, somebody out there still knows how to read. Since the first baby boomers sat transfixed before the first television set, the book publishing industry has multiplied by a factor of 10.

Under a broader definition, even physical products can be a kind of information in physical form. For example, when catalog companies like Brookstone and The Warming Trend put out catalogs of products showing how to save energy using weather stripping, wood stove accessories, firewood choppers, etc., they are really purveying tangible information on how to outwit the high cost of heating. And The Banana Republic, which sells funky clothing by mail and store, is really built on the excellence and enjoyability of the information it provides about each garment.

The Proliferation of New Products

Seeking to beat their competitors to the punch, companies have been swamping the market with new products and line extensions backed by ads, coupons, premiums, and sweepstakes. A *Business Week* article pointed out in 1983, "Of the 261 varieties of cigarettes for sale today, about half are 10 years old or less."[9]

Altogether, some 28,000 nationally advertised branded products are for sale in the United States. Companies must therefore wage a fierce fight not only for public awareness but also for shelf space. Marketing consultant Lawrence C. Burns points out that "stores are eliminating slow movers and won't take on new products unless they are assured of good inventory turns and margins. They want proof that a product really is a success, and the only way companies can provide that is through more regional roll-outs and more test marketing."[10] Proof is often hard to come by, because so many of the new offerings are basically parity products, those with little unique advantage.

Between 1970 and 1979, 6695 new grocery products were introduced. Only 93, or 1.4 percent, achieved $15 million or more in annual sales. And the cost of introducing a new product has soared. It is said that at least $50 million is needed to establish a national brand in a major category.

Still, manufacturers must keep going because they are caught in a vicious circle. To maintain and increase their share of market in a category, they must pour in new products. . . . But the flood of new products tends to shorten products' life spans, which in turn sets up a demand for more new products.

The answer is not to produce more of the same but to custom-design special products for special audiences and to open up new channels of communications and distribution for them.

Multiplication of Distribution Channels

Back when East was East and West was West, most companies distributed to the consumer through one of three more-or-less watertight channels: retailers, sales agents, or directly by mail. This purity of distribution was a canon of marketing.

But just as floodwaters flow to the sea any way they can, the torrents of new products and services in the demassified society have refused to be confined to traditional channels. The mind-set that insists on only one method of distribution is giving way to a new open-mindedness about multiple distribution. With this new attitude has come the dawning realization that distribution is not merely a *consequence* of marketing, it is a *component* of marketing. The question is no longer, "How should we distribute?" Rather, "How *else* should we distribute?"

Changing households and lifestyles have also demanded new thinking about distribution. How can you sell door-to-door when in 7 out of 10 homes no one is at home during the day and people are afraid to open their doors at night? How can you sell a $600 exercise machine in a store when the sales clerks are too busy or untrained to demonstrate it? How do you catch up with a highly paid career couple who work long hours during the week and then dash off to their country home on the weekend?

In answer to these questions, extraordinary new forms and combinations of distribution are emerging:

- Avon built from scratch a $150 million division selling fashion apparel directly to the consumer by mail-order catalog, bypassing the Avon representatives.

- Reader's Digest announced that it plans to sell Metropolitan Life Insurance to its subscribers, and Metropolitan boasted in institutional ads of "leading the industry in a search for more and more innovative distribution techniques."

- Johnston & Murphy sells shoes direct to the consumer in its own catalog, opens its own retail outlets, and meanwhile continues to sell through traditional dealers.

- AmWay developed a billion-dollar business in gifts ordered from catalogs toted to homes by its agents.

- IBM sells its personal computers through thousands of independent dealers as well as its own sales channels.

- Liberty Mutual has started peddling its insurance in Stop & Shop supermarkets.

- Aquascutum opened its own store on Fifth Avenue, and Ralph Lauren is selling his fragrance by mail.

- Catalog firms like Brookstone, Royal Silk, and Williams-Sonoma are opening nationwide networks of their own stores.

It's a new ball game. To meet this challenge, every company's marketers, no matter how large or how small the company, must now consider every channel of advertising and distribution with completely open minds.

The Explosion of Couponing

A little more than 10 years ago, 27.6 billion cents-off coupons were distributed annually. Today that figure has grown to nearly 200 billion.

In 1971, when Nielsen conducted the first national survey on couponing, 58 percent of all households were using coupons; 65 percent were using them in 1975, and 76 percent were using them by 1980. These figures do not include fast-food restaurant coupons, which don't have to go through redemption channels. A. C. Nielsen does not include them in its industry tally.

The trouble is, when everybody does it, nobody wins (except perhaps the public, and even that is not always true). Advertisers suddenly find themselves in a no-win couponing trap.

The short-term challenge is to find new ways to make couponing more cost-effective, more than just disguised discounting to existing customers. The long-range solution must look beyond couponing and dependency on couponing for better ways to gain an advantage in the marketplace.

The Slippage in Network Television Advertising Efficiency

Ever since the majority of U.S. households got a television set, network television has been the driving force behind the marketing of package goods. Its power to reach and influence the mass market has been awesome. Marketing planners have found that, other things being equal, a given "weight" in gross rating points translates directly to a predictable share of market. (Unfortunately, other things—such as the power of the commercial or the aggressiveness of the competition—are seldom equal.)

Since the mid-seventies, charges for television commercials have gone up faster than the rate of inflation—and meanwhile the sizes of the audiences for the programs have gone down, and the audience for the commercials has shrunk even more. The reasons? They sound like the name of a law firm or an advertising agency—Clutter, Zap, Flip, and Tug.

The *clutter* of commercial messages that bombard the average household (some estimate 50,000 messages a year) is causing many viewers who own videocassette recorders (VCRs) and record off the air to *zap* past the commercials with the fast-forward control during playback—and the number of television households with VCRs was estimated to have reached 33 percent by the end of 1985.

The additional channels now available on cable not only offer other program options; they also allow viewers to *flip* during the commercial break and watch a snippet of news, weather, or music video. Some of the new generation of restless viewers have even developed the knack of watching two programs simultaneously, by frequently flipping back and forth between the two.

The *tug* of other attractions is tempting people to spend less time watching network shows. By spring of 1984, Paul Klein of PKO Television, a former programming head of NBC pointed out that the number one network was no longer NBC, ABC, or CBS—it was AOT, all other television—cable, independent stations, PBS, superstations, videocassette viewing, pay television. By the end of that year, AOT was averaging a 32 to 33 percent share, leaving the other three networks to divide up smaller pieces of the pie.

In the early 1980s, as sales of VCRs boomed, the advertising trade press was filled with warnings and reassurances about the threat to network advertisers of Clutter, Zap, Flip, and Tug.

At a symposium in July 1985, an executive of General Foods estimated that by 1990 there would be a 30 percent audience loss because of "physical" zapping (viewers leaving the room during the commercials), a

13 percent audience loss from electronic zapping, and a 4 percent audience loss as a result of VCR play of programs with commercials. He stated:

> The net result of all factors is an average prime time commercial audience of 53 percent by 1990, and it translates into an erosion of advertising value.
>
> We pay more every year for network time. Fewer viewers are delivered, resulting in skyrocketing inefficiencies. Add to this the increasing loss of viewers at the commercial break and you begin to wonder *at what point it is no longer worth the price.* [Italics ours.][11]

As the cost of television time continued to rise, the networks began to permit companies to run a "split 30"—two 15-second commercials for two products in a 30-second time slot. Then, beginning with CBS, the networks began to offer 15-second "stand-alones" at about 65 percent of the cost of a 30-second slot. However, many advertising executives predicted that it was only a matter of time until the 15s would cost as much as the 30s cost in 1985.

By introducing stand-alone 15s, the networks apparently hoped to make television advertising more affordable to smaller advertisers. What seemed to be happening instead is that many of the big advertisers and their agencies wanted to trade in their 30s for 15s. As one media executive put it, "It's an opportunity to get better cost-per-thousand efficiencies at a lower out-of-pocket investment while achieving the same level of rating points."[12]

But then what? If the number of network television commercials aired each week rises from 4000 or 5000 to 6000, 7000, 8000, or 9000, will the weary viewer be able to remember them or put up with them? No wonder national advertisers are reviewing their options.

Early in 1985, Polaroid planned to increase its $40 million advertising budget by 15 to 20 percent. But according to *Adweek*, "Along with its increased ad commitment, the company plans to focus its advertising on a wider variety of media vehicles." A company executive commented: *"Our goal is to get away from the stranglehold of the TV networks."* (Italics ours.)[13]

In March 1985, it was Campbell Soup's turn. "We're going to be exploring a lot of things with media," said company president R. Gordon McGovern about their $150 million advertising budget. "We're not going to keep paying the high network prices."[14]

And in April, it was a similar story with General Foods. With the introduction of many new products came a 20 percent increase in their $210 million advertising budget for packaged goods, but—"we'll become more diversified in our media programs," said a company executive. "We'll become more localized, and that will take away from our network-TV commitment."[15]

If you have been dependent on network television advertising, where do you now turn to influence share-of-mind on a cost-effective basis? If you have never been able to afford the astronomical cost of such advertising or if your niche in the marketplace cannot support a television-advertising budget, can MaxiMarketing offer alternatives?

The New Playing Field

Taken individually, any changes we have touched on can profoundly affect the success or failure of a business in reaching its marketing objectives. Taken together, these changes represent nothing less than a new playing field with a new set of ground rules for business decision makers. This unfamiliar terrain requires that companies look with new eyes at every step of the marketing process—from preliminary research to product development and pricing, all the way through to formation of advertising and promotion strategies.

None of the steps in the marketing process will be transformed more profoundly by these changes than advertising and sales promotion. With expenditures for advertising reaching $100 billion a year, and sales promotion estimated as high as $60 billion, U.S. businesses must reexamine the advertising, promotion, and marketing assumptions that seemed to work so well just a decade ago and to test them against the new realities.

Those who do not, risk falling behind competitors who are already exploring the explosive opportunities of a new approach to advertising and sales promotion. This new approach uses new media technologies to target the most likely prospects, insists on accountability for each advertising expenditure, and links the advertising to a private database used to convert prospects into "triers" and to transform triers into heavy users.

The Bottom Line

The marketplace is changing dramatically, whether you like it or not. Whatever steps you have taken to meet these challenges may not be enough. Demographic and lifestyle changes have delivered a heavy blow to mass marketing and brand loyalty. Ours is a multioption society, and the individual consumer is king.

Deregulation has splintered the financial, travel, and communications sectors into a shopper's paradise of choices.

It is becoming affordable for any company to keep track of an individual's preferences and purchases and respond to them. Thanks to the computer, marketers can reach out to customers and competitor's customers with special products, services, and offers tailored to the personal information accumulated in public databases and in private customer databases.

The toll-free telephone call, the 6 to 10 credit cards per household, the retail transaction computer terminals, and the targeting of direct mail to individual lifestyles and psychographics are all reshaping consumer shopping habits.

There are new considerations on every side: The service economy. The information society. The flood of "me-too" products. The new distribution options.

Nowhere have these changes destroyed more assumptions than in advertising and sales promotion. The proliferation of couponing is neutralizing the effectiveness of the No. 1 sales promotion tool. The slippage in network television advertising efficiency is causing a basic rethinking of media budgets. The fascination with "creative" advertising is giving way to a concern for accountability and responsiveness.

The good news is that there are proven or highly promising new ways to meet the challenges of change—bold innovations by companies and organizations able to throw off the shackles of conventional thinking about outmoded advertising and promotion practices. And that's what we're going to explore with you in this book.

2

The Essence
of the
MaxiMarketing
Solution

The Big Picture

The drastically changed marketplace sketched out in the previous chapter demands a basic shift in thinking about advertising, promotion, and all other steps in the selling process.

Demassification is transforming yesterday's monolithic consumer markets into smaller and smaller fragments. The computer, the credit card, and the toll-free call are drastically changing the very nature of the sales transaction. And now the new world of database marketing offers the opportunity to get closer to your customers and gain incremental profits after the sale is made.

Just when nothing seems to be what you would expect, a new reality is emerging—a reality in which direct interaction with indi-

*vidual prospects and customers is replacing the mass-market men-
tality of the past. The new reality is replete with new opportunities:
You can make your advertising and sales promotion more accountable than ever before. You and your computers can talk to each
customer in response to personal needs and wants. You can replace
the discontinuity of the old marketing—where each step in the
selling process went its own way—with an organic continuum. You
can make your advertising do double duty by inviting a response
from your best prospects while increasing general awareness of your
product or service. You can leap across the distribution barriers
that set arbitrary limits on your company's growth.*

*All this is possible with a new way of thinking about the selling
process. We call it MaxiMarketing. This chapter will give you an
overview of the MaxiMarketing concept—a model that can serve
as a guide to your own company's strategic planning. Then the
following chapters will examine each MaxiMarketing step in detail.*

*MaxiMarketing is a universal concept you can apply to the
challenges facing your company now. You can follow the Maxi-
Marketing path whether you are the marketer of a product or a
service, whether you are the manufacturer or the retailer, whether
your product is sold in stores, by direct mail, or by a personal sales
rep. What we are offering is a shift in thinking about the way goods
and services are sold—a new direction in advertising and promotion strategy for the closing years of the twentieth century.*

If you are a decision maker with marketing or management responsibilities, you have certainly been aware of the sweeping changes outlined
in the previous chapter, even if you have never stopped to consider them
all at the same time. Your company has undoubtedly already responded
to or been directly affected by a number of them in various ways.

Maybe a special committee of your top people has sat around the
conference room table and concluded, "It's a very different world out
there now. How should our company be behaving differently?"

And if a full realization of the new realities is still lacking at the top in
your company, maybe you have been thinking "How can I take action at
my level anyway?"

You have seen big, impressive corporations—including some cited for
their excellence by Waterman and Peters's *In Search of Excellence*—slip
backward or fall apart. If your own results are slipping, you certainly are
concerned about the warning signals of what might follow. And if your

product, division, or company has been experiencing growth and profit increases, you know this is no time for overconfidence. So it's likely that you and your company *are* changing and experimenting and groping for new answers.

But you may have never undertaken a systematic review and questioning of all the assumptions in your marketing thinking. You and your associates probably have been too absorbed in meeting and dealing with the immediate challenges at hand. Then there are the familiar problems of inertia and mind-set that trouble so many companies. It is only human to develop an emotional investment in "the way we've always done things around here" and to experience great difficulty in reexamining beliefs long considered sacred truths.

It took years to drag department stores, kicking and screaming, into the age of MasterCard, Visa, and American Express. General Foods is still stinging from their slow recognition of the potential represented by the development of frozen, gourmet, and natural foods. The Montgomery Ward "big book" is gone because management refused to accept a fragmented market's desire for specialty catalogs.

So, it is understandable if you have a nagging feeling in the pit of your stomach that your company should be doing something more to change with the times, but you are not sure exactly what.

From our years spent in planning and preparing advertising which calls for responses from—and communication with—individual customers, we have become increasingly convinced (as have many others) that coping with the great marketing changes of our time involves a more personal kind of marketing for all companies. As Professor Theodore Levitt expressed it so pointedly in *The Marketing Imagination,* "The future will be a future of more and more intensified relationships, especially in industrial marketing, but also increasingly even in frequently purchased consumer goods."[1]

Already many major service industries—banking, insurance, airlines, telecommunications—have seen a revolution in the way they deal with their customers. Vast databanks control a constant stream of communications that maximize sales and contacts with their best customers by mail and phone and single out likely prospects with the same characteristics as their best-spending buyers. AT&T recently announced a $100 million budget for just one of their data-based customer incentive programs. AT&T is spending far more today advertising to their private database of customers than in "reaching out" to the country with awareness advertising.

The customer relationship revolution which started in the service sector in the late seventies has now begun to sweep package goods, fast foods, high-tech industries, and every consumer product category. But we have observed a wide variation in corporate responses to the avalanche of change. Some companies seem to have performed brilliantly. And some are still living in the past.

Most companies are somewhere in the middle. They have responded by piecemeal reforms. They are doing many things right, but they have not yet fit these right things into a new comprehensive view of the marketplace, and they are missing some important pieces.

Because we saw so many smart, successful companies engaged in a curious combination of smart and not-so-smart practices—exploiting some opportunities skillfully but fumbling others—we decided there was a need for a universal model of the new direction in advertising and marketing.

Whether your company is large or small, is manufacturer or retailer, or completes transactions face-to-face or by mail or phone, you need a frame of reference to review your own practices at each step of the selling process. A universal model could help you see which parts of your advertising and sales promotion strategy were taking new developments into account and where gaping holes and cracks allow opportunities for additional sales to slip away.

We began by reviewing and diagramming the way things have always been done (in recent decades, anyway) in the four traditional selling modes. The result was the four diagrams you see in Figures 1 through 4.

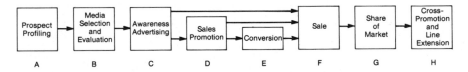

A   B   C   D   E   F   G   H

FIGURE 1.   Brand Merchandising.

Brand merchandising usually starts with PROSPECT PROFILING (A), employing market research to learn as much about the prospect as possible. Then quantitative and qualitative yardsticks are applied to MEDIA SELECTION AND EVALUATION (B).

AWARENESS ADVERTISING (C) is created to carve out the product's position in the marketplace and to condition prospects to want or prefer it. Sometimes SALES PROMOTION (D) is used to activate the prospect—to turn vague buying intention into measurable action. (This book deals with sales promotion *advertising* only. A vast world of additional sales promotion activity—store displays, dealer allowances and deals, etc.—is beyond the scope of the book.)

Sometimes, but less often, additional advertising is interposed between the awareness advertising or sales promotion and the sale. At the request of the prospect, more information—CONVERSION literature (E)—is provided in an effort to convert mild interest into buying intention and SALE (F). Repetition of this process over a time results in a SHARE OF MARKET (G) or consumer brand franchise, however large or small.

This share of market is a corporate asset, albeit a tenuous one, that creates the possibility of CROSS-PROMOTION AND LINE EXTENSION (H). A company with a line of successful products can use one of them for cross-promotion to another through on-pack, in-pack, or joint promotion. The built-up popularity of the brand name can sometimes (not always, alas!) rub off onto the introduction of new products with the same brand name.

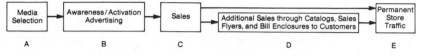

A   B   C   D   E

FIGURE 2.   Store Retailing.

The retailer, selling merchandise of either general or special interest, advertises to just about everybody in the market area and uses quantity and quality guides for MEDIA SELECTION (A) from the available local choices.

Retail advertising may promote some AWARENESS of a favorable image of the store or the advertised product (especially through co-op advertising supplied by the manufacturer). This is often combined with some ACTIVATION ADVERTISING (B) (such as bargain sales or promotional offers) to turn the customer's interest into immediate store traffic and SALES (C).

The sales may result in a mailing list of customers, usually of charge-account customers only. This list may be used to promote ADDITIONAL SALES THROUGH CATALOGS, SALES FLYERS, AND BILL ENCLOSURES TO CUSTOMERS (D). Even though the mailing list is surely on computer these days, it usually serves as only a primitive database because it provides no information about—or access to—each customer's individual characteristics or buying history. Repeated advertising and repromotion of customers then helps build a base of PERMANENT STORE TRAFFIC (E).

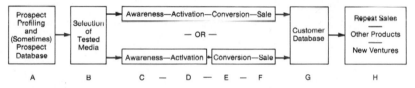

A   B   C — D — E — F   G   H

FIGURE 3.   Mail-Order Merchandising.

Mail-order merchandising is essentially nonstore retailing, whether by the originator of a product or service or by a direct marketing merchant engaged in buying from the originator and selling to the end-user. It starts with detailed PROSPECT PROFILING (A). It is based sometimes on classic market research but more often on analysis of past direct-response results and customer buying behavior in relation to the same or similar products. Increasingly, mail-order may also begin with the construction of a PROSPECT DATABASE (A), which contains prospects identified not only by name and address but also by a number of other known and desirable characteristics.

SELECTION OF TESTED MEDIA (B) is accomplished not so much by cost per thousand as by cost per response. Even in a launch, when the product has no response media experience to draw on, the response history of various media used for other direct-sold products provides a means of selecting tested media for the test schedule.

Old-fashioned mail-order advertising usually focused on making the sale without regard to the advertising's effect on the company's image. Today the largest and most successful direct marketers know the importance not only of making the first sale but also of beginning a profitable continuing relationship. These marketers are very interested in public awareness of the lasting company or product image created by their direct-response advertising.

A direct-response advertisement by a mail-order company may contain AWARENESS (C), ACTIVATION (D), CONVERSION (E), and completion of the SALE (F) all in one (such an advertisement "pulls for the order"). Or it may contain only awareness and activation (it "pulls for the inquiry"). The process is then completed with conversion and sale in a follow-up mailing or phone call.

The sales then lead not just to the creation of a customer list but to the start of a CUSTOMER DATABASE (G). This database can be used to stimulate REPEAT SALES (H) of the same product, the sale of OTHER PRODUCTS selected or customized to fit the prospect's individual interests, tastes, and financial means, or the launching of NEW VENTURES, sometimes with almost push-button ease.

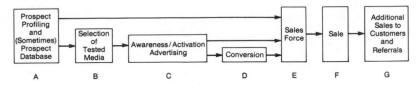

FIGURE 4.   Personal Selling.

Personal selling to consumers has traditionally taken one of two routes: The first is cold-canvass selling to consumers by agents for companies such as Avon or Tupperware, with *no* prospect names provided to the agent by the company—and often with little or no awareness advertising to pave the way for the agent. The second route is selling by agents to a prospect list generated by inquiry advertising.

Advertising designed to provide leads for personal selling obviously must begin with careful targeting or PROSPECT PROFILING (A). When responses to the advertising provide sales leads, they can provide an index of the efficiency of the various media sources. So it could be said that SELECTION OF TESTED MEDIA (B) occurs, although one would be entitled to a strong suspicion that some companies are careless about measuring the responses, cost per response, and conversion ratios of their media sources.

The stimulation of AWARENESS and ACTIVATION are usually combined in the inquiry-producing ADVERTISING (C), although this might be supplemented by awareness-only advertising. The inquirer may receive CONVERSION (D) literature, either before or during contact by a member of the SALES FORCE (E) who seeks to complete the SALE (F). This sale may be followed up by ADDITIONAL SALES TO CUSTOMERS and REFERRALS (G) and their friends and relatives, either by the sales agent or by the company.

Waste and Inefficiency—
A Fact of Life

All four standard ways of doing business depicted in the figures have a great deal of waste and inefficiency built into them. Why?

In business as in medicine, we live in the age of specialization. As organizations get bigger, skills and tasks get more specialized, and this specialization has its weaknesses as well as its strengths. Specialists can become so focused on their narrow view of the problem and generalists so focused on one or two points of leverage that millions of advertising and promotion dollars can spill through the cracks in the floorboard, and the opportunity for millions of dollars in sales can be lost.

Another source of inefficiency involves the societal and technological changes of the last decade or so. These changes have been so swift and so huge that the marketing community has not had time to adjust to the rapidly changing landscape.

In addition, enormous waste is inherent in mass advertising. For example, if Hertz spends $25,000 to advertise its Florida car rental rates on the back cover of *Travel and Leisure* and only 10 percent of the readers of that magazine vacation in Florida, Hertz is actually getting only $2500 worth of functional advertising for their money.

But many important new breakthroughs are taking place on the business scene. By developing a master plan, it is possible to provide a framework into which they can be fitted. Thus many seemingly unrelated improvements in advertising and marketing efficiency can be assembled into a meaningful pattern to combat the waste and inefficiency.

The Three Common Denominators of the Selling Process

To develop such a master plan, we first reduced all the steps in these four traditional ways of doing business to the simplest terms possible, to their three common denominators (Figure 5):

- *All* marketing must reach out to satisfy needs and wants of prospects, whether blindly or thoughtfully.
- *All* marketing must make the sale—converting the prospect's interest into buying intention and actual purchase.
- And *almost all* marketing should seek to develop an ongoing relationship with the customer after the first sale by encouraging additional purchases or continued loyalty.

FIGURE 5. The Three Common Denominators of the Marketing Process.

The MaxiMarketing Model

Proceeding from these common denominators, it is possible to construct the MaxiMarketing model (Figure 6). In the model, the advances in advertising and marketing we have observed (plus our own refinements and additions) have been fitted into a master sequence that you can follow to maximize your own company's business opportunities.

1. Maximized Targeting

The ideal selling process begins with the traditional step of learning as much as possible about your prospect. But it includes, whenever and wherever desirable and possible, a prospect database that allows you to approach your target prospects as individuals.

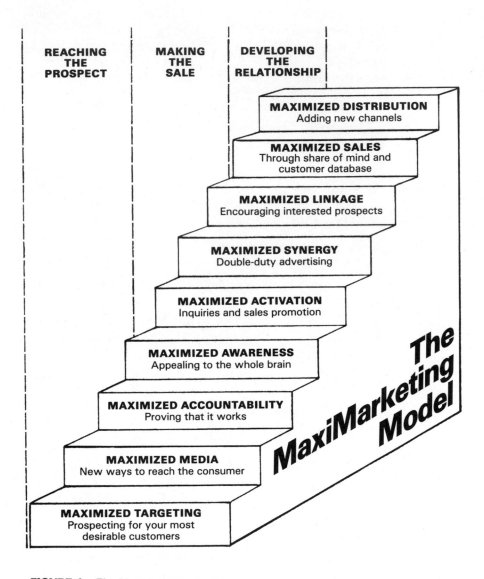

FIGURE 6.   The MaxiMarketing Model.

This database ideally contains not only the names and addresses of likely prospects but also a number of other bits of revealing information about each prospect. It may be a public database which happens to contain or can yield the information you need, a private database which you have constructed from responses to your advertising and sales promotion, or a composite of both.

The most cost-efficient object of your advertising and promotion expenditures is the individual who needs or wants your product or service and is ready and able to buy it. Singling that person out of the mass consumer market is more easily accomplished at less cost with each year of the computer era.

2. Maximized Media

In pursuit of your rapidly moving, ever-changing target, you will want to examine carefully—and to explore as your budget permits—the dazzling, almost bewildering array of new media options which are either available now or soon will be.

But you will want to keep this exploration under control. Most media tested should be held directly accountable and made to prove their value—whenever feasible, by tabulated responses. Testing media effectiveness is surprisingly easy when you use the tools perfected by direct marketers in measuring responses to each print insertion, each direct mailing, and each television commercial.

3. Maximized Accountability

The proliferation of media choices and the escalation of media costs have increased the need for accountability in advertising expenditure. Until recently conventional wisdom for general advertising dictated that media be evaluated by the advertising cost per impression and readership studies, and copy by audience opinions and recollections or by artificial simulations of the marketplace.

In the increasingly fierce competition for customers, the winners will be those who make their advertising expenditures more accountable. They will evaluate and rank media and media buys by the proven advertising cost per prospect response or purchase. And they will improve copy by comparing how two different promises or treatments in the real advertising environment actually affect consumers.

4. Maximized Awareness

Stimulation of favorable awareness is common to all advertising, even the response advertising used by mail-order merchants, since prospects can't buy your product or service unless they are first made aware of it. But a great deal of awareness advertising suffers from a high degree of misguided creativity. MaxiMarketing addresses the need to maximize the impact of awareness advertising by giving more careful attention to the duality of human thought processes.

The new level of sophistication in awareness advertising will often appeal equally to the left and right brain (that is, to both the rational and nonrational sides of our nature). The highest creative challenge will be to appeal to the whole brain of the prospect.

5. Maximized Activation

Activation includes but is broader than sales promotion. Activation simply means making something happen by means of your advertising. That something might be a purchase, or it might simply be taking the prospect a step closer to the purchase by asking for some specific action:

- When brand advertisers say, "Send for more information" or "Redeem this cents-off coupon," they are promoting activation.
- When a retailer advertises "On sale today—Friday only," that, too, is a way to get activation.
- When a direct marketer says, "Reply coupon must be returned by September 30" or "Affix token to reply card," that is activation.

There is a growing consensus that a great deal of activation aimed at promoting retail sales is merely wheel spinning. Frequently, sales promotion cuts into the profit margins on sales to loyal customers while failing to win new customers.

MaxiMarketing calls for applying the same stern yardstick of efficiency and accountability to promote activation in advertising as well as to gain awareness in advertising and to target the prospect.

Surprisingly enough, even direct marketers, the supposed masters of activation, are sometimes lax. European catalog firms are by and large much more enterprising than their U.S. counterparts when it comes to stimulating the prospect or customer to pick up the catalog already received and order or reorder.

6. Maximized Synergy

By making your advertising do two or more jobs at the same time, you can achieve a synergistic explosion of energy and profitability. You might simply add new twists to the familiar concept of combining awareness advertising and sales promotion. Or you might combine your message with that of a compatible fellow advertiser to share the cost.

Maximizing synergy might involve advertising a separate profit center in a way which also promotes your brand name, promoting two channels of distribution simultaneously, or stealing space or time from your advertising to promote an event or cause in a way that is also helpful to your company.

With the rise in media costs, it becomes increasingly urgent to review your advertising plans and ask yourself how the cost might be spread over—and justified by—more than one purpose.

7. Maximized Linkage

Too often, awareness advertising leaves the prospect dangling, with no idea of what to do next, where to buy, or how to obtain more information. At the very least, the ideal advertising and marketing process should bridge this gap between the advertising and the sale by offering—and providing—additional information. We call this "linkage."

Linkage means more than just plugging a gap in the advertising continuum. It is also a way of focusing more advertising effort and dollars on the most desirable, most interested prospects.

Instead of spending, say, 80 or 90 cents out of each dollar in the advertising budget on advertising to a broadly defined target (mostly on television as far as many national advertisers are concerned) and less than a penny to send something to those individuals who happen to write or call for more information, MaxiMarketing would use the mass advertising to locate, interest, and get a response from the strongest prospects and then spend as much of the advertising dollar as necessary to turn these prospects into customers and loyal friends.

We foresee that the importance of bridging the gap between the upfront advertising and the cash register will be increasingly appreciated.

8. Maximized Sales

All the steps in the MaxiMarketing process outlined so far should, if well planned and executed effectively, result in a significant increase in sales and profits. But MaxiMarketing does not end with the first sale to a new customer. What happens *after* that sale can also have a profound effect on the bottom line.

As President Coolidge is famous for having observed, "When too many people are out of work, unemployment results." In the same vein of wisdom, when you sell lots of product to the public over and over again, you achieve a certain share of market and share of mind.

But MaxiMarketing adds something new to the picture: a customer database. Once you start saving the names and addresses of inquirers, warranty card returners, rebate applicants, coupon redeemers, sample requesters, charge account and credit customers, etc.—and use the latest tools of targeting and segmentation to add other identifiable characteristics to each name and address—you possess a powerful new marketing instrument.

You have a private advertising medium you can promote for repeat sales. And you can begin to apply the magical concept of lifetime customer value (LTV) to make every sale lead to two, three, or four additional sales that you weren't realizing before.

You can use your share of mind and customer database to:

- Stimulate repeat sales and consolidate market share
- Increase the chance for success of line extensions
- Cross-promote different products in your line
- Build lasting loyalty of your best customers
- Help open up new channels of distribution

Market share alone can *help* achieve all these goals; market share *plus* customer database can greatly increase your chances of success. The two combined can double and triple the lifetime value of each new buyer you attract.

Finally, a customer database can help you in ways that market share alone cannot. Suppose you want to launch a new product, service, or business, but trying it out in a regional test market would be very costly and would tip off your competitors immediately. Through database marketing, you can quietly and privately test the idea. You can sift through the database to find the ideal prospects, and these can serve as bellwethers who will lead other likely prospects in the direction of your new product or business.

9. Maximized Distribution

How can your company continue to grow when your retailers refuse to offer you any more shelf space? Or your personal-selling agents can't find or get appointments with enough new prospects? Or your mail-order catalog is swamped by a horde of competitors in the mail box?

Many companies have found the answer in opening up a new channel of distribution. It's like extending your business activities to another continent—without the complication of foreign language, customs, and distribution methods. This may involve using a database built from your present customers, using the share of mind built up in one channel to support another, or using some other advertiser's database. Often, although not always, this creates a synergistic reaction between two or more distribution methods. What you may get is truly the best of two worlds: You establish a new form of distribution, and the new distribution channel nurtures the way you have always done business before.

How the MaxiMarketing Steps All Work Together

An intriguing and significant aspect of the MaxiMarketing approach to marketing is how the various parts fit together and work together. The common thread is a measurable *response* from the individual consumer to whom you want to sell or have already sold:

- *Responses* can tell you if your advertising is correctly targeted.
- *Responses* can provide an index to the comparative efficiency of different media, different product images and benefits, different offers.
- The technique of allocating more of the advertising budget to self-identified interested prospects depends on first getting a *response* from them.
- *Responses* are the foundation of an in-house prospect-customer database.

Response is so much a part of improving performance in the face of the new marketing realities that the term *responsive advertising* should begin to get the kind of attention bestowed in the past on so-called *creative advertising*.

We object not to creativity but to the overuse of the term to the point of absurdity. In advertising meetings and in the trade press, the term *creative advertising* is used repeatedly with no reference whatsoever to the sales effectiveness of the advertising under discussion. Usually what is being lauded as creative is related to whatever advertising fad or advertising agency happens to be in vogue at the moment.

The new marketing imperatives will demand *responsive advertising*. First and foremost, this advertising must demonstrate measurable responsiveness to the marketing objective. It will always be held accountable for the results achieved. It will insofar as possible find ways to determine cost effectiveness by weighing expense against performance. It will always support the positioning of the brand and the desire to reach out and get as close as possible to the real needs of real prospects.

Creativity in pursuit of responsive advertising will be most welcome. Creativity in pursuit of justifying its own creative reputation should no longer be tolerated.

The Self-Examination Process

As we examine each step in the MaxiMarketing process in the following chapters, bear with us if some details do not seem sufficiently related to your immediate problems. (For instance, if you are a retailer, the discussion of conversion or sampling may not seem relevant to your situation. But don't be too sure!) If you become familiar with the entire process, you will be better able to use whatever part does fit your company's current situation.

And keep in mind that MaxiMarketing is essentially a *self-examination*—an opportunity to look at some of the critical marketing points that influence your business success. We will not tell you, "Here is what you should be doing," because every business and the position of each company in that business are different. So our purpose is simply to stimulate you to ask at every step, "What can I learn from what is happening here? Is there something—or something more—we could be doing about this? If so, what?"

Then, we hope, *you* will become a master MaxiMarketer and participate in leading *your* company into the nineties!

The Bottom Line

MaxiMarketing does not *mean giving up what your company is already doing. It means examining every step of your selling process, from visualizing your prospect to what you do after the sale is made in order to maximize profits. It means adding powerful new capabilities to what you already do very well.*

MaxiMarketing puts you in a one-to-one relationship with the consumer. The responses you get from likely prospects and your contacts with end-users of your product can add a new reality to your decision making and a new ability to measure the effectiveness of your advertising, promotion, and marketing practices. You will enter the new world of "responsive advertising" and focus attention on getting measurable responses from the people for whom you developed your advertising message.

With MaxiMarketing you will begin to appreciate the difference between getting a sale and getting a customer. Today you may be accustomed to spending as little as one-twentieth or as much as one-third of the amount of a sale to make it happen. In the world of MaxiMarketing, you may expend three or four times the amount of a sale to get a long-time customer—and consider it money well spent when you apply the lifetime customer concept.

3

Maximized Targeting: Prospecting for Your Best Customers

The Big Picture

Targeted marketing is all the rage in the demassified market, but it is seldom clearly defined. Our working definition here is that targeted marketing is the art and science of identifying, describing, locating, and contacting one or more groups of prime prospects for whatever you are selling.

The various methods for targeted marketing can be reduced to five basic patterns. Three are old wine in new bottles, and two depend on the magic new elixir known as "database marketing."

Maximized targeting is the essential first step in the Maxi-

Marketing model. In today's marketplace, if you don't know who, what, and where your true prospects are, or if you fail to go after them as individuals, you will lose ground to competitors who do.

Whether the advertiser or the advertising creator realizes it (and sometimes they don't), all advertising begins with the prospect. Since all advertising of goods and services presents an answer to the need of someone, somewhere, the advertiser is always talking to an individual within an identified segment of the total population.

There is no such thing as a universal product, that is, one for which everyone is a prospective buyer. That's rather astonishing when you think about it. You might ask, "What about universal essentials like soap, toilet paper, light bulbs?" But if you live in a communal setting like a college dormitory, you are not a prospect because these things may be supplied. Or if you are an adult member of a household, you may not be a prospect if you are not the one who shops and therefore you don't much care what brands the household uses.

So, for as long as there has been advertising, there has been targeting, whether conscious or unconscious. Copywriters may *think* they are merely writing *about* the product, but, unavoidably, they are also writing *to* some people who will be more interested than others. In the days of mass advertising and mass products, this was a matter of less concern to the biggest advertisers. "Everybody" was interested in owning a black Model T Ford.

But product proliferation also means prospect proliferation. And the more different kinds of prospects there are, the more waste is built into advertising that continues to talk to "everybody" (even though a certain amount of that may be necessary).

So today advertisers are taking a hard look at both new ways and old ways to keep from wasting their advertising money on nonprospects. And the computer is helping, by making it possible to describe, locate, and engage in dialogue with prime prospects.

Today we see essentially five ways to find and talk to your best prospects: "fishing" (targeted messages), "mining" (targeted media), "panning" (list segmentation), "building" (in-house database), and "spelunking" (niche marketing). The first two have been around for a long time, but are taking on a new importance. And the second two represent a powerful new marketing force that is having a profound effect on traditional marketing strategy. The last is a traditional form of marketing being given a new lease on life by the computer database.

As we go through these five basic ways of prospecting, try force-fitting your own company's or product's prospects into each and see what ideas emerge for you.

1. Fishing for Prospects

Fishing for prospects is as old as advertising itself. It involves attracting an individual out of the total audience and delivering a message that is highly meaningful only to that prospect.

Fishing with Graphics

Fishing can be done with pictures as well as words. For example, a recent series of ads for Players cigarettes shows what seems to be a singles bar crowded with Yuppies having a wonderful time—many of them smoking, naturally. The wordless message is, "If you are this kind of person, you will have a wonderful time with this kind of cigarette."

Fishing with Words

Two classic direct-response advertising headlines ran for years and defined and attracted prime prospects. One was, "Do You Make These Mistakes in English?" (The prospect was someone who made mistakes in English *and was self-conscious about it.*)

The other was, "We're looking for people who like to draw." (The prospect was that one person out of—how many?—who has had an almost genetic compulsion toward sketching since the first grade in school and who is therefore a prime prospect for a home study course in art.)

Failure to visualize who the advertising is attempting to reach and to *call out* to prime prospects as they turn the page is the single greatest and most wasteful fault in print advertising today. (Chapter 6 discusses this issue in greater depth.)

The clever, punning headline which conceals the advantage or benefit offered by the advertising attracts people who enjoy cleverness and punning, including some prospects, but many other, busier prospects hurry on past, unaware that something of interest to them is hidden in the advertisement. Advertisers caught in the squeeze between rising media costs and declining audiences can no longer afford this luxury.

Chapter 9 will show how fishing can be combined with linkage to expose your prime prospects to many pages of advertising for only a fraction of what it would cost to schedule that many pages of publication advertising.

Fishing for Users of
Competitive Products

In a mature market with little room to expand, advertisers who want to grow are forced to try to steal customers from their competitors.

One fiendish way of fishing for competitors' customers is to offer a reward to a prospect who sends in proof of purchase of your *competitor's* product.

L'Oréal, for instance, ran an ad offering a free sample of its Avantage semipermanent haircolor lotion: "Loving Care users: L'Oréal wants you to change they way you color your gray. For free." And the reply coupon offered a free sample in exchange for a panel from Loving Care hair coloring *only.* ("Front panels from any other haircolor or Avantage cannot be accepted.")

This was L'Oréal's second use of the technique—they used the same technique a year earlier for their Preference permanent hair coloring. Reportedly, the success of the first campaign led to the second one.

The Values of VALS

Sometimes it is not enough to know that a prospect is someone who uses your kind of product. Within a product category, what motivates some prospects to choose one brand and some to choose another? Is there not some *psychic predilection* based on a prospect's value system that can be uncovered and targeted?

This question has led to the development of VALS (values and life-styles)—a method of classifying people according to their values and identifying their geographic distribution by neighborhoods. VALS can be used both for fishing and for "panning" for prospects.

Prior to the development of VALS, various efforts were made to classify consumers into psychological types. For instance, the advertising agency Benton & Bowles interviewed 2000 homemakers and identified six personality types; Outgoing Optimists and Conscientious Vigilants were two.

As an aid to developing a new laundry detergent for Procter & Gamble, Young & Rubicam classified homemakers as Practical Women, Convenience-Oriented Women, the Economy-Minded, the Traditionals, and the Experts. Needham, Harper & Steers identified five male and five female types, including the Self-Made Businessperson, the Frustrated Factory Worker, and the Militant Mother.

More recently, ATC, Time Inc.'s group of cable television companies, divided its prospective subscribers into four groups and targeted a different message to each: the Young and Busies, the TV Lovers, the

Prove-Its, and the Older Resolves. Each group received direct mail with special copy attuned to its different needs and attitudes.

The VALS system of classification, the best-known approach to typology, grew out of many years of study by Arnold Mitchell and others at the Stanford Research Institute (SRI) who were examining the effect of lifestyles and values on consumer buying decisions.

Throughout the early 1970s, Mitchell studied what effect the values of the baby boomers would have on the marketplace, and he searched for a way to classify them and other consumers. Finally, during a weekend in 1976, a light bulb went on in his mind—rather literally. Mitchell developed a bulb-shaped diagram constructed of nine different types of consumers. Borrowing terminology from David Riesman's *The Lonely Crowd,* Mitchell then grouped these types according to whether they were Need-Driven, Outer-Directed, or Inner-Directed.

At the base of the bulb were the two Need-Driven categories, the Survivors and the Sustainers. Above them, on one side, were the Outer-Directed types—the Belongers, the Emulators, and the Achievers. On the other side were the Inner-Directed folks—the I-Am-Me's, the Experientials, and the Societally Conscious. Finally, at the top of the bulb were the Integrated—those fortunate few who had it all together, who "meld the power of outer-directedness with the sensitivity of inner-directedness."

Mitchell developed the concept with elaborate portraits of each type, but it was still just a theory.

In 1980 the VALS project at SRI set out to validate the hypothesis with a field survey. They administered an 85-page questionnaire to 1635 subjects and developed a million bits of information about this cross-section of U.S. consumers.

A vast number of fascinating correlations emerged: Sustainers drink more instant-breakfast products than any other group. Emulators read more classified ads. Belongers go bowling three times more than I-Am-Me's. Societally Conscious are more likely to own dishwashers, garbage disposers, and food processors. Achievers play golf, drink cocktails before dinner, and have a lot of credit cards.

Armed with these data, VALS set about developing a number of services by which businesses could use this typology; by the mid-eighties it was a $2 million operation with 151 clients and a staff of 19.

By linking their findings with the census tract classification techniques of the mailing list services, VALS became able to tell you to which neighborhoods to mail if you wanted to reach a rich concentration of Belongers or Achievers. You could now analyze a cross-section of the best customers for your product, determine their psychological type, and then go looking for media and mailing lists with a high concentration of those VALS types.

VALS has influenced the thinking and decisions of a considerable number of advertisers.

Dr. Pepper had fought its way to number-4-brand position soft drink in national sales by 1980. But then Coke and Pepsi brought out sugar-free and caffeine-free line extensions and promoted them vigorously. Dr. Pepper sales began declining. So in 1985 the old "Be a Pepper" theme, aimed at Belongers, was traded in for a "Hold Out" campaign of zany humor commercials aimed at the Inner-Directed types.

Anheuser-Busch broke out VALS-based campaigns for Michelob and Michelob Light beers that pitched Michelob to Emulators ("Where you're going, it's Michelob") and Michelob Light to Achievers ("Oh, yes, you can have it all").

But you don't have to be a brand advertiser to use VALS. Although its classifications are open to criticism as arbitrary and overlapping—after all, some Achievers are Societally Conscious, for example, and so are some Belongers—the system is a useful way of thinking about a broad range of consumer marketing problems and targeting the consumers by psychological type. For instance, a home builder in San Antonio used the VALS system to design and sell 1400 homes.

Ray Ellison Homes conducted focus group research with three VALS types—Belongers, Achievers, and Societally Conscious. On the basis of the reactions of panel members to various proposed home features, the builder then designed a house for each type and developed a different targeted advertising campaign for each.

The Achiever campaign emphasized "sensible luxury." The Societally Conscious advertising showed a woman and her boyfriend sitting on the floor sharing a spaghetti dinner. The Belonger commercial featured a Hispanic family and was filled with the feel of tradition and family.

However, useful as it may be as a way of thinking about and approaching a marketing problem, VALS provides knowledge only about types of people, not about individual prospects and customers. VALS is a good place to go fishing for your kind of prospect, but, as you will see later, a more sophisticated method of targeting will now allow you to know more about your prime prospects, not as groups but as individuals.

2. Mining a Rich Vein of Prospects

Mining is the art and science of digging where there is a rich vein of prospects, that is, through specialized media. Obviously you are going to do better selling yachts in *Yachting World* than in *The New York Times*. For this reason, although the large general magazines such as *Life, Look, Collier's,* and *The Saturday Evening Post* were stricken by the onslaught of television, specialized magazines multiplied like weeds in the rich soil of the demassified market—everything from *Family Motor Coaching* and *Trout* to *Muscle Digest*.

But what if you are selling toothpaste or floor cleaner? There is no *Toothpaste Gazette* or *Floor Cleaning Digest*. Even if there were, the circulation would be rather small—and within it would be advertising by all your competitors. And so brand advertisers are increasingly turning to a brand-new marketplace, the "public database."

The Rise of the Public Database

A public database has already done most of the hard work for you. It has identified by name and address just about every household worth bothering with that *uses your product category but does not use your brand. Or has exactly the hobbies or equipment or lifestyle your product or service call for*. Talk about a rich vein of prospects! You can't get a richer concentration than 100 percent. You can coupon them, sample them, send them private advertising and not waste a drop.

Furthermore, your competitors don't know what you're doing, since your private message is hidden from view, so they can't neutralize your effort with a deliberate counter-promotion.

About the time that VALS was entering the marketplace, several companies acquired mainframe computer capability and offered such a public database by compiling data on the product usage, brand preferences, and family makeup of millions of U.S. households by name and address.

Lifestyle Selector handles the processing of warranty cards for dozens of major manufacturers. They have expanded their database by eliciting information on the families, pursuits, hobbies, and lifestyles of more than 12 million respondents who have returned warranty cards. In creating a database for the manufacturer, they obtain the right to make the information provided by the buyer available to other companies. Thus for a golf resort they can furnish lists of people who travel and who play golf.

Select and Save distributes questionnaires to 50 million households via Valassis free-standing inserts and targeted direct mail. Consumers are promised price-off coupons and/or samples for filling out and returning a questionnaire. The questionnaire inquires about category usage, brand preference, volume of consumption, length of purchase cycle, number of users per household, multiple-brand users, and special usage information such as size of the family pet. All this information is entered in the company's database. Then in co-op mailings, advertisers can enclose custom-tailored offers that reflect how the advertiser wants to treat each name. For instance, people known to be users of a competitor's product might receive a coupon with a larger cents-off value.

Donnelly's Carol Wright direct mail co-op, which reaches approximately 45 million households in 351 metro markets, now offers advertisers a targeting service called Share Force. Questionnaires on product and brand usage are distributed through the Carol Wright co-op twice a year. The response rate is about 14 percent, providing data on 6 million households. Respondents are rewarded with a small box of samples and coupons. In this way advertisers can give samples or coupons to self-identified nonusers of their products.

Even local supermarkets, drugstores, and other retailers can use this new technique of no-waste marketing. Until now, most supermarkets have joined with brand advertisers in wastefully distributing coupons or circulars to both customers and noncustomers throughout an entire market area.

CSI Telemarketing does telephone surveys of homes in a given area around a supermarket that wants to build its customer base. Respondents are asked what supermarket and drug store they patronize and what brands they use. Then only noncustomers can be selected to receive a mailing of coupons designed to woo them to pay the store a visit. Retailers pay CSI about $1 for each name of a competitive store's customer, manufacturers pay about 10 or 12 cents for the name of the user of another brand. CSI recently went public and hoped to expand its survey base to 10 million in 1986 and 20 million in 1987.

Although CSI obviously has a great deal of accumulated skills and expertise, if you are a retailer, nothing should prevent you from adapting this basic principle to your own needs with your own local resources. You can determine by telephone survey which households in your trading area are patronizing a competitor's store, and then send targeted direct mail to those households with special new-customer offers.

Twenty Million Households You Can Know by Name and Shopping Habits

JFY is responsible for perhaps the most ambitious undertaking in profiling households by name and address. This company began in 1979 with a pilot database of 20,000 households which had answered a questionnaire about product and brand usage. By 1983 JFY was mailing out a fairly elaborate questionnaire to 40 million households a year and getting back 8 million replies (response is stimulated by a vague promise of coupons and samples).

Which toothpaste do you use? Which coffee? How many smokers are in the family and which brands do they smoke? Do you color your hair? Do you diet? Do you own a dog? Do you often order things by mail? How many credit cards do you carry? Which ones? Do you have a universal life insurance policy? With which company? Do you plan to buy a new American-made car in the next 6 months? A house? A personal computer? A trip to Europe? How old are family members? What is the family income bracket? All this and more is entered in the JFY database for use by mailers.

Advertisers can obtain the names and addresses of respondents in their category on an exclusive or nonexclusive basis. Unlike one-time list rental, clients receive a computer tape of the names and addresses which they can keep and use as often as they wish.

Even a database of 8 million households with information on which services and products each uses is not large enough to interest some advertisers with full national distribution. Thus in mid-1985 JFY's president, Harry Dale, announced that by using both mail and phone surveys the company could now make available data on 14 million households and expected to increase that number to 20 million in the future.

Among the early users attracted by JFY services were R.J. Reynolds, Seagram, and General Foods.

An Impressive Example of No-Waste Advertising

The revolutionary potential of this new marketing tool was demonstrated in a test that broke new ground for a leading pharmaceutical company.

Menly and James tested four ways to reach the target audience for Ecotrin, an aspirin product specifically for people who suffer from arthritis. The goal was to get target prospects to try Ecotrin medication and then to remain loyal.

The control was a coupon ad in free-standing inserts in Sunday newspapers. Three direct-mail packages were tested against the control. They were mailed to a list of arthritis sufferers provided by JFY.

Certain details of this case history have not been made public, but we can assume that the packages were mailed to arthritis sufferers who were not currently using Ecotrin medication, since the purpose was to get new customers.

The three direct-mail offers and the response rates were:

1. Free sample enclosed, plus coupon good for 50 cents off the price of a full-size package—over 50 percent redemption

2. $1 coupon enclosed—over 50 percent redemption

3. Send for a free sample—75 percent response

A startling result of these offers was that the cost per redemption of the direct mail with the $1 coupon was as low as that of the free-standing insert (fsi)—and that is cost *before* the waste in the fsi ad due to misredemption is figured in. The results debunk the notion that direct mail is necessarily a more costly medium for distributing coupons.

The other shocker was the 75 percent response to the offer of a sample. Although direct-mail response generally varies widely by list and offer, response is commonly assumed to be no more than a few percent. The 75 percent response to the Ecotrin medication sample shows that the arithmetic of direct-mail promotion can be favorable for even a low-price shelf product like Ecotrin. If the mailing cost $375 per thousand or less (including JFY's charge) and produced 750 responses per thousand, that means it cost Menly and James only 50 cents each to obtain the names and addresses of keenly interested nonusers of their products.

What use is being made of the names and addresses of the people who requested a sample has not been revealed. The MaxiMarketing way would be to seek to convert them to loyal usage with a series of private messages and promotions. Telephone surveys of a random sample of the names could determine if this strategy were succeeding.

The Arithmetic of Marketing Directly to Known Users of Competing Brands

To mass marketers accustomed to thinking in terms of reaching and influencing millions of magazine readers or television households, prospects and nonprospects alike, the traditionally small percentages of direct-mail response may not seem worth the bother. But the new art of marketing directly to consumers known to use your competitor's brand requires an entirely new way of thinking about direct mail and of interpreting the results.

Figure 7 is a visual forecast of the possible result of a mailing plan for promotion of an expensive brand of liquor. Let us assume this brand sells for around $20 a bottle. The advertiser has secured through JFY the names of 100,000 drinkers who used two leading competing brands selling for around $12 a bottle. We prepare a mailing inviting these drinkers to try our brand and see the difference and we enclose an $8 gift certificate to pay the difference.

Figure 7 depicts our working assumption that 5 percent of the recipients of our mailing would accept our offer and use the certificate. (This

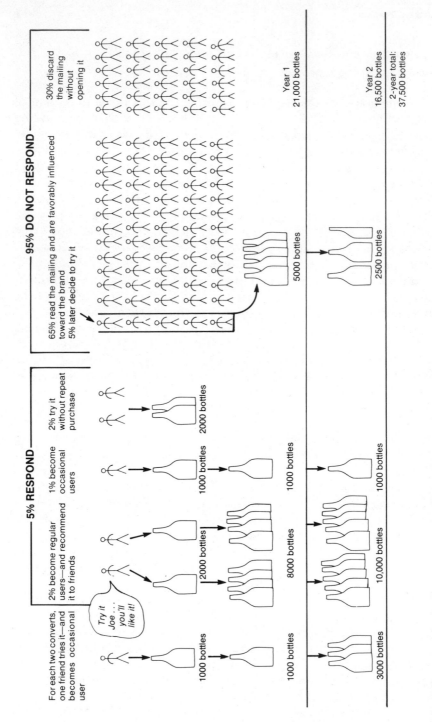

FIGURE 7. A Possible Outcome of Mailing to 100,000 Known Users of Your Competitor's Brand of Liquor.

42

is a conservative assumption—remember that the Menly and James mailing saw the enclosure of a $1 coupon produce a response 10 times as great—over 50 percent redemption. We chose a much more conservative estimate here because a bottle of premium liquor is a more serious, costly purchase.)

Now a 5 percent response, or a sale of 5000 bottles to 100,000 names, doesn't sound like much. But, as the figure shows, there is much more involved. At the extreme right of Figure 7 are the 95 percent who did not respond. Of these, we assume that 30 percent tossed away the mailing without even bothering to open it. The remaining 65 percent opened the envelope and glanced through the mailing. They did not use the certificate, but 5000 of them—just 1 out of every 20—received a favorable impression of the brand from the mailing and eventually purchased one bottle anyway. (This aspect of direct mail—the *advertising impression made on nonresponders*—is receiving increasing attention in marketing circles.)

Of the 5000 mailing recipients who did respond, our forecast predicts that 2000 will merely use the certificate and then return to their old brand, 1000 respondents will be sufficiently pleased by their trial to buy 1 more bottle, and 2000 respondents—just 2 percent—will become converted enthusiasts. After their trial, each will buy 4 more bottles. Furthermore, because of their enthusiasm, their word-of-mouth advertising will be quite effective and half of them—1 enthusiast out of 100 mail recipients—will influence 1 friend to buy 1 bottle.

That's just the first year. In the second year, the enthusiastic converts each buy 5 more bottles. The persuaded friends each buy 3 more bottles. The semienthusiasts each buy 1 more bottle. And half of the favorably impressed nonrespondents who had purchased 1 bottle each now buy 1 additional bottle.

So we end up with a projected grand total of 37,500 bottles sold in the first 2 years as a direct result of the mailing to 100,000 liquor consumers—quite a different picture from the 5000 bottles sold that might be superficially assumed to be the total sales return.

Note that we are not talking here about just plain-and-simple distribution of sales promotion by solo direct mail. It is obviously uneconomic to mail out a discount coupon at random for perhaps $200 per thousand or more when it can be distributed by co-op or fsi for as little as $5 per thousand.

Four factors in the hypothetical liquor mailing outlined here set it apart from routine sales-promotion direct mail and make it cost-effective:

1. There is zero waste circulation. We are mailing only to prime prospects—known users of competing brands.

2. In addition to the gift certificate, the mailing contains a four-page letter with potent, persuasive brand advertising. So it influences the buying attitude of many nonrespondents as well as respondents.

3. The total sales effect of the mailing on respondents, friends, and nonrespondents over a 2-year period is estimated and factored in. (Postresearch could pin down the numbers.)

4. Names and addresses of respondents are captured by entry in a customer database where they can be used in the future for reinforcement direct advertising, research, holiday gift promotion, and the other uses of a customer database you will read about in Chapter 10.

An Interesting Cost Comparison

In this example, the net profit from the accountable sales comes close to returning the cost of promotion—and the advertiser gains up to 9000 new users for each 100,000 direct mailings.

JFY has done an interesting analysis comparing the true cost of delivering one 30-second television image with the cost of delivering what they call a "tangible sales kit" (a direct-mail package) to a targeted prospect known to use your category but not your brand.

JFY started with the assumption that one showing of a 30-second prime-time television spot costs around $138,000, including amortized production costs. After subtracting (1) the number of households in which the sets were turned off, (2) the residents who were watching noncommercial television, and (3) the households that were recording the program for later viewing and zapping the commercials out during playback, JFY then divided the remaining households over three networks. They ended up with a hypothetical audience of 11.5 million households. So the cost per thousand households watching the commercial ($138,000 divided by 11.5 million multiplied by 1000) would be $12.

However, two additional factors erode this figure: (1) Not every household is a user of the product category advertised, and (2) according to the research firm, Burke, the average "day-after recall" of a commercial is only a little more than 20 percent. (In the interest of simplicity, let's call it exactly 20 percent.) How these additional factors affect the cost per thousand prospects influenced by one showing of our 30-second spot is shown in the table on page 45. As this table shows, if only 25 percent of the households who are watching use your kind of product, your cost of delivering to them just one 30-second commercial they can recall the next day is $230 per thousand—about the cost of a simple

Category incidence (percent)	Households using category (millions)	Households recalling commercial next day (20 percent) (millions)	Cost per thousand category user households recalling commercial next day (dollars)
100	11.5	2.3	60
75	8.6	1.7	81
50	5.8	1.2	115
25	2.9	0.6	230

direct-mail package. And a flight of 100 commercials will cost $23,000 per thousand prospects or $23 per prospect!

The kind of information in a public database such as JFY's was once prohibitively expensive to maintain on a timely basis. Now even the company whose market share and ad budget are tiny when compared with the leaders in a category can use a wealth of individual buyer data as the basis for innovative marketing strategies. What could *you* do with the names of thousands or millions of your competitor's product or service customers in hand?

There is another kind of public database which is not new but which should not be overlooked—the mailing list. List brokers have thousands of lists for rent, names of people compiled from public records and of people who have responded to an offer or a plea. If your price and margin are high enough to afford direct mail's high cost per thousand, somewhere there are lists of people who closely match your target profile. And it may be more efficient to reach them simply by communicating directly with them (instead of through broadcast or publication advertising) whether you want them to buy directly from you or from one of your retail outlets.

Madison Avenue has been slow to realize the potential for dramatic sales increases provided by public databases and targeted mailing lists. Marketing directors, ad managers, and their counterparts at the advertising agencies would much rather focus attention on the highly visible world of television advertising, where reputations rise and fall on the "creativity" of the latest campaign to be placed by the new ad agency just hired to replace yesterday's creative shop.

Just think what you could be doing to steal a march on your competition by focusing your agency's creativity on the task of talking directly to your best prospects and using the wealth of information now readily available to make your private advertising break new ground and new sales records.

3. Panning for Pure Gold Prospects

The third way to reach targeted prospects is *panning*, which involves sifting promising names through ever-finer screens until only nuggets of pure gold remain in your pan.

To take an extreme example, suppose you are marketing expensive high-style jeans for petite female redheads. Your market research or past sales tell you that only in Texas and California are female redheads interested in high-style jeans. Trying to reach them with mass advertising would be prohibitively wasteful and inefficient, but there is no existing list of affluent, petite, female jeans wearers living in California or Texas. What to do?

Well, sophisticated list compilers could help you. They might start by locating rental lists of mail-order customers of petite fashions and renting only those names and addresses on the lists that are in Texas and California. Then against this list they could overlay or "merge-purge" computerized lists of mail-order purchasers of jeans of all sizes and lists of females residing in affluent neighborhoods. They might even contact Clairol and L'Oréal to work out a reciprocal exchange (you provide your names later) to identify the redheads. The final result would be a compiled list of people who closely fit the description of the prospect. (A *merge-purge,* for the uninitiated, is exactly what it sounds like. You merge two computer files of names and addresses into one and then purge from the combined list all of the duplicates of the names that appear twice. Thus you are left with a combined list of unduplicated names. The purged duplicates, or "multihit" names, form a separate list of people who have the characteristic of *both* lists.)

When *INC. Magazine* was about to be launched, its innovative publisher, Bernard Goldhirsch, faced an unusual problem. He perceived a need for a magazine to advise and guide smaller entrepreneurial companies which couldn't afford the battery of attorneys, financial advisors, and marketing consultants that giant corporations were able to employ.

The ideal prospects for the magazine would be subscribers to something like . . . well, like *INC.*! In other words, the ideal prospect list or audience for the magazine—owners and top executives of small entrepreneurial companies—did not yet exist. The gold nuggets would have to be assembled by panning. With the help of Donn Rappaport, chairman of American List Counsel, Inc., they assembled, merged, and purged many likely lists of people who had responded to related offers.

As you continue to merge and purge, the names dwindle down to a precious few. If you then apply the relentless arithmetic of direct-mail response to an opportunity to purchase something, which means that ordinarily at best only a few people out of 100 accept your offer, your precious few dwindle down to a few percent of a precious few.

Goldhirsch knew he needed substantial circulation right away, in order to interest advertisers. However, simply to mail to a large compiled list of thousands of small- and medium-size companies would not produce the desired numbers, since compiled names (as in a directory) never respond as well as lists of somebody else's customers or responders.

So, in a master stroke of database marketing, Goldhirsch's staff merged the list of *The Wall Street Journal* subscribers and a list of U.S. companies identifiable by annual volume. Then they purged nonbusiness *Journal* subscribers and subscribers connected to large companies. What remained was a solid-gold list of *executives of smaller companies who had proven their responsiveness by subscribing to The Wall Street Journal.*

Altogether, it took *2 years* to compile the prospect database of 1.2 million names. Even with that many prospects, the normal response rates of 3,4,5, or even 6 or 7 percent you would expect from a subscription offer for a new magazine still would not have provided the impressive circulation figures that Goldhirsch needed. So, in another daring stroke contrary to what magazine experts would ordinarily advise, he began to send sample copies to portions of the database in rotation. This accomplished two things: It added to the number of monthly circulated copies he could promise advertisers, and it produced a phenomenal response—not 4, 5, or 6 percent but 20, 30, and 40 percent. In its infancy the magazine was able to zoom to a paid circulation of around 400,000, a heavy number in the business publications field.

The New Powers of List Segmentation

Companies like Claritas, National Decision Marketing, CACI, National Demographics and Lifestyles, Donnelley Marketing, and R. L. Polk have been able to classify the households in the United States's 36,000 zip zones and 206,000 carrier routes into a number of describable homogeneous socioeconomic family groups. For instance, Claritas has identified 160 zip zones it calls Black Enterprise clusters, inhabited by "upscale, white-collar black families in major urban fringes."

List segmentation by type of neighborhood is only the second generation of targeting by mailing address. The third generation, just emerging, describes and locates not just homogeneous groups but individual households by name and address.

Persoft, Inc. has introduced a $375,000 mainframe-based software package for large mailers that can predict with impressive accuracy which individuals on any mailing list are most likely to respond. Applying such factors as geographic and demographic characteristics and buying history, they can rank each individual on the list by likelihood to respond. Theoretically, the system can score by as many as 1000 characteristics. Early in 1986, Persoft drastically lowered the price of entry for small business customers.

The first season Brookstone used the Persoft system to select names for their catalog mailing, they were able to get 70 to 80 percent as many orders by mailing to only 50 percent as many names. This resulted in a significant increase in profit contribution per catalog mailed.

This technology has so far interested chiefly large direct-marketing companies, but it is undoubtedly the wave of the future for many kinds of advertisers. For example, retailers can now avail themselves of this capability through new software which tracks in-store purchases the way a catalog merchant tracks the history of a mail-order customer. Higbee's, a retailer with 13 stores in Cleveland and surrounding areas, is among the retailers now using this new approach.

The program enables the retailers to keep detailed information on a customer's recency, frequency, total dollar purchases, type of merchandise, and preference indicators by taste, price levels, and size ranges. By adding census data, the retailers can then determine (1) where their best and worst customers live, (2) what census characteristics they have, and (3) which types of census tract are therefore most likely and least likely to respond to certain mailed offers. This allows a store to mail profitably beyond the limits of its charge-card list.

4. Building Your Own Prospect Database

The ultimate in sophisticated database prospecting is to construct and maintain your own permanent in-house prospect database. As you add names and bits of information to each name, you learn more and more about who, what, and where your prime prospects are. Out of this database you can build a subgroup of prospects for any specific marketing objective.

In considering this option, keep in mind that direct mail is no longer a costly medium with relatively low response rates best suited for high-margin direct-marketing offers. Rather, the new targeting capabilities of public and private databases make possible response rates that make direct mail a cost-effective medium even for low-cost, low-margin products. (Next time you are considering your media options, call in a database marketing specialist for advice on what the suddenly glamorous new world of direct-mail targeting might be able to accomplish for you.)

Tourism Canada, a branch of the Canadian government's Department of Regional Industrial Expansion, offers an outstanding example of in-house database marketing. To attract U.S. tourists, the department had been sending mailings to prospects in the United States, principally to prospects who hunt, fish, or engage in other outdoor activities. Around 1982, they decided they weren't realizing the full potential of the program, and they brought an experienced professional on board, Aimee Britten.

One of Britten's first moves was to confer with their agency, Business Services Inc., asking how to expand the program and get better results. Might there be a sizable market of people who were not active outdoors? What about tourists who wanted to visit Canada for its cities, history, and culture? Were trips self-planned or arranged through a travel agent? How were tourists traveling?

To begin answering these questions, Tourism Canada restructured one mailing to prequalified prospects to include a detailed reply coupon and questionnaire. It asked respondents for their age, occupation, travel frequency, travel interests, and so on.

The information provided by the replies was entered in the database, along with the keyed source of the advertising that generated the response. This database is updated constantly, and allows Tourism Canada to tailor mailings and ads to appropriate market segments.

No longer do families that plan their own trips receive mailings that tell them to contact their travel agent. Nor does a 60-year-old librarian who is interested in visiting Montreal receive brochures about fishing and resorts. And the source code identifies exactly which mailing piece, list, publication, or ad produces the best results from specific target groups.

Results aren't results until a prospect becomes a customer. An ingenious feature of the campaign tracks actual visits to Canada by respondents in the database. A prepaid business reply card is enclosed with each fulfillment package. Returning the card makes the respondent eligible for a premium or a prize, but to qualify, *the card must be mailed in Canada.* This tells the department not only which and how many of the inquirers actually visited Canada, but also exactly where they went.

Most U.S. state tourist bureau programs are not as sophisticated. State legislatures are glad to spend money on advertising to tout their state's attractions, but they don't understand enough about MaxiMarketing to spend an additional amount for the prospect database system needed to get full value for their advertising dollars.

Chrysler Corporation used a semipermanent prospect database that was compiled annually to promote its new Laser in 1983, a sports car designed to compete with such models as the Camaro, Firebird, and Mazda RX-7. From their annually compiled prospect database, they selected households which (1) owned competitive make cars, (2) bought new cars frequently, (3) switched makes when they bought, and (4) lived in areas with dealer coverage. These names then received not just a mailing but a mailing campaign, including the local dealer's name and address and a reply card which could be used to order the Laser catalog.

Kimberly-Clark's Huggies disposable diapers division offers perhaps the most dramatic example of the shift toward selective database marketing by a packaged-goods marketer. In Kimberly-Clark's consumer products group, operating profit rose 40 percent in the first quarter of 1985 compared to the previous year. The increase was attributed almost entirely to Huggies, which was reported to have captured 25 percent of the $2.7 billion disposable diapers market. They gained 10 share points in a single year against the formidable opposition of Procter & Gamble's Luvs and Pampers diapers, which together had dominated the market.

How did they do it? By a number of innovative moves, including a revolutionary departure from traditional marketing strategy. Out of a total advertising budget of around $35 million, the company reportedly spent $25 million on awareness advertising in broadcast and publication media and $10 million on database direct-mail marketing to new mothers.

They have constructed a database program which can identify by name 75 percent of the 3.5 million new mothers each year. They start by getting the name of the expectant mother from the hospital or doctor. The mother receives very personal letters which include beautifully prepared educational pamphlets about caring for a new baby—communication which builds a relationship with the mother. When she has returned home with her new baby and needs diapers, Huggies cents-off coupons arrive to cash in on the good will created by the mailings.

Furthermore, Kimberly-Clark now had a priceless by-product, a huge and annually growing database of information about parents and children by name and address. This database is as much a company asset as factories and forests. It can be used, if they choose, as a market for many products other than disposable diapers. For instance, they could, a few years later, offer the mother a series of beginning readers for the kindergarten child . . . printed, of course, on Kimberly-Clark paper!

But isn't such a program prohibitively costly? Kimberly-Clark, by thinking in the MaxiMarketing mode, changed the rules of the game. They based their arithmetic on the fact that a family that uses premium-quality disposable diapers spends $1300 on them in the first 2 years of the child's life. By focusing on the *lifetime value* of a customer (total sales) rather than the value of a unit sale, the company found that if the entire loyalty-building program increased the number of regular Huggies diaper users by just 1 percent, it would pay for itself. Reportedly the program is doing much better than that.

Murphy Realty/Better Homes & Gardens of Bergen County, New Jersey, has developed what is surely the last word in a prospect database. It is a database of *future* home-buying prospects.

In 1975, Murphy sent out a mailing to 75,000 Bergen County households offering information on Murphy's services. It included a questionnaire with such questions as, "What type home are you presently living in? How long do you intend to stay in your present home? What factors make a move unlikely within 5 years? What factors would influence you to move? If you do plan to move in the future, what type of home will you be looking for?" Signing the questionnaire was optional. Within 3 weeks of the mailing, Murphy had received a 4 percent reponse, and half of these were signed with the names and addresses of respondents.

Murphy was now in a position to accelerate the buying decision (and to get to the prospect long before the competition!). If an appropriate property came on the market, Murphy could approach a likely future prospect and say, in effect, "Look, I know you said you weren't planning to buy a new house until a year or two from now. But since market conditions and interest rates are favorable right now, and I have something that is right up your alley, I thought you might like to consider it." (Plus, undoubtedly: "And don't worry about selling your present house. We can take care of that for you too.")

It was reported that Better Homes & Gardens was so impressed with the system that they planned to introduce it nationally. Doing so could effect a major change in the way residential real estate is bought and sold.

Chevrolet has tested a similar strategy in magazine advertising aimed at career women. The ad sought to involve and reassure the reader *before* she "comes on the market" as an active car shopper.

To accomplish this, they developed an innovative ad consisting of four pages in color plus a full-page card insert. One page promoted a jazzy model that a young career woman might fancy—the Celebrity Eurosport. One page was devoted to fashion- and career-oriented "you" copy. And two whole pages were devoted to supporting the card insert, which happens to be a credit application that folds up to form a postage-paid reply mailer.

If the application is approved, the prospect can take her letter of approval to her Chevy dealer with the reassuring knowledge that "you're a preferred customer before you walk through the door." If the car she wants is in stock, she "may be able to drive it home the same day," a mighty exciting and appealing notion.

Like Murphy, like Chevrolet, try to develop a relationship with your target prospects before your competitors even know they are prospects (and maybe even before the prospects realize it themselves!).

5. Spelunking for Prospects

Spelunking is the exploration of caves. A cave is really a deep niche, right? Ergo, "Spelunking for prospects" is our name for *niche marketing*. There are essentially two kinds of niche marketing:

1. Find a new niche for your product.

2. Find products for a niche waiting to be explored.

Searle's Metamucil campaign in the early eighties afforded a fascinating example of finding a new niche while not endangering or confusing the existing market. It is also an outstanding example of MaxiMarketing, incorporating many of the principles in this book. Among other things, Searle exhibited an intelligent use of targeted couponing, in striking contrast to the wasteful mass couponing we see so often and will discuss in a later chapter.

Traditionally, Metamucil Laxative has been popular with the laxative market—largely elderly people and lower-income people with poor dietary habits who have problems with "regularity." But there is a much larger niche, if it could be reached and persuaded, of people who do *not* necessarily have a health problem. On the contrary, they are health and fitness conscious and may be into dieting, jogging, working out.

Many of these people have already been persuaded that a "fiber supplement" is part of a fitness program. If Searle could reposition Metamucil as a fiber supplement, part of everyday fitness, a whole new market could open up. But it might be at the expense of the old market if the repositioning were done in media to which Metamucil's usual customers were exposed.

To resolve this dilemma, Searle turned to private advertising and database marketing. They targeted three groups:

1. *Dieters,* to whom the appeal would be "feel fuller, eat less, and get the fiber your dieting body needs."

2. *Laxative users* selected from the JFY database as more upscale and urban than the typical Metamucil user and known to use a competitive product.

3. *Young urban professionals* who don't habitually use a laxative but are aware that their bodies need fiber and that they may not necessarily be treating their bodies right. If this niche could be persuaded to make Metamucil a daily habit, like taking a multivitamin, the sales potential could be huge.

The economics of the program allowed about $3 for acquisition of a customer. A customer was defined as a person who would buy two boxes of Metamucil Instant Mix at retail within a year.

A test mailing in the form of an economic self-mailer targeted to its specific audience was sent to a random sample of each group. The post-paid reply card offered free samples, a "calendar of coupons" (40 cents off each month for a year), and a booklet of health tips.

The overall response rate was more than 15 percent. Thus the advertising cost per inquiry was a little more than $1. If only one out of three of the respondents became customers, the program would be a success. And the percentage of respondents who did become customers was probably much better than that, since the respondents had already demonstrated a keen interest in what the product had to offer just by responding to the offer.

How would Searle know which respondents actually became customers? The name and address of each respondent was assigned a serial number, which was printed on the back of every one of the 12 monthly coupons. As these coupons trickled through the retailer and coupon clearinghouse, the serial numbers were picked up and recorded, allowing an ongoing observation of the effectiveness of the program. This gave Searle not only the macro results you ordinarily get by counting coupons but also the names and addresses of tryers, buyers, and multiunit buyers of their product. Searle could then use one kind of offer to turn non-tryers into tryers and another kind to turn tryers into regular users—and increase the lifetime value of each new customer.

Halbert's provides an impressive example of finding a product for a niche. Their niche would probably never occur to you and might not sound very promising, but Halbert's has managed to parlay it into a $20+ million-a-year business. Their niche—with many alcoves—is simply families with the same Irish surname.

Four times a week, a group of 50 people (just enough to fill one tour bus) leaves the United States and Canada for a 10-day Halbert's tour of Ireland. All 50 have the same Irish surname.

Tour group members are signed up by computer-customized mailings: "Dear Friend: On behalf of the Ancient and Royal Clan McCLURE and the men, women, and children of Ireland, it gives me great pleasure to invite you and your family to attend the historic Grand Reunion of the

McCLURES in Ireland. . . ." Those who respond by asking for more information receive a follow-up conversion mailing and, if necessary, a phone call.

The company started filling up four busloads a week this way in 1981, at a charge per tour of $1995, and later indicated it was planning to extend this strategy to other ethnic groups. A little simple arithmetic—$1995 × 50 people × 4 groups a week × 52 weeks—indicates an annual sales volume of $20 million from this one application of highly targeted niche marketing. In this age of the personal computer, small businesses can often find and fill a niche that is not big enough for larger companies to bother with.

Murder by the Book is a small mysteries-only bookstore in Portland, Oregon, started by Jill Hinckley. She has observed that many mystery fans are addicts who devour two or three mystery novels a week. Usually they have distinct tastes in types of mystery—some enjoy locked-room puzzlers; some, hard-boiled private eye yarns; some, realistic police detective stories; some, international spy thrillers; and so on—and have difficulty finding enough titles that won't disappoint them. So the bookstore is planning a national advisory service which will classify subscribers into perhaps 20 types by computer and keep the readers in each group informed on titles suited to their individual taste.

Of course, the catalog field is filled—indeed, jammed—with examples of entrepreneurs who have found products for a niche and are reaping the rewards. There are catalogs with products for retired people, children, invalids, gourmets, cooks, gardeners, large women, large men, petite women, hunting and fishing enthusiasts, gadget freaks, kite flyers, book lovers, do-it-yourselfers—and every season somebody finds another niche that needs to be filled.

Is there an undiscovered niche lying in wait for your product or service? Or an empty niche for which you could create a brand-new product or service? Why not get out your miner's headlamp and go spelunking and see?

The Bottom Line

Before you do anything else, you need to find out who and where your best prospects are and what are the most efficient ways to reach them. A market research firm can help you develop the profile of your best prospects. So can psychographic classification systems like VALS. So can the actions of your prospects and customers, through the kinds of appeals they respond to and the information they can provide on questionnaires.

You can invite your likely prospects to identify themselves by responding to targeted appeals and offers in the available media. And you can go straight to the best prospects by selecting them either from a public database or from a one-time, semipermanent database you construct from available list data.

By following one or more of the five basic patterns of targeting, you will take the first step toward minimizing the waste of your advertising dollars and maximizing the effect of your marketing strategy.

4

Maximized Media: The New Embarrassment of Riches

The Big Picture

Along with the proliferation of products and services and the segmentation of types of prospects has come an extraordinary proliferation of media. There are new kinds of media, new developments in the traditional media, and new uses for media. Increasingly, the new media are tools for targeting rather than for blanketing the mass market. As we review these new media possibilities, ask yourself, "Is there something here for my company?" Just one or two new kinds of buy could breathe new life into long-standing media buying habits.

You can't use them all, but you need to know the wide range of choices that exist in order to make the most intelligent and cost-effective selections. And because there are so many choices, the need for greater accountability and a means to measure comparative cost-effectiveness when you try the new media becomes acute.

The Winegrowers of California test-marketed a new television campaign in the Northeast in the fall of 1985. California wines make up about 60 percent of national wine sales, but sales in the East had been below 50 percent and going down. Imported wines had been able to compete on price because of the strong dollar and foreign government subsidies.

The two 30-second spots tested featured Julia Child giving suggestions on the proper wines to serve at lunch or dinner. The spots included a toll-free number that consumers could call for free, non-brand-specific wine tips. Inclusion of the number would also "provide a gauge on how the ads are being received," according to the management supervisor of the advertiser's agency.[1]

From our point of view, this test is a step in the right direction in the new world of advertising media. The advertising involves the consumer, and it provides a method of measuring real-world consumer reaction to the message and medium being used.

But we would like to see the Winegrowers of California go even further. A complete MaxiMarketing strategy would include *comparing* the responses from two or more messages and/or from two or more media.

The reason for this is that evaluation of effectiveness is much more difficult without some kind of yardstick. Over the long pull, the test campaign might be able to prove its cost effectiveness in actual sales in the test market. But what if it didn't? How would you know which piece in the strategy needed fixing? Comparative response data could provide clues.

Another MaxiMarketing refinement would be to enter the names of callers in a database. After all, these are prime prospects, people concerned enough about the correct choice of wine to make a phone call for more information. Then the Winegrowers could go to its member vintners and say, "Let's do a co-op mailing to these people. Prepare your own leaflet on your own brand, and we'll insert it in our co-op mailing envelope and mail it for you for just a penny or two per prospect." Finally, the co-op could include offers and rebates on specific brands and provide a basis for measurement of sales.

We have focused on the hidden possibilities in this test campaign to make an important point about the MaxiMarketing approach to media. In the demassified market, you must deal with an extraordinary proliferation not only of market segments and of products created to satisfy them but also of ways the prospect can find out about the product. These ways include not only new ways to use old media but also entirely new media.

Edsel Ford II, general marketing manager of Ford's Lincoln-Mercury division, complained in a talk to an auto writers group that he didn't know of an advertising medium that he considered effective enough for reaching women. He pointed out that 40 percent of new cars sold are registered to women and an additional 50 percent of sales are strongly influenced by women.

Ford expressed doubts that women's magazines were the answer. "I believe there is another way," he said, "but I don't know what it is."[2]

"The advertising industry, whether it likes it or not, will have to come to grips with a whole new way of advertising," says an entrepreneur named Stuart Young. His own particular "whole new way" is "ambient video" or "video wallpaper"—moving images to be displayed continuously in discos, bars, restaurants, cruise ships, and international flights, with or without advertising messages woven in.[3]

Hardly a week passes without another media innovation like this, proposed or proved, making news. The advertiser wandering in this wonderland of media possibilities without a cold-blooded method of evaluating sales effectiveness can be like a ship ploughing through dark waters without a compass.

Furthermore, you must steer between the Scylla and Charybdis of timidity and foolhardiness. If you are too timid, your competitor may race on ahead of you. But if you are too bold, you may fritter away your precious advertising resources on the latest novelties in media and end up with nothing to show for them.

We cannot provide here a definitive treatment of all the available media opportunities today. What we *would* like to do here is to open your eyes to some of the startling developments in media, and to stimulate you to consider which might apply to the product, service, or business you wish to promote.

You will find that many, probably most, of the media possibilities mentioned here are too "far out" for what you are selling. But if you get just one exciting, profitable idea, then looking at all of them will have proved to be well worthwhile. Gaining familiarity with what is available can arm you with the right questions to ask the next time a so-called media expert stops by to sell you on staying with the tried-and-true familiar choices.

However, if you find you are too tempted by too many of these avenues, we urge you to apply, whenever and wherever possible, some strict test of accountability in experimenting with these new media opportunities. Without such accountability, in the form of measurable sales or responses, you may never know whether you have spent your money wisely.

Campbell Soup Company has pioneered in exploration of unconventional media while insisting on measurability. "As TV prices continue to escalate," Paul Mulcahy, president of Campbell's in-house agency, pointed out, "advertisers operating on marginal budgets will have to find somewhere else to go."

Campbell's has been spending up to $3 million a year on such experimental media as parking meters, church bulletins, shopping carts, radio snowstorm reports, ski lift tickets, and in-store ads. But, insists George Mahrlig, the company's director of media services, "Our media choices may be unorthodox, but they're not serendipitous. *The common denominator is their measurability.*"[4] (Italics added.)

We will start with new developments in established media, and then briefly survey a number of other new forms which have varying degrees of promise.

What's New in Newspaper Advertising

TMC and SMC.   Total market coverage (TMC) and its sexy cousin, selective market coverage (SMC), are the biggest developments in newspaper advertising since free-standing inserts. Most daily newspapers cover about 60 percent of their markets. That's fine if you're aiming at an upscale market. Compared to television viewers, heavy newspaper readers include more than twice as many college graduates and households with more than $25,000-per-year incomes.

Daily newspapers also make a very desirable medium if you want to add weight to a national ad campaign which has a foundation of network television. Newspaper advertising enables you to focus on the prospects your television spots may be missing in major markets where sales are greatest.

But many advertisers, including aggressive retailers, want 100 percent coverage of the market. So to drown out the siren song of direct-mail services and free "penny saver" newspapers that offer 100 percent coverage at an attractive price, more and more newspapers have developed a TMC vehicle. By 1984 there were an estimated 1000 to 1200 TMC or "alternative distribution" systems. Today at least 9 out of 20 daily newspapers offer such a service.

Some TMCs are simply an expanded special edition of the daily published a certain day of the week and mailed or delivered free to nonsubscribers. Some are a kind of community weekly or feature magazine distributed free to nonsubscribers. Some are simply a bundle of advertisements delivered with or without a wrapper to the homes of nonsubscribers. But all can give you the additional reach into homes not covered by the paid circulation.

Those TMCs with some kind of editorial format argue that they offer you a significant advantage over direct mail, "shared mail," or co-ops, because people say they feel more favorably inclined toward newspaper advertising than toward co-op mail. TMC advertising may also offer you a cost advantage over shared mail because the newspaper portion of the total coverage is delivered more cheaply than direct mail.

However, if you are an independent retailer, you may be even more interested in the opportunities offered by SMCs. For instance, the *Los Angeles Times* has divided its market area into 109 geographical grids. An advertiser can select 1 grid, covering 6000 homes, or as many as the entire 109, covering 2.8 million homes. In addition, the newspaper offers 15 suburban editions. So a neighborhood retailer, by advertising in the suburban edition covering its market area, and then supplementing it with SMC shared mail to nonsubscribers just within its immediate area, can easily arrange a concentrated punch at a manageable cost. "Our sales double for at least three days after we use it," according to a retailer in Santa Monica quoted in an advertisement for the service.

Ethnic SMCs are a new tool for targeting an ethnic market. In September 1985, newspapers in cities with large Hispanic population began including in selected neighborhoods a four-color magazine section called *Vista*. It kicked off with a minimum of 427,000 copies and claimed to be the largest circulation periodical ever for the Hispanic market, a community that numbers 20 million and represents annual purchasing power of $70 billion.

Free-Standing Inserts. Free-standing inserts (fsi's) began appearing around 1968 and now come pouring out of the Sunday paper like a cascade of autumn leaves. They offer an aggressive retailer an opportunity to use quality color printing and to display an entire catalog of sale merchandise. (Through newspapers and shared mail, K-Mart has been distributing as many as 120 million inserts per *week*!) And the multiadvertiser fsi's with price-off coupons and mail-order ads provide brand advertisers of package goods with just about the cheapest distribution of coupons available. The newspaper industry has been lobbying the Audit Bureau of Circulation to permit it to feature on the front page the total value of the coupons inside.

Now, because of the fsi's low cost ($7 per page per thousand or less), some national advertisers are beginning to use it for a brand-building advertising message *without* a coupon. For instance, the makers of Glad bags ran an ad headed, "Glad lowers prices on trash and garbage bags so you don't need a coupon to save."

The Spadea Wraparound. This medium is popular with many retailers and is gaining recognition from national advertisers. It might be just what you are looking for if you want some of the impact of your own fsi without the high cost. Designed by the Greater Buffalo press, which prints 65 percent of the nation's comic sections, it is a single page folded vertically around the spine of the comic section, covering half of the front and half of the back pages. Retailers use both sides for sale items and coupons and find it highly responsive and less costly than a fsi.

Sunday Newspaper Comic Sections. These sections are the most overlooked, underutilized sections in newspapers today. Studies indicate they are often the first section people turn to. A full page costs 20 to 50 percent less than any other section in the newspaper. Over 250 papers can be purchased locally, regionally, or nationally through Puck or Metro comics.

Television Advertising for the Information Society

As rates continue to go up, and audiences continue to dwindle, lured away by cable and VCRs, network commercials are destined (or should we say doomed?) to get shorter. In August of 1985, CBS made the 15-second spot official by announcing it would now accept it as a stand-alone ad, not just as half of a 30-second buy by an advertiser. Curiously enough, there is no rush to make commercials *longer* except for a few brave experiments on cable. (Or perhaps not so curiously, in view of the horrendous cost of commercial time.)

Until recently, the Federal Communications Commission (FCC) had sternly forbidden more than 3 commercial minutes out of every 15 minutes of programming and indeed had banned several advertisers from doing programs that smacked of being all-commercial. Then came the era of deregulation in Washington. Today the FCC leaves radio and television stations to set their own limits on commercial time.

Just as many Catholics found it hard to adjust when the Pope decreed that it was now okay to eat meat on Fridays, stations and advertisers have hesitated to experiment with their theoretical new freedom. And yet— think of it—it would cost a station no more to permit 30 minutes of commercial time than it would to limit advertisers to 6 minutes. And it would be many times more productive to the advertiser.

All-commercial programs may sound like repellent viewing, but a tasteful "infomercial" could be more appealing and enlightening than a great deal of the junk programming and reruns now offered. For instance, many years ago a correspondence school, Famous Artists School, was able to buy time in a number of markets for its informative 15-minute film about the school. It was highly absorbing for anyone interested in being an artist and not unappealing just for the average bored viewer.

In the golden days of radio, several mail-order advertisers got excellent results with a series of programs especially written to promote the product. For instance, one of the authors of this book was involved in the promotion of a respectable book called *How to Stop Killing Yourself,* by Dr. Peter Steincrohn. To sell it via radio, we prepared and produced a series of interviews with Dr. Steincrohn. Each program was 15 minutes, including direct-response commercials for the book. It made interesting, rewarding listening, in no way offensive, and yet far more effective, of course, than a stand-alone commercial could have been.

Are you old enough to remember the commercials on the Kraft Music Hall in the early days of television? They simply showed hands preparing some tempting dish using Kraft products, while Ed Herlihy's soothing voice described the dish and offered to mail the recipe. It was a model of what "infotising" can do and be.

A few years ago, Rapp & Collins was considering producing a series of television programs in which various mail-order catalog firms could, in return for sharing the cost, send a representative to appear on the program and show and offer their most intriguing items. It would be all commercial, but would have the kind of entertainment value of a Johnny Carson or Dick Cavett showing viewers an intriguing new item.

We asked a number of independent television stations if they would be willing to accept this theoretically all-commercial programming. (There are now 214 independent stations, up from only 71 in 1972.) About a third said they would, and the number probably would have been much higher if we had appeared on their doorstep with the program in one hand and the cash in the other.

Viewers may be weary of 50,000 commercials a year. But *prospects* are hungry for information, enjoyably presented. Infotising and infomercials, on over-the-air television as well as on cable, are a revolution waiting to happen. If you have a product or service that could use a lot of explaining and you know how to make the explanation enjoyable, the medium is worth exploring.

Low-power television can also mean low-dollars television, especially for advertisers who want to reach upscale 18- to 40-year-olds. Broadcasting over a limited range, these low-power stations are free of regulations and not required to carry any particular programming. About 157 are currently in operation, and another 850 have received construction permits.

Low-Power Technology Inc. of Austin, Texas, was operating 2 such stations in 1985 and hopes to build a 50-station national network. Their ingenious strategy is 24-hour broadcasting of music videos, which major record companies are happy to supply, and local news. And the price is right for advertisers: One station charges $25 for a 30-second spot that covers a market of 250,000 households.

Target Marketing via Radio

Although some hefty national advertisers use radio, it is not their medium of choice. In 1984, less than 7 percent of all advertising expenditure went into radio, and three-fourths of that was spent by local retailers.

Chapter 3 touched on the targeting capability of the nation's 9600 radio stations and 19 different formats. The following are some companies which are using radio to their advantage:

- *Campbell Soup* targets skiiers with commercials for its soups adjacent to skiing condition reports.
- *Taco Bell* builds dinner business by running mouthwatering commercials to catch homeward-bound motorists during evening drive time.
- *Ciba Vision* scheduled radio when they found that women aged 18 to 34 were prime prospects for their new Softcolors tinted contact lenses and that this target group listened to radio frequently, especially rock and soft rock programming during morning and evening driving time.
- *Ford* promotes pickup trucks on—what else?—country music stations.

If you are an insomniac, you may have discovered the fascination of the new all-talk call-in radio programs; the radio station's 24-hour day is divided into segments hosted by experts in finance, gardening, psychology, etc. This is a new gold mine for the most enterprising doctors, dentists, lawyers, accountants, locksmiths, and other professionals and tradespeople in each market area who have discovered the special effectiveness of advertising their services on these programs. The host expert comes across as tremendously believable and trustworthy, and the commercial delivered by the host becomes a powerful endorsement. National advertisers appropriate for this medium have been slow to wake up to its enormous potential.

Needless to say, broadcast sales representatives will be glad to help you match what you are selling to the right audience and programming. You can thus reach prospects you perhaps can't afford on over-the-air television and can't find on cable. (Although it will never be like the good old days, when an Atlantic City station used to broadcast a special program for nearby Ocean City listeners and would sell spots to Ocean City merchants—for 50 cents each!)

Magazines Fight Back

Can magazines survive the video revolution? Past revolutions in communication suggest that they can. In fact, the public is buying more magazines than ever before—312 million paid copies per issue in 1984.

Movies didn't kill stage plays. Free music on radio didn't kill recordings. Free dramas on television didn't kill Hollywood movies. And television viewing didn't kill listening to the radio or reading magazines, newspapers, and books.

In each case, however, the medium under attack did change radically to survive. And this will happen—is happening—to magazines.

More Specialization.   There are now over 1400 consumer magazines, the great majority of them highly specialized. If you use them as an advertising medium, you may pay a higher cost per page per thousand *readers* compared to a large general magazine, but you will pay a far lower cost per thousand *prospects*.

More Regionalization. Editor Clay Felker almost single-handedly started a revolution in magazine publishing with his brilliant *New York* magazine. By 1970, there were 23 city and regional magazines, and by 1984 the number was up to 147. In many cities ambitious publishers are attempting to slice the pie even finer with magazines designed for special-interest segments within the city.

A city magazine gives you a chance to address readers who are more emotionally involved than those reading a national publication and who may keep the publication around for a longer time than they do the local newspaper.

A Big Splash for a Few Bucks.   How would you like to run a full-page black-and-white ad in *TV Guide?* Well, it would have cost you about $75,000 at the 1984 one-time rate for the national edition, but you could have advertised in just the Cleveland metropolitan area edition for only $350!

This is an opportunity many local merchants overlook. You can buy just local or regional circulation of weekly magazines like *TV Guide,*

Time, Newsweek, U.S. News & World Report. You'll pay much more per thousand—up to twice as much if you buy the smallest circulation possible. But in dollars it may still be a modest sum. And you may impress the heck out of your customers and your mother-in-law.

For direct-response advertisers, this is a secret weapon—especially *TV Guide.* You can do split tests in regional editions at modest cost and then roll out the winning ad in the national edition.

New Technology.   In 1985, France's leading newsweekly, *Le Point,* published what was called the first electronic print ad. It was a 4-page IBM ad that lit up and played music. A year earlier, a software company bound an actual demonstration disc in the pages of a computer magazine. In Britain, magazine publishers are attaching free samples to their front covers. For example, a cover of *MizzPu* had a sample of Gentle Touch Foaming Face Wash attached. Honeywell spent $1 million just printing, die cutting, and assembling a spectacular pop-up ad inserted in *Business Week.*

The Customized Magazine.   We have already seen the customized magazine's beginnings. R. R. Donnelley & Sons Company, a printing firm, has developed a process called Selectronic, which harnesses the computer to the printing press to print tailor-made individual copies.

Farm Journal was the first to take advantage of this capability. It adjusts the editorial and advertising contents of each copy to what individual subscribers raise on their farms. The magazine published 8896 different versions of the May 1984 issue!

Games magazine's October 1985 issue had each of its 550,000 subscribers' names printed on individual covers, and a message was addressed to each subscriber by name in a Chevrolet ad. In addition, 100,000 known mail-order buyers received 32-page catalog inserts in their copies. Another 250,000 buyers not quite as likely to buy got 16-page inserts. The remainder got single pages containing an offer of the full catalog.

What if you would like to list your dealers in your ad but hate to spend the money for the additional advertising page or pages? By using subscribers' zip code data, the Selectronic process can even print in the ad the name and phone number of the reader's closest dealer.

If you have an idea for a new kind of magazine advertisement—no matter how impossible it may seem—don't be too quick to conclude that it can't be done.

Cable TV

When cable television first began to grow, in the early 1970s, the advertising agencies were greatly excited about this extraordinary new advertising medium. At last it would be possible to cast off the severe restrictions on over-the-air television advertising and let imagination and creativity run wild.

Two things quickly cooled their enthusiasm. In comparison with a network share, the audience for any one advertiser-supported channel was pathetically tiny and poorly measured. And even when special cable advertising was prepared on the cheap, production costs were still so high in ratio to the time charges and audience ratings that preparing special material just for cable didn't seem to make economic sense.

By 1986, even though most of the major cities were still underwired because of political delays in awarding franchises and building systems, over 46 percent of U.S. television households had cable, and wiring had begun in all of the top-20 television markets that did not have cable.

But despite a number of brave experiments, cable-TV advertising has been viewed by most national advertisers simply as a way to provide what one agency representative called "cheap tonnage"—more exposure for commercials prepared for network television. Some of the experiments:

- *General Foods,* one of the brave pioneers, has experimented with a new cable advertising format it calls "shortcuts"—2-minute spots that combined 90 seconds of entertainment and kitchen tips with a 30-second product pitch sandwiched in the middle.

- *Dr. Pepper,* reaching for young individualists, has sponsored rock music trivia quizzes on MTV.

- *Goodyear Tire & Rubber Company* was planning in the spring of 1985 to test a 15-minute infomercial in four cable markets against traditional 30-second spots in another four markets. Then it planned to compare sales and retailer feedback in each market.

The Challenge of Cost Control and Creativity.   The problem posed by production costs arises from an entrenched system based on network-television advertising costs and thinking. The cost of network-television time has been so astronomical that no one wanted to quibble about production costs. As the advertising director of Kraft, Inc., pointed out, "If we're spending $10 million to buy TV time, we shouldn't threaten creative integrity just to cut production costs to $145,000 from $150,000."[5]

He is quite right in theory. But by the same token, why limit the cost to $150,000? Why not permit $160,000? $180,000? $200,000? $500,000? (Jackie Gleason was reportedly paid $500,000 as the talent charge alone for just one MasterCard commercial.) Where do you draw the line?

The pressures pushing costs up have been greater than the pressure to hold them down. "Clients," one agency head has wryly pointed out, "want to spend less money for commercials, but they also want extravaganzas to stay ahead of one another visually."[6] And agencies want to win awards. And people representing the client, the agency, and the production company may all like the idea of going on location, especially to a sunny climate in the winter time. Madison Avenue grinned knowingly at the story of the advertising genius who announced that he was flying off to Tahiti to shoot a commercial on roller bearings. Why? Because "I've just discovered a place on one of the islands that looks exactly like downtown Akron!"

The cost of making commercials grew 99 percent between 1979 and 1984, more than double the growth rate of the consumer price index.

Cable advertising cries out for a new kind of creativity, a creativity that will include creative ways to control costs while conveying entertainment, information, and persuasion to the viewer all in one package. Then its potential as a new advertising medium will be fully realized.

Quality versus Quantity.   Keith Reinhard, president of DDB-Needham Worldwide and a steadfast cable believer, has argued that less attention should be paid to poor cable ratings and more attention given to the quality of the audience. "If cable gets only one-tenth of the audience, but delivers an audience that is ten times more involved and receptive, or ten times more interested, the numbers will work out fine."[7]

Most cable advertisers have failed to realize that how few people are watching your advertising almost doesn't matter if they are the right people. Ordinarily, audience size is not under your control. But certain kinds of infotising, involving subject matter of enough interest to enough people, can offer you some control over the size of the audience.

If your subject matter is denture adhesives, forget it. It's not likely you can get viewers to remember to tune in. The subject is simply not compelling enough. But if you are dealing with a subject of compelling interest, even if to only a small percentage of the total population, you can significantly enlarge the target audience for your message and make it pay.

Print-Supported Cable.   Print-supported cable is the secret. Canny entrepreneurs are already using this secret. Sooner or later major advertisers will catch on. "Tune in" ads, in the newspaper television listings, the Sunday television magazine, the local edition of *TV Guide,* or the cable magazine go fishing for interested prospects in the sea of general humanity and pull them in to watch special-interest cable programming.

Let's go back to the question of denture adhesives. We said no one would take the trouble to tune in on a discussion of denture adhesives. *But what about a discussion on the possibility of eliminating the need for denture adhesives altogether?* If you were an unhappy denture wearer, that would be worth taking the trouble to tune in, wouldn't it? And if the programming were aired on a cable system of a million homes and attracted only 1 viewer out of every 1000 households, the audience would still include 1000 people—not many by television rating standards, but pretty darned good if you're filling a lecture hall.

This is essentially the advertising approach used by a Manhattan dentist who ran fractional-page display ads in a free television guide which said: "If you are one of the millions who suffer with removable dentures, bridges, or loose and missing teeth . . . watch Dr. Leonard I. Linkow, D.D.S., pioneer in dental implantology, being interviewed on 'Meet your Health Professional' on this new and interesting subject. Dental implants can make your life wonderful again!" We'll wager that a number of interested prospects did tune in and that the program converted a fair number of them into patients of Dr. Linkow.

Paul Simon, real estate expert, has run a fair-sized ad in *The Wall Street Journal* urging readers to tune in to his 2-hour cable-TV special, *Get Rich with Real Estate.* It listed the viewing times in all four time zones for three different airings on two cable networks, and urged readers to call the local cable system to find out how to tune in.

A New York bank has used this same technique. It ran an ad in the entertainment pages of *The New York Times:* "Don't miss this show. Your employees may be watching. 'Employee Benefits and the Small Company.' Tonight at 8:00 on Channel ——."

The Thirty-Minute or Sixty-Minute Commercial. With or without support from tune-in print ads, hour-long commercials are one of the unexplored frontiers of cable advertising. Clever entrepreneurs are buying program-length chunks of time to present a compelling self-help lecture interwoven with direct-response commercials for a home-study course on the same subject. (Actually, of course, the entire program is a commercial.)

Media Arts International pioneered this approach. They developed seven canned lectures for which they bought cable program time: *Get Rich with Real Estate, Get Rich with Foreclosures, How to Master the Art of Selling, How to Win at Blackjack, A Millionaire's Secret to Wealth, 60*

Minutes to Success, and *Breakthrough to Weight Loss.* Each sold a home-study course on the featured subject for around $295.

The lecture on real estate chalked up more than $1 million in gross sales in just 2 days from three exposures on SPN and one on The Nashville Network (at 3 a.m.).

Image-conscious national advertisers may sniff at the style and content of these brash and possibly unscrupulous promotions. If they do, however, they are missing the point: *A 30-minute or 60-minute commercial watched by a comparatively few viewers who are prime prospects may be a better buy than 30 seconds sprayed at everybody, including a few prime prospects.* And we know from the Media Arts experience that many cable systems can be persuaded to sell time in 30-minute and 60-minute chunks.

Local Cable Opportunities.   If you are a local advertiser, cable can provide an entrée into television homes that you might otherwise not be able to afford.

Bob Westall, a Toyota dealer in surburban Virginia, invested $3200 in ninety-six 30-second spots on three channels of two local cable systems. By the end of the first month of advertising, he had sold 100 cars—a 30-day high achieved only twice before in the dealership's 25-year history.

A car dealer in Gastonia, North Carolina, persuaded his pastor to do a testimonial spot for use on local cable. The dealer said he didn't know how many cars it sold—at a cost of $6 per 30-second spot, he wasn't too concerned! (Of course, television advertising is not all beer and skittles in Gastonia. Local cable advertisers must also pay a production charge ranging from $250 to $390.)

Computerland in Grand Rapids, Michigan, sponsored a 28-minute infomercial produced by Apple Computer. It was promoted via newspaper ads and took advantage of cable's potential for providing a detailed explanation of a product.

Until recently, many of the nation's 6000 cable systems didn't know how to sell local advertising, but they are learning. Total sales of local cable commercials were estimated to have risen from just $8 million in 1980 to $193 million in 1986.

The New Direct Mail

Chapter 3's discussion of public databases touched on the development of direct-mail co-ops and of private advertising mailed directly to self-identified prospects. Here are some more important developments in direct mail.

Shared Mail. Shared mail is the direct-mail answer to the daily newspaper's TMC—or is it the other way around? Assorted advertising by participating advertisers is bundled together and mailed to selected households.

Advo-System, the undisputed leader in shared mail, is the largest private mailer in the world. It has the most comprehensive mailing list in the United States: 87.5 million addresses, fully computerized, and updated weekly. It was actually used by the U.S. Census Bureau for its census questionnaire mailings.

Advo serves more than 20,000 advertisers and processes over 10 billion pieces of advertising material annually. Their "marriage mail" goes out weekly and enables retailers large and small to reach as many as 40 million households or as few as 25,000. Their "network mail" is a monthly program that delivers money-saving coupons on nationally advertised brands to 50 million households and lets local retailers tie in.

What is staggering about the Advo system is that they are able to customize the contents of the direct mail packages received in each of the 36,000 zip zones. Thus if you are a small retailer, you can choose as little as one zip zone—the 25,000 nearest households in your immediate trading area—and send a coupon or message to them for as little as 2.5 cents each or $675 altogether!

Or if you are a giant franchise chain, you can push one button and distribute coupons, each imprinted with the location of the local franchiser, in just about every household in every one of your trading areas.

Direct-Mail Co-op Packages. With participating advertisers splitting the costs, direct-mail co-op packages are a precise and economic targeting tool. The different kinds of co-ops and gift packs available from the leading suppliers (with their annual frequencies in parentheses) include: Hispanics (3), blacks (5), preschool (4), children aged 5 to 12 (2), teens (6), seniors (4), upper-income adult (1), sports (2), college (2), newlyweds (12), expectant mothers (12), new mothers (12).

Card Decks Card decks are probably the fastest-growing form of co-op mail for advertisers looking for direct response. According to the *Response Deck Reference,* more than 88,000 businesses spent $86 million in card deck advertising in 1983. There are now 620 different card decks available!

They began as card-stock booklets affording each advertiser a business reply card, but they soon evolved into a plastic bag containing a stack of loose cards, each with an advertising message and fill-out reply portion on one side and a business reply face on the other.

Today you have a choice of specialized card decks for gardeners, computer owners, senior citizens, executives, doctors, investors, etc., available usually for $15 to $25 per thousand—compared to perhaps $250 per thousand for a solo mailing.

Product samples are now appearing in card decks. Warner-Lambert has included hand lotion samples in packs that were mailed to 250,000 nurses and to 500,000 women in other professions.

America with Distinction is a deluxe card deck using fashionable four-color cards to sell to the affluent. The founders, Kathleen and William Sneckenberg, started in Chicago by obtaining lists of residents in affluent zip zones and manually selecting from them the addresses they wanted. When they spread into other cities, they used a sophisticated computer program which scanned the markets at block level for such indicators as $63,000+ income, homes worth $200,000+, and ownership of expensive automobiles.

Local Names from National Lists.   Although not always easily obtained, these names can be a productive source of local business. *The Amoskeag Savings Bank of New Hampshire* pulled a 4.3 percent response from a mailing to 3482 New Hampshire subscribers to *Business Week.*

Driving Customers to Your Retailers.   Solo direct mail is usually used by direct marketers seeking direct-response inquiries or orders. But not always, and not necessarily. An astonishingly underutilized form of direct mail with a great future is mailings sent to selected target prospects to get them to buy your product at the nearest retail outlet.

This form is underutilized because advertisers shudder at the thought of paying 30 cents or 40 cents per "impression," instead of the half-cent or penny in other media. But a direct-mail piece is not just an impression, it is a whole campaign. Viewed in that light, it may be your best media bargain—depending on what you are selling.

Bollinger Champagne was successfully introduced in new test markets by Julius Wile Sons & Company thanks to an innovative direct-mail campaign by the Howard/Marlboro Direct agency—winner of the 1984 Henry Hoke Award. A handsome holiday greetings mailing contained a card that played Christmas music when opened and an offer of a replica of an eighteenth-century French champagne cork puller for proof of purchase. Selected dealers in the test markets were told that the mailing would be sent in their trading areas if they agreed to order three cases and install the special floor display. The mailing was then sent to 20,000 subscribers to *Food & Wine* magazine in the test market areas. The mailing generated a 12 percent response, and the participating dealers sold out. Sales averaged $50 per customer.

Panasonic sent out a mailing for its Sr. Computer which provided a model of how such promotion can and should be done. The mailing may not have been profitable because of the savage competition and price wars going on in the computer field at the time, but that does not detract from the thoughtfulness and professional excellence of the mailing.

It looked like a powerful direct-response mailing and was undoubtedly created by a direct-response professional. The outside envelope teased the reader to open it with "Inside—The personal computer our competition wishes we would keep a lid on—Plus a special 25th anniversary gift offer for you."

Inside, a four-page letter and four-color 11 × 17-inch circular did everything—explained everything—showed everything—about the computer and the offer—explanations that computer-advertising critics have so often claimed were missing in so much computer advertising.

But then, instead of asking for a direct order, the mailing provided a complete list of Panasonic computer dealers nationwide. As an action stimulant, a reply form displayed on one side the premium—a Panasonic earphones stereo radio—and on the other side an order blank for requesting it, to be mailed back with proof of purchase.

A variation of this technique is what might be called the "non-mail-order catalog" being supplied by fashion designers to department stores. The latter affix their own logos and mail the brochures to their customers.

Anne Klein II has pioneered in this kind of promotion. It produces three different brochures per season, each with different clothing. In a given market, the retailer that sells the most Anne Klein II gets the first choice of brochures and corresponding line, the number-2 store gets second choice, and the third store takes what's left. In this way, the company can put the line in several outlets and still grant each store exclusivity.

A total of 20 stores sent out 3 million such mailers for the Fall 1985 collection. Instead of inviting mail orders, the copy urges "Come In! Try On!" A company spokesperson credited its "tremendous" growth in recent years to the direct-mail campaign as well as to its television ads. Ralph Lauren, Albert Nipon, Perry Ellis, and Norma Kamali have been trying a similar approach.

Merle Norman Cosmetics, a beauty products company for over half a century, has 2600 licensed studios across the country. Until the late 1970s, the company acted simply as a supplier, leaving retailers to do most of the promotion and advertising.

In 1978, the company decided the time had come to start building support for its licensees and embarked on an aggressive advertising program with studio locations listed in the advertising. Then, in 1984, it decided to go a step further.

To introduce their new skin-care line, they obtained over 2.5 million names from their licensees' card files and sent out to each address a mailer with an unrestricted $4 gift certificate for the addressee and another $4 certificate for a friend. Customers did not even have to buy anything to redeem the coupon.

The redemption rate for Merle Norman patrons was estimated at 18 percent and 9 percent came from friends of patrons, making an overall redemption rate of 27 percent and bringing in 100,000 completely new customers. Furthermore, past patrons spent an average of $14, and friends spent an average of $12.

Instead of nothing more than hundreds of card files in the hands of their licensees, Merle Norman now has a powerful customer database which can be expanded and used repeatedly for the benefit of both the company and its licensees.

Videocassettes

With VCRs in over 38 percent of television households by the end of 1986 and 66 percent expected by the end of the decade, the time has come to take videocassettes seriously as an advertising medium. As a medium, it is the advertiser's dream. It offers all the power of television's hypnotic visual communications without television's time limitations.

Instead of being forced to conform to the frantic mind-spinning pace of the 15-second commercial, you can take as long as needed to tell your story or show your wares. And instead of worrying about whether your captive audience will resent your intrusion, you enjoy the delicious awareness that your viewers *want* to see and hear your advertising and have made an effort to get it.

The advertising videocassette is not just the medium of the next century or the next decade. It's here—right now. Advertisers are using it successfully. And it's a medium you can test tomorrow, especially if you are selling a high-ticket product or service that could benefit from a lot of demonstration or visualization.

Soloflex, Inc., makers of a $495 home exercise machine, provided one of the most impressive early examples of the videocassette as a selling tool. Soloflex's founder and president, Jerry Wilson, couldn't get sales personnel in sporting-goods stores to demonstrate his machine properly, so he took it out of retail distribution and started selling it directly to the public.

Then, after purchasing a videocassette recorder for his family, he suddenly realized that here was the perfect advertising medium for his product. He spent $150,000 to produce a 22-minute demonstration on videotape and began offering it free (as well as a brochure for those who didn't have VCRs) in his magazine and television ads. Each "video brochure" costs the company $6.50 for materials, dubbing, packaging, and postage.

By 1985, after 6 years in business, the firm was reported to have sold 100,000 units. It had mailed out over 60,000 free videotapes. They found that up to 40 percent of those who requested the demonstration videotape eventually bought a Soloflex, an astounding sales conversion percentage, compared to 10 percent conversion of those who received only the brochure.

The Circle Gallery in New Canaan, Connecticut, faced an unusual problem in finding collectors for the limited-edition kinetic light sculptures of artist Bill Parker. The sculptures are glass spheres filled with ionizing gases. An electrically charged rod excites the gases and creates brilliant bolts of light in a variety of colors.

The director of the gallery felt that conventional direct mail couldn't do justice to the sculptures, so he mailed out ten thousand 7-minute videocassettes presenting the artist, his work, his background, and his kinetic light sculptures in action to lists of affluent prospective buyers.

Rivergate, a luxury rental apartment building in Manhattan, developed videotapes about the building and the neighborhood that prospective tenants could take home with them, to help them weigh the decision in the privacy of their homes.

Videologue Marketing Corporation launched the first catalog on videotape in the summer of 1985. Subscribers pay $12.95 and receive a series of tapes displaying, explaining, and offering attractive catalog merchandise. The first direct mail to VCR owners and others brought in 5000 subscribers. The videocassettes are being duplicated in Hong Kong at a cost of $8 each. Within months, Videologue had signed up 25,000 subscribers, and companies like West Bend and Black & Decker were paying $3000 for a 30-second commercial on each tape.

Advertisers and their agencies are studying the possibility of sponsored videocassettes, but they are nervous about whether viewers fleeing from heavily commercialized television programming will accept advertising on tapes.

Red Lobster Inns has sponsored a home video based on Dr. Robert Haas's best-seller, *Eat to Win.* The program content does not include any commercials, but the Red Lobster logo appears on the package and billboards at the beginning and end of the tape, identifying Red Lobster as the sponsor. Red Lobster is mentioned in the program, as when Dr.

Haas instructs actress Judy Landers on healthful restaurant foods and she says, "But just don't tell me I can't have lobster at the Red Lobster." (Sure enough, he doesn't.)

Glenmore Distilleries and Karl/Lorimar Home Video began selling "The Mr. Boston Official Video Bartender's Guide" for under $20 in both video and liquor stores. Like the Red Lobster videotape, it carried no overt commercial but depended largely on favorable association and logo-type exposure. However, since it was at the very least self-liquidating (and it should do better than that), it was hard to see how Glenmore could lose as long as enough were sold to amortize the production cost.

Eastman Kodak has introduced in photography buff magazines a daring concept in video advertising: the Kodak Video Exchange, a library of 43 video cassettes on photo how-to and travel subjects.

Although conducted by phone and mail, the business is operated exactly like the typical video rental store. You pay a membership fee of $29.95—you get two free rentals and a free tripod for joining, and then you pay $6.95 each time you exchange a video cassette for another. You can purchase those you want for your permanent collection for only $19.95. Kodak seems to have killed three birds with one stone:

- Self-amortizing exposure and image building for the Kodak name
- Expansion of the market for film and developing by educating and encouraging camera owners to take more pictures
- A new profit center—admittedly a pretty small one in this $10 billion corporation, but if you watch your millions, the billions will take care of themselves—and the venture permits Eastman to get its feet wet in an important medium of the future

Video Tours has run mail-order ads offering seven tour descriptions on your choice of seven video cassettes for only $8.95, barely more than the cost of a blank cassette. "Once you've watched the program," the ad copy points out, you can "use the tape as you would any high quality blank video cassette." So the video program is virtually free.

Air France has offered in its advertising a videocassette preview of such travel packages as its tour of Paris and the Riviera, with a trailblazing method of covering the cost. You were asked in your response to provide your credit-card number. Then you may *either* return the video cassette within 14 days and pay nothing *or* keep it and your credit-card account will be automatically billed for $29.95. This is an innovative application of the negative-option principle used by book and record clubs to a free rental or purchase of a video.

At last report, Air France had produced nine different videos and was receiving 2500 requests a week. Most people return the tape rather than pay $29.95 for it. Many "steal" it by making a copy, which must make Air France cry all the way to the bank.

Nikon has taken a step into the future with a videocassette instruction book and photography course offered free with the purchase of one of their cameras. Anyone who has ever strained to read and understand one of those instruction booklets in tiny type ("Match dot on lens barrel with dot on flange near cable release socket") would be thrilled at the ease of understanding Nikon's video explanations and demonstrations.

The next obvious step for Nikon and other advertisers of high-tech, high-price products will be (in fact, by the time you read this, it is undoubtedly already happening) to provide prospective customers with a demonstration videocassette not after the purchase is made but *before*. Videocassettes could be offered for the actual cost of manufacturing and dubbing (between $5 and $6) with a credit certificate good for that amount on purchase of the product.

The high production costs of topnotch videocassettes may intimidate local marketers at present. But this will change rapidly.

The new generation of "camcorder" home video cameras is going to produce an accompanying new generation of video whiz kids everywhere who will be able to shoot and edit with professional skill, in some cases combining their material with slick computer graphics and computer-generated music. Then even in smaller cities the local real estate developer, lawn service, or health club will have a new marketing tool.

Hank Johnson, when he was president of Spiegel and the man responsible for repositioning the catalog firm as a high-fashion upscale marketer, has shared with audiences an extraordinary vision of how luxury automobiles may be sold *by mail* and videotape in the foreseeable future. (And the future is closer than you think!)

> I want to begin by introducing you to John World, a Spiegel customer of the not-too-distant future. Dr. John lives in a small town in Midwestern America. He has a thriving practice, but today is Wednesday, his usual day off.
>
> Spiegel is aware of this, so we've arranged for him to receive a small, attractive box from us in his morning mail. A little puzzled, since he hasn't ordered anything from Spiegel recently, he opens the box to see what's inside.
>
> He's even more surprised when he finds that "America's Fine Department Store in Print"—Spiegel—has sent him a video cassette tape with the intriguing title . . . "INVITATION TO ADVENTURE."
>
> Enclosed with the video cassette is a short letter from me. In it I explain to John that he has been a terrific Spiegel customer. I list two or three of the major items he has purchased from us and tell him that since I understand he is a doctor with a thriving practice in a small community—and since cars

and driving are one of his passions—he might find the enclosed tape worth viewing.

This is not just a guess, one we hope will be lucky. Spiegel knows that Dr. John loves sports cars, and that he can afford one. We understand that he cannot find the luxury autos he likes in his small hometown. And we predict that he will be curious enough to pop that cassette into the tape player we know he owns . . .

The video tape highlights the mystique of the British built personal luxury car—the Jaguar. The tape takes John from his living room chair and drops him in the driver's seat. He is behind the wheel of a sleek sedan, touring some of the most spectacular roads in America. The tape then takes him to England, to the plant where the Jaguar is assembled. He sees the care and craftmanship that go into each model. He hears Jaguar engineers and assemblers talk about the love and dedication that go into each step of the creation and building of a Jaguar. And he relates these vignettes to his own longing for a sports car.

The tape ends with an offer that John can't resist. By calling a special Spiegel number, John can arrange to have the Jaguar of his choice, color and equipment exactly the way he'd like it, delivered to his home for a 30-day trial period.

If he wants to return the car at the end of the month, he pays a $500 rental charge. If he decides to keep the car, he receives a free bonus gift—an all-expense paid vacation for two to the countryside the Jaguar in the videotape toured so dramatically.[8]

This is MaxiMarketing supreme, encompassing segmentation, targeting, database, innovative distribution, promotion, and a daring new approach to media. Says Johnson flatly, "It is an exciting scenario—and it will happen."

If we had to name one medium that will show the most exciting and spectacular growth between the time this is written and the time you read it, it would be commercial applications of videocassettes in one form or another.

The Boom in Telephone Marketing

While you were looking the other way, the telephone became the nation's third-largest advertising medium, passing up direct mail around 1984 to take its place in the big three with television and newspapers.

In 1980, an estimated 4500 people were involved in telemarketing and telephone sales. By 1985, the number has grown to an estimated 300,000. *U.S. News and World Report* has predicted that by the year 2000 the number will rise to *8 million!* Between 1980 and 1984, the number of telephone marketing agencies grew from 15 to about 100 full-time, full-service agencies and another 1200 agencies of lesser capability. In-house telephone centers grew from approximately 1500 to around 30,000. Direct Marketing Association research in 1983 pointed to total telemarketing sales in 1984 of $100 billion.

What do all the impressive statistics mean to you? They mean simply that if you are not maximizing use of the telephone in marketing the product, service, or business you are promoting, you are in danger of being left behind. And if you are accustomed to thinking of telemarketing simply as calling up somebody to sell something, you are missing half the story. Inbound telemarketing is fully as important as outbound telemarketing, perhaps more so for many businesses, and now it is easily within the capability of almost any business.

Outbound Telemarketing

If you are thinking of using telemarketing to contact prospects or customers, here are several important considerations:

- Each call will cost you about ten times as much as a direct-mail solicitation, and, if successful, will produce about ten times more results. However, this kind of success in calling consumer lists is usually possible only when the caller has already established some kind of cordial relationship with the respondent. Thus outbound telemarketing has been used successfully in magazine subscription renewal campaigns and in fund-raising appeals to previous donors asking for a repeat donation. Time-Life Books was able to do massive outbound telemarketing of its libraries because so many U.S. families had had a highly favorable experience with one or more of their libraries in the past.

- Don't try a do-it-yourself operation, any more than you would ask an inexperienced secretary to put together a direct-mail effort. Outbound telemarketing is a job for a professional agency. They will be able to write a skillful professional phone script for their trained operators and, through feedback from respondents, will refine it to a high level of effectiveness. And there should be significant cost advantages compared to paying your own line charges and full-time operators whose work load might vary widely.

- The lower the response rate expected, the higher the unit of sale must be. A magazine seeking a $15 subscription renewal can afford to invest $3 per completed call if a third of the respondents renew, bringing the advertising cost per renewal up to a tolerable $9. But a company or organization that made a sale from only 10 percent of its completed calls would have an advertising cost per sale of $30, not so good if the amount of the sale is only $20.

And there is an Emersonian Law of Compensation at work here: Other things being equal (which of course they never are), the higher the price, the greater the sales resistance. So there is no magic answer, but a professional telemarketing agency and a well-designed test can provide a realistic answer.

- You can install a machine called an automated dialing and recorded message player (ADRMP) to automatically dial a list of prospects and deliver your taped message—but we hope you won't! A stockbroker in Washington installed this new technology and found he could get 3 to 5 percent of the respondents to leave a reply message asking him to call personally. The trouble is, the more this is used, the sooner that various state legislators will hear from angry consumers and pass laws forbidding unwelcome commercial calls.

Inbound Telemarketing

Many companies may think that simply answering the phone is not marketing at all, but it is, and many opportunities are often overlooked.

Referring Customers to Dealers and Vice Versa. Chapter 9 discusses in detail the importance of building a bridge between the advertising and the sale. A basic way to do this, used by many advertisers with spotty distribution, but blatantly ignored by at least as many others, is inclusion in the ads of an 800 number that readers can call for dealer information.

If you do this, be sure you do it well or you may offend more people than you sell. As a spot check from time to time, try calling the number yourself, pretending to be a prospect, and see how you make out.

On a high-ticket item, it often pays to set up a system of also sending the name of each inquirer to the nearest dealer and assisting the dealer in establishing a local follow-up system.

List Building. Every incoming call is an opportunity to build your database of inquiries and prospects. A few tactful questions from a phone-answering script will enable the operator to enter not only the name and address but also revealing demographic and psychographic details for later customized follow-up promotion.

Adding a Service to Your Product. In a marketplace jammed with similar products, the product that includes a service becomes in the eyes of the consumer a more valuable product.

Since 1974, Procter & Gamble has listed on its products toll-free numbers consumers can call with questions, and the company handles around half a million calls a year. General Electric expected to receive 2.8 million calls in 1985.

Reportedly, large companies like this have not made any effort to save or use the names of callers. This will undoubtedly change as they begin to realize they are discarding a valuable resource.

Line Extension. Companies that think they probably can't use telemarketing are probably wrong. For instance, how in the world could Tropicana Orange Juice? Very simply—they advertised gift packs of high-quality citrus on their cartons and listed an 800 number you could call to place an order.

Call-In Sweepstakes. Here is a very creative use of the 800 number that really paid off big. Quaker Oats ran a sweepstakes for its Cap'n Crunch cereal with 5000 Huffy bicycles as prizes. Each cereal box contained a pirate treasure map and an 800 number to call. If the location on the map coincided with the right 800 number, the caller was a winner. The company received *24 million calls,* requiring 400 operators to handle, and increased its residual market share by 15 percent!

Upsell. If you have operators taking orders on the phone, good training and/or a good script will enable them to increase the size of each order. Many report that offering a deluxe or specially packaged version of the product at higher cost works about 25 percent of the time. Others offer a quantity discount if the customer will buy two or more.

Sell during "Hold." What won't they think of next? A company called Audiocom prepares tape cassettes to your specifications, so you can give callers a sales message while they are on hold. Clients have included Sears, Montgomery Ward, National Cash Register, and Spiegel. The company says that Polaroid generated between a 16 and 20 percent response rate from its promotions on hold tapes. Nationwide Insurance tested promotion on hold and found that the number of hang-ups decreased by about 6 percent, and about 88 percent of the callers found the messages interesting and asked for more information.

Dial-a-Message. You can use either an 800 number or a 900 number (see below) for creative use of recorded messages.

Flyfaire, a travel wholesaler which does business through independent travel agents, advertises its tours in the *Sunday New York Times* travel section. So do major competitors like Liberty Travel and Empress Travel, and they operate their own retail outlets, many of which are open on Sunday when most independent travel agents are closed.

So Flyfaire's agency prepared an ad proclaiming "Free, listen to fantasy holidays on tape." The ad listed a different phone number to call for each prerecorded description of a specific vacation package—sometimes even a different number to call to receive the message in a different language—plus another number to call for an explanation of the benefits of booking through an independent travel agent.

The first day the ad appeared, Flyfaire received 2000 phone calls. Our direct-marketing experience tells us the total must have been several times that much—an extraordinary response.

Inbound 900-Number Telemarketing. AT&T's Dial-It 900 service is an intriguing service that marketers still haven't figured out how to use widely. Callers pay 50 cents (on their phone bills) to dial and get a recorded message. The message sponsor pays a $250 setup charge and 25 cents a call if the number falls below 2000 a day. Above 2000, the sponsor is paid a few cents per call on a sliding scale.

The service got a major launch during the Carter-Reagan debates. Viewers were invited to call in and register their opinion on who won: 727,000 people each paid 50 cents to call in.

Newspaper ads for the Paramount movie *D.A.R.Y.L.* invited readers to dial a 900 number and "Learn D.A.R.Y.L.'s secret. Find out how you can qualify to win a free gift." More than 440,000 called during the 11 days of the promotion and were told how they could get a free poster at theaters on opening day. A Paramount spokesperson hinted that Paramount's share of the revenue from the calls paid for the posters.

Columbia created a similar tactic in promoting the Burt Reynolds movie, *The Man Who Loved Women*. Moviegoers were invited to call a 900 number to hear a recorded message by Reynolds. When a commercial aired during USA Cable Network's *Night Flight* promised that Burt Reynolds would personally return six calls, 75,000 people called within 1 hour.

Andrea West, marketing manager for the 900-number service, has suggested a clever application. Instead of charging 50 cents per call, charge $25! In other words, a fund-raising organization could invite callers to respond, and callers would be charged $25 instead of 50 cents on their next phone bills, the money to be turned over to the fund-raiser by AT&T.

Affordability. In 1985, AT&T lowered its minimum charges for 800-number service to $36.80 per month plus a one-time installation charge and a charge per call. In addition you get a free listing in the AT&T 800-number directory. Any company that does business out of state and receives or could receive calls from customers can now use this service.

The Cloudy Future

In telemarketing, it's possible that nothing fails like success. There is no limit to the future of inbound telemarketing because the public wants it and likes it. Outbound telemarketing is another story. In 1985 a record number of bills were introduced in state legislatures to restrict outbound telemarketing in various ways. For instance, use of ADRMPs would be outlawed or restricted. Or phone companies would be required to offer their customer the option to forbid sales calls by having an asterisk placed next to their names in the directory.

The Direct Marketing Association has established a Telephone Preference Service, similar to its successful Mail Preference Service, permitting customers to put their names on a list of those who do not wish to receive sales calls. The association is lobbying vigorously for this self-regulation as an alternative to restrictive legislation. Meanwhile, all marketers who use outbound telemarketing must do so with utmost respect for the consumer, or they will kill the goose that is laying many golden eggs.

Electronic Shopping— The Whiz Kid of the New Marketing

The following discussion is guaranteed to be at least partially obsolete by the time you read it. What matters is not knowing everything about everything being tried everywhere but getting your feet wet doing something, somewhere.

Most electronic shopping today is not much further along than aviation was at Kitty Hawk. But because of the accelerating rate of change, the picture could change overnight. The technology is available and affordable. Now is the time to think about conducting your own electronic marketing tests.

Video machines about the size of an arcade video game are being placed in shopping malls, airports, and other high-traffic areas. They use a videodisc on which 54,000 frames can be stored, and through computer technology they can display stills or movies in high-resolution color.

Avon is using the machines to find new customers not being reached by its sales force. Each machine displays a catalog of over 180 Avon products from six major categories—women's fragrance, men's fragrance, makeup, skin-care, jewelry, and gifts. The user touches the screen to select the category of interest. At the end of the demonstration, screen messages invite the user to order by inserting a credit card and typing in name and address for delivery.

The machines can also collect valuable data, even when viewers don't make a purchase. They can record how long a user stays at the machine and which product categories and products are examined (and for how long), providing valuable market feedback.

ByVideo of Sunnyvale, California, supplied Avon with the machines on a turnkey basis for about $15,000 each. The cost of the software and service depends on the sophistication of the program. ByVideo estimates that a machine must generate $150 per day in revenue to pay for itself.

The Florsheim Company started in 1985 to test an interactive display terminal in one Florsheim Thayer McNeil shoe store and three mall locations. They called it the Express Shop and billed it as "the world's smallest shoe store with the world's largest selection of shoes." It allows a customer to choose from the entire Florsheim line of 250 men's styles in sizes 5AAA to 15EEEEE. Most of their stores carry only 100 styles. Shoes are ordered by credit card and keyboard, a receipt is issued, and the order is electronically forwarded to Florsheim's central warehouse in Jefferson City, Missouri. The shoes are shipped the same day, and, if not satisfactory, they may be either shipped back or taken to the nearest store for refund.

In its first month of operation, the machine installed in the Florsheim store in Fort Lauderdale, Florida, accounted for three or four orders a day and was expected to pay for itself within a year.

If this sales figure seems disappointing, keep in mind the factor of early public awareness. Remember, credit cards got off to a slow start. It took time for people to get comfortable with using a card instead of cash.

By 1985 there were Florsheim Convenience Centers in eight malls nationwide. Some of the terminals even have an electronic foot-measuring device.

Sears, in a joint experiment with IBM, has tested electronic information kiosks in a number of its stores. According to a company executive, the kiosks allow consumers access to very complex sources of data. For instance, Sears has 14,000 different types of window coverings! The consumer can see and hear about a complete assortment of products— how to achieve a decorator look; determine the quantity of merchandise and hardware needed; and get a printout of sizes, stock numbers, and prices.

Also growing is use of noninteractive video simply for point-of-purchase promotion.

L'Oréal, in a first for the cosmetics industry, offered an in-store video to food, drug, and other mass merchandise outlets. In exchange for putting up and maintaining a store display and ordering a certain number of units, stores received a 3-minute continuous video loop, "A Day in the Life of Deidre McGuire" (the L'Oréal model). Over 300 stores were running the video monthly, and the brand manager reported "overwhelmingly positive" results. Pathmark stores reporting moving "truckloads" of units due to the video display running in all its stores. (Later, however, Pathmark dropped the program—because, they said, of problems in maintaining the hardware.)

Check-Out Line Television, Inc. offers 30-second commercial videos for supermarkets to show customers waiting in the check-out line. Says a regional sales manager for one of the advertisers, "If one person looks at the screen, sees the commercial for turkey dressing and says, 'I need that,' we're doing the right thing."

There is a confusion of electronic shopping companies that have names beginning with *compu-*. Because you'll be hearing more about all of them in marketing news reports, let's take a moment to sort them out:

- *Comp-U-Card* is a giant service for discount shopping via telephone and computer. By 1985, they had nearly 60,000 different consumer products in their database and 900,000 individual members plus a number of groups—altogether they claimed 2 million members. Those using computers were said to be spending an average of $700 a year through the service. A computer owner can access and compare products, features, and prices and then type in an order.

- *Comp-U-Store* is Comp-U-Card's in-store video kiosk, using interactive videodiscs to display merchandise on the screen. The first Comp-U-Store tests were for manufacturers such as J. P. Stevens, who wanted to try offering a full line in a department store. In 1983 Comp-U-Card started putting machines in places like A&P, Ben Franklin Variety, and Eckert Drug to sell its own catalog merchandise at a discount, giving the store a cut.

- *CompuServe* launched in February 1985, in partnership with L. M. Berry & Company, a service called the Electronic Mall. It is a co-op advertising medium aimed at computer owners who subscribe to CompuServe. There were 200,000 subscribers in the spring of 1985, and they were growing at the rate of 8000 a month. And the service had 55 advertisers or "tenants." Some advertisers invited direct orders, some pulled for inquiries, and some merely furnished information. Production costs per advertiser ranged from $50 to $400 per thousand.

Of the 6 million homes with personal computers at the time, 1.5 million were equipped with the modem needed to contact a database like the Electronic Mall. Future Information Systems predicted that the sale of modems would grow by 40 percent each year through 1988.

- *CompuSave* installs a video called Touch-n-Save in retail stores. Inside, on videodisc, there's a warehouse with 24 departments stocked with up to 3000 durable goods, offered at claimed discounts of 30 to 40 percent. The retailers pay $5000 for a machine and get to keep 5 percent of all sales revenue.

The company hoped to have 3000 machines installed by the end of 1985—first in supermarkets, but eventually in other kinds of locations as well, such as beauty salons, gymnasiums, drug stores.

If you're a retailer selling noncompetitive goods, the CompuSave machine could be an extra source of revenue for you.

If you want to get experience selling products or services to computer owners, then the Electronic Mall sounds like a good place to test.

And if you want to promote or sell your own brand in your own machine at your own locations, then you would shop for hardware and software with a company like ByVideo.

More Ways to Break Out of the Media Box

There are other surprising ways to advertise you probably never heard of before—because they didn't exist until recently. But it's a trend big enough to have rated a full-page news treatment in *Business Week:*

> The average woman in Baltimore looks at the parking meter for 14 seconds as she deposits the right change. In that time, she can check when the meter will expire—and read an advertisement from Campbell Soup Co. or Minolta Corp. Both companies recently began marketing their products on message boards mounted atop meters.
>
> Parking meters are just one of the many unusual places where advertising is popping up with increasing frequency. In New York City, electronic ads light up in front of taxi passengers; in sports stadiums, giant video screens display ads to fans; and in supermarkets, shoppers' carts are plastered with tiny billboards.
>
> "There's no question that more of our ad dollars are going to nontraditional media," says George Marhlig, Campbell's director of media services. Campbell currently spends about $1 million on alternative advertising, compared with virtually nothing five years ago.
>
> Campbell and other big marketers have a compelling reason to look for new advertising vehicles. They have been jolted by a dramatic rise in the cost of television spots at a time when the network audience share is steadily shrinking.[9]

One reason for the burgeoning of new media, the story pointed out, is changing lifestyles. For example, as more women leave home to work, advertisers can no longer reach them through daytime TV.

"As there is less opportunity to reach women through television, our media mix is changing," agreed Jay Uhlmansiek, director of advertising services for the Drackett Company, a Bristol-Myers subsidiary responsible for such household products as Windex, Endust, and Vanish cleaning products.[10]

Here is a quick look at some other emerging media. No matter how strange some of them seem, remember, we are entering a new era, and this is a thinkbook. Something here may spark in you an entirely unrelated idea for a new way you can sell or a new medium you can offer.

Floppy Disks for the Home Computer. This new channel of communication shows promise as an advertising medium of the future. Over one out of every six households now report owning a home computer.

Chevrolet has experimented with use of this medium in an ad headed, "Shopping for a New Car or Truck Just Got Easier." The text states: "As a PC owner, you know that knowledge is power. And we're out to give you more new car and truck buying power. Our FREE Chevy Tech software program 'specs out' popular Chevy cars and trucks. So you can build the Chevy you'd like to buy. . . . We've even included a short video game. It's easy, it's fun, and it's free." The accompanying order coupon calls for a payment of $3 for shipping and handling and asks the respondent for name, address, phone number, type and make of vehicle owned, and buying intentions.

A test of the diskette in California's Silicon Valley produced impressive results. Of the 1800 computer owners who requested a diskette after seeing an ad in a San Jose newspaper, 26 percent had gone in to see a dealer within 2 months and another 27 percent intended to do so.

In view of the stiff information requirements in the coupon, we would have eliminated the $3 charge. The best way to evaluate a marketing question like this is to consider the follow-up cost as part of the advertising cost per inquiry. Then it's easier to see whether you should charge and, if so, how much. For example, let's say Chevrolet's cost to make and mail the disk was $5 and their advertising cost per response was $15. They would be out $20 per response minus the $3 cash income, for a net investment per prospect of $17.

Look what might happen if they eliminated the $3 charge: The advertising cost per response might go down to $12. Add to that the $5 for making and mailing the disk, and the investment in each prospect would still be $17—but, because of the greater response, they would be reaching more prospects.

The nature of the offer plus the request for additional information should be enough of a qualifier to screen out mere curiosity seekers. So what if some of the respondents are teenage computer whiz kids? They are the Chevrolet prospects of tomorrow.

Furthermore, what if eliminating the $3 charge increased the responses still more and the advertising cost per inquiry went down to $9? Then the total investment per response would be only $14, and Chevrolet would be getting *more* inquiries at a *lower* cost per response.

Teleconferencing.   Companies like Videonet and Videostar will enable your company to make "live" video presentations to prospects or dealers simultaneously at various locations around the country. Vector Graphics used a video teleconference to introduce a new product to dealers and sold $150,000 worth of product right on the air.

Advertiser-Sponsored Entertainment and Sports.   Sponsorship has become big business. In 1985, about 2500 U.S. corporations spent over $1 billion sponsoring an estimated 3000 festivals and other special events. The 1985–1986 Virginia Slims World Championship Series encompassed more than 55 events worldwide and more than $12 million in prize money.

Skytray.   Skytray is a computer built into the seat-back tray table of commercial passenger planes, providing enjoyable two-way communication between advertisers and passengers.

Street Selling.   Street selling can be a respectable and effective advertising medium. Walton Productions organized a street campaign to sell long-distance phone service for US TEL. Smartly uniformed, well-trained young people tended colorful booths set up at high-traffic locations, and many of them signed up over 100 customers a day.

Doorhangers.   Doorhangers are an advertising vehicle that every recipient has to take in hand and examine at least once. Ferrington Place, a condominium in Charlotte, North Carolina, hung them on doorknobs of rental apartments to snag homecoming tenants with a riveting message: "Don't pay the rent." ChemLawn used doorhangers as a follow-up in marketing their lawn services in California: "I came by to find a solution to your landscape problem. See inside for results."

Actmedia.   Actmedia reaches 40 million households through the small billboards its army of 5000 trained part-time employees place on the ends of shopping carts. "I can't think of a better time to remind customers of your product than when they are actually making a purchase," said Jay Sloofman, marketing manager at Pepsi-Cola USA Inc. Actmedia affixes ads to nearly 2 million carts in 7700 stores, giving it broader reach than commercials on telecasts of the Super Bowl. In 1985, Actmedia introduced another new medium, Aislevision, a 20- by 30-inch space on aisle directories in 2700 supermarkets, as well as in-store sampling and demonstration service.

On-Pack/In-Pack Advertising.   Quick, which advertising medium has the greatest circulation of all, even greater than television, yet imposes no media charge? It's on-pack and in-pack advertising, which is also the most neglected advertising medium. Think about it—a package of *something* is in every home in the United States!

This medium is currently used mostly for premium promotion, product and institutional sell, and cross-sell. But it has enormous potential as an additional profit center, because it can be used to distribute advertising for related ventures at no advertising distribution cost. For example, most large boxes such as breakfast cereal or dog food have various advertising and promotional messages on the sides of the box, but they have *nothing inside* except perhaps a price-off coupon.

Because of low price and slim profit margins, the net profit per package sold might be only 10, 20, or 30 cents—or even less. But suppose inside there was a sales flyer or minicatalog inviting purchase by phone or mail of a related item or items, or membership in a monthly shipment club? And suppose the average gross sale to those who responded was $10, and the cost of merchandise and fulfillment was $3? *If just 1 percent of those who bought a package responded to the offer inside, it could add 20 percent to the profit on the sale of the packages.* And if your package sales are several hundred million dollars, that 20 percent increment would be lotsabucks.

Hasbro/Bradley, Inc., over a period of 3 years, developed a database of 1.5 million customers who had ordered additional toys by mail from the company—all as a result of minicatalogs inserted in the packages of such big Christmas sellers as GI Joe and My Little Pony. A company spokesperson said that the overall response rate was around 5 percent.

The company was said to have rented the list to more than 100 different companies. If each rental had been for the entire list, income of close to $5 million would have been generated just from the list rental.

The items sold by mail were line extensions not available at retail—such as a Parachute Pak for GI Joe—and were positioned as sale stimulators. They could be ordered for a modest price plus "points" printed at various places on the purchased package.

The company is obviously a very small step away from turning the operation into a profit center, if it isn't one already. There is no law against turning a profit on a premium, and if the Parachute Pak is self-liquidating at $1.50, charging $2 should turn a profit of 50 cents without arousing consumer price resistance or dealer opposition. The company spokesperson dropped a strong hint: "We see it as a way of helping retail by stimulating sales and *by giving us entry into a whole new area, a whole new channel of distribution.*"[11] (Italics ours.)

And what if your product is packaged in a jar? American Labelmark of Chicago has developed a new method of labelling that allows you to carry up to a yard of printed material in the space now used for one label. It's a multipage leaflet tucked under the front panel. When the consumer cuts along the dotted line, the leaflet pulls out, accordion-style.

Movie Theaters.   Remember that famous "1984" commercial for the Apple MacIntosh that ran just once, during the New Year's Day Super Bowl broadcast, and cost $1 million?

We'll bet you didn't know that before its television debut, the commercial had already been seen by *12 million people.*

The theater exposure was handled by Screenvision, the only U.S. company to distribute commercials to movie houses on a national basis. With 4000 first-run screens in nearly 2000 affluent surburban locations, Screenvision reaches some 24 million people, the majority of them aged 18 to 34, over a 4-week period. The average cost is $375,000 for a 4-week minimum national scheduling of a 1-minute commercial—less, the company points out, than it would cost to buy two 30-second spots on a top-rated and prime-time show.

More important, it's a good way to reach younger upscale people, especially college students, who may be out doing things with their friends rather than sitting at home watching television.

The commercials are usually longer, more elaborate, and softer-sell than on television. One advertiser, Eastman Kodak's film division, did research to find out if audiences resented the advertising and found little adverse effect.

Mail-Order Catalogs.   These catalogs are becoming an advertising medium. With the help of Catalog Advertising Sales, Bloomingdale's started selling space in 12 forthcoming catalogs in 1985, and within a short time was 70 percent sold out, generating $1.8 million in revenue. The Sharper Image soon followed suit.

Shipping Cartons.   So often stacked in store aisles, shipping cartons are becoming an economical point-of-purchase advertising medium, thanks to dramatically improved printing methods.

Owens-Illinois, one of several packaging companies in the field, expected to supply 50 million cartons with the upgraded graphics in 1985, a tenfold increase over the year before. A field marketing manager for Stroh Brewery Company said use of the vividly printed cartons in a display program in the Boston area helped boost sales of Erlanger, a Stroh's specialty superpremium beer, from a normal 150 cases to more than 800 cases.

Lamp Posts. So you have a tiny service business with a staff of one or two, offering something like word processing or painting or carpentering, and you think there is nothing here about maximizing media for your business? Well, you're wrong. In Manhattan, a new form of folk advertising has arisen, and if you can scrape up $25 or so, you can try it.

Small services in Manhattan are plastering lamp posts and telephone poles with hand bills advertising their services. That's not new. But what *is* new is that along the bottom is printed a row of little vertical coupons, with vertical slits separating them. Each coupon has the service's telephone number on it—some also carry a brief advertising message. This fringe of coupons along the bottom of the handbill waves in the breeze like a hula dancer's skirt. If you like the idea of the service described in the handbill, you tear off one of the little coupons as a reminder to telephone them.

Don't laugh. It's cost-effective. It's measurable. It calls for a response. This, too, is MaxiMarketing!

Matchbooks. Don't forget that humble but persistent traditional medium, the matchbook. As one supplier has pointed out, with 20 matches to the book, advertisers get exposure of a message that lasts much longer than a 30-second commercial. And it's cheaper too. You usually have to buy a minimum of 5 million, but that many would cost you only around $6000 or $1.20 per thousand. In quantities of 100 million, the price can drop as low as 40 cents per thousand.

Edward Horn, a New York attorney, advertises his law firm by distributing over 6 million matchbooks a month, each bearing his name, phone number, and an offer of free consultation. He says it costs him less than $1000 a month, and it more than pays for itself.

And there are plenty more media ideas where those came from—travelling billboards mounted on flatbed trucks, bus shelter ad panels, Jim Bouton's baseball cards, the video jukebox with built-in commercials, wall posters in fitness clubs, moving signs on boats and blimps and taxis, and even posters in the men's rooms of taverns.

You can't afford to try them all, unless you are a giant advertiser like Procter & Gamble or Campbell Soup Company. None of them may be right for you, but we hope they will make you think about how the world of advertising media is changing and how your thinking about media must start changing too.

The Bottom Line

In media, it's a whole new ball game today. You need to keep informed of what *is available to reach your target audience, and must also mobilize your creative resources to work out* how *to best use the bewildering variety of media choices today.*

And if you're not careful, you can lose your shirt twice. Once on intriguing new media or media uses that didn't work, and once again on costly research to find out why *they didn't work.*

We admit that adding a response element to shopping-cart advertising is not very practical. And we also admit that shopping-cart advertising may nonetheless be a good idea and a good investment for some advertisers. But we advocate and urge adding a response element to all media explorations whenever and wherever it is possible. It is the only completely accurate way to compare the advertising effectiveness of a variety of media sources and find out which can do the job for you. And the responses you get can begin your one-to-one relationship with a prime prospect or new tryer whom you can convert into a lifetime customer.

5

Maximized Accountability: Proving That It Works

The Big Picture

All advertising campaigns—even those seeking mail orders—begin by fostering a favorable awareness of the product or service advertised. The big difference in this respect between direct and indirect advertising is that the latter must create and build up lasting *awareness. Awareness must linger in the prospect's mind until the opportunity or need arises at the retail level to do something about it.*

In advertising by direct marketers, we know at once if the attempt we have made to create a favorable awareness of what we are selling has been successful. The public tells us right away, by its response. When we fail, we can find out where we have failed by isolating the various parts of the message and testing each separately.

In advertising designed to build a lasting image of a brand, a *company, or a service, it takes much longer—sometimes $5 or $10 million longer—to find out what has failed and why.*

How often have you read in the weekly advertising press of the failure and abandonment of a campaign theme which had been introduced with such enthusiasm and confidence a year or so earlier? How often have you winced at embarrassing excesses of cleverness in advertising and wondered what was wrong with their research?

The problem is that attitudes and attitude changes are much more difficult to measure than actions. The effect of awareness predisposition and image-building advertising depends not only on its content but also on weight and frequency of its exposure, and thus prediction of attitudinal changes over time is a very tricky business.

If your selling process is to be maximized at every step, you must maximize the power of your awareness advertising or the awareness-fostering elements in your advertising. And that calls for greater accountability and more precise measurement of advertising while it is happening.*

It also calls for more—and more exact—comparisons of advertising alternatives. Not just the old campaign versus the new campaign, but comparisons of a number of possible new campaign approaches and of different elements in the advertising tested against each other.

The question of the actual sales effectiveness of a given advertising effort can be removed from both the realm of opinion and the imprecise evaluations of traditional advertising research. But it requires an open-minded exploration of the new options by an advertising fraternity wedded to the past assumptions of the mass marketing era.

Although exact numbers would be difficult to come by, it seems a fair guess that as much as half of the roughly $100 billion in annual advertising expenditure in measured media is devoted to pure *awareness advertising.* And yet, despite the $1.5 billion current annual expenditure on advertising and marketing research (or more—just the top 40 firms in

---

* Chapter 4 discussed the value of adding a response element to your advertising as a means of evaluating and ranking the cost-effectiveness of your media buys. Keep in mind as you read this chapter that everything we say in it about the worth of measuring copy effectiveness through direct response is equally true of measurement of media effectiveness.

the field were paid $1.449 billion in 1984), *no one has been able to accurately measure the effect of any given awareness advertising on sales.*

The Naked King: Today's Advertising Research

Yes, advertising effectiveness can be measured in a general way: "We ran this campaign in a test market. Sales went up 20 percent. It must have been the advertising." What is missing is the capability to *improve* the advertising by scientifically measuring the effectiveness of one single advertising effort or impression versus another. And by "measuring," we don't mean observing what people *say* they intend to do, or suggest that they *might* do, or *seem* to have done, or *ought* to do based on their opinion of the advertising. We mean precise measurement of their actual response to real advertising in a real-life situation.

Direct-response advertising is the secret weapon that has enabled direct marketing to grow from its modest beginnings, small mail-order ads in farm publications in the nineteenth century, to the major marketing force that it has become. (Based on a Simmons study of direct-marketing transactions in July 1984, commissioned by Rapp & Collins, we estimated that the total volume for 1984 of all goods and services purchased and fund-raising contributions made as a result of mail and phone responses to direct-marketing advertising could have been as much as $170 billion.)

Yet direct response is a weapon that is conspicuous by its absence in almost all awareness advertising. Instead, great reliance is placed on research methods which the experts themselves admit (as we shall see) are woefully inadequate.

The truth is that a great deal of advertising and marketing research that is devoted to advertising effectiveness is a king who, a child can see, has no clothes on—or at least a king with his pants down and his knobby knees showing! To switch metaphors, an author's prerogative, most advertising accountability research is conducted by an army of brilliant, knowledgeable, sophisticated, blind people, equipped with fiendishly ingenious procedures and technology, doing their darndest to observe and describe an elephant they have never seen.

So the answer may come out, "Very big, tough hide, and what appears to be two tails." And sometimes it turns out not to have been an elephant at all, because it laid an egg and none of the blind people had observed the creature's internal reproductive process.

Do we exaggerate? Of course we do. Obviously $1.5 billion in research yields large amounts of valuable information. About desirable product attributes. About brand image and positioning and ranking. About share of market and share of mind. About almost everything except "How many sales will this particular advertising produce?" Or "How many *more* sales would this *other* advertising produce?" Or "How does our advertising in this media source compare with this other media source in actual effect on the public?"

Limitations of Research Frankly Confessed

Let others make the case for us. Stephen Fajen is media director of Saatchi & Saatchi Compton, in New York. In a brief piece in *Advertising Age*, he expressed with biting wit his obvious sense of frustration:

> Recently I reviewed a media plan. It was pretty simple. After IDing the target with demos and geos, it was refined with Clusterplus, VALS and a group of psychos. Then we looked at the reco.
>
> An adequate number of occasions were scheduled on the three nets, which is more than many of us can say about our personal life. We even fed some occasions because of a copy split test. We maximized our recall adjusted GRPs as much as possible. While we still can't measure CA's, our AA's held up well (as simulated on the MAGIC run off NTI data). R and F's were high enough, with a decent FDE, especially at a 3+ level.

And so on, for several more mind-spinning paragraphs of jargon. Then he concludes poignantly:

> In other words, we executed a plan that should work. There are however two remaining, rather important questions:
>
> 1. "Does everyone understand everything we are talking about?"
> 2. "Will this plan help sell more product?"[1]

Good questions—especially the second one. And that's just media. Look at what marketers have to wrestle with in copy research, as related by Stanley E. Moldovan, director of creative research at SSC&B Lintas Worldwide:

> When we began to think about our own copy-test procedure, there were a variety of what Shirley Young had called "magic numbers" that we could have used: everything from "basal skin response, brain waves, eye movement, pupil dilation, and physical activity; unaided and aided recall score, noting scores, copy-point recall, visual and slogan recall; interest and attitudes toward the brand, product attributes and benefits, buying intentions, coupon redemption, and simulated sales response."

We could have used a number of different research designs: pre-post versus post only, single versus multiple exposure, projectable versus non-projectable samples, and natural exposure versus forced exposure.

Forced exposure could have been varied: in-home, theatre, trailers, or mail situations. We could have tested individually or in groups. We could have tried to attempt to simulate a natural setting by introducing distracting or competitive advertising, program material, or simply gone straightforward.[2]

And still the question hangs in the air: "Will this plan help sell more product?" Listen to a most eminent authority on the subject, Dr. Edward M. Tauber of the University of Southern California, Los Angeles, editor of the *Journal of Advertising Research:*

"How will this copy perform?" That is the never-ending question asked by advertisers around the world. It is a question that researchers must address *in spite of the inadequacies of our tools to give a thoroughly satisfactory answer.* [Italics ours.][3]

This question is almost, although not quite, as old as the century. By 1923 advertising research was far enough along for Albert Lasker, the master builder of Lord & Thomas (later Foote, Cone & Belding) to grumble that it revealed only "that a jackass has two ears when we knew all the time that a jackass had two ears."[4]

One cannot help being stuck by this observation in reviewing the copy-test procedure that Stanley Moldovan and his associates did develop for SSC&B Lintas Worldwide, as he recounts in the 1984–1985 special issue of the *Journal of Advertising Research* on copy testing. Faced with a mountain of data derived from thousands of respondents, 37 variables, and hundreds of commercials, they boiled measurement of effectiveness down to six factors (using a "varimax" procedure in which the factors are "orthogonal").

The main (dependent variable) factor was persuasion, because that's what it's all about, intent to buy. The five independent variables were clarity, tastefulness, empathy, stimulation, and credibility.

Actually, the items scored under each factor are fairly sensible. For instance, under clarity a commercial is scored on items like "Did a good job of making its point. Clear. Informative. A good way to show the product." Under tastefulness: "Good taste. Not offensive. Enjoyable. Appropriate. Nothing disliked. Likable."

But one can't help wonder: Wouldn't a jury of all the employees at the offices of the agency or client be able to tell the creative director whether a commercial was "clear" or in "good taste"? And where is it written that a high score on all these factors inevitably leads to sales, reasonable as the assumption may seem?

Remember Rosser Reeves? His hard-sell commercials wouldn't score very well by the above standards, especially "good taste" and "enjoyable." But a "hard-sell advertisement," he preached to horrified ears, "like a diesel motor, must be judged on whether it performs what it was designed to do. Is a wristbone ugly? An ear? Or are they beautifully functional?"[5]

As Reeves later recalled (thanks to Stephen Fox's engaging history of advertising, *The Mirror Makers*, for reminding us), his Anacin boxes in the skull "were the most hated commercials in the history of advertising." But, Fox pointed out, in 18 months they raised Anacin sales from $18 million to $54 million.[6]

Please don't misunderstand—we are not arguing for a return to Rosser Reeves's hard sell. Times have changed, and so have consumers. (However, lest you think that Rosser Reeves's thinking is completely obsolete, we would like to point out one of the conclusions in a study by David Stewart of the Owens Graduate School of Management and David Furse of the Nashville Consulting Group. In an impressive analysis of 1059 commercials for 356 brands, they concluded: "Many years ago Rosser Reeves argued that every commercial should include a unique selling proposition. Our results would seem to suggest that he was right."[7])

We simply want to emphasize that research often goes to great lengths to measure irrelevant things, including people's *opinions* about advertising or their *memories* of it rather than their *actions* as a result of it. An objective observer might begin to wonder if U.S. business is spending hundreds of millions of dollars supporting a copy-research complex almost as wasteful as the military-industrial complex.

Don't you wonder how Richard Avedon's Brooke Shields commercials for Calvin Klein jeans would have scored with Mr. Moldovan's system?

For those who are interested, a succinct account of the origins of today's market research was presented in the *Journal of Advertising Research* by Dr. Benjamin Lipstein, chairman of National Scanning Services. Most significant for this discussion was his conclusion: "The issues raised more than half a century ago are as relevant and thought-provoking and in many instances the same as the issues we are raising today. *All of the investigators of the past recognized that their copy-testing efforts and measurements were just a surrogate for actual buying behavior.*"[8] (Italics ours.)

Self-Doubts in the Trade Press

Serious questions about copy research were raised at an American Association of Advertising Agencies regional conference in the mid-1970s.

"We've substituted palpable nonsense and simplistic shortcuts" for meaningful copy research, *Advertising Age* quoted panelist Arthur Pearson, at that time Clairol's marketing services director and vice chairman of the Advertising Research Foundation. "After all is said and done, there is no nice, neat analog to advertising's effect on sales."[9]

The magazine's report continued: "Mr. Pearson's conclusions hardly came as news to the session's audience of research experts; few voices were raised to dispute Mr. Pearson or other panelists holding the same view. Yet copy testing—research designed to find out which ad or commercial will move the most merchandise—is a $75 million annual industry that *continues to rely largely on assumptions, if not wishful thinking*."[10] (Italics ours. Of course it's much more than $75 million today.)

And Larry Light, then BBD&O research director, was quoted, "We've learned that all copy testing techniques have an inherent degree of unreliability greater than most users would like." Suppliers, he observed, "assure us that their techniques are reliable, valid, and furthermore are a bargain at twice the price." But when he paired different testing techniques against each other, he said, different methods picked different winning commercials 77 percent of the time. "We were concerned that research companies were getting richer than our clients."[11]

And how had the situation improved 10 years later? Listen to Alvin Achenbaum of the marketing consulting firm of Canter, Achenbaum, Associates Inc. He is an advertising veteran with impressive credentials: His previous positions were as director of marketing services and corporate planning at J. Walter Thompson and executive vice president in charge of marketing and business services at Grey Advertising. On February 7, 1985, at a breakfast conference of the American Marketing Association in New York, he fired a volley that should have echoed up and down the canyons of Madison Avenue (and Park, and Third, where more agencies are located today):

> Copy tests are in my opinion no better than market tests in their performance. To take the most prevalent technique used today—so-called recall tests—irrespective of the number of studies done which show that recall measurements are irrelevant, that they are not in fact related to consumer purchase proclivities or purchasing behavior, marketers continue to use and rely on that measuring stick. . . . But copy tests lack for more than a relevant measurement device. The fact is that they fail on almost every aspect of good research design—from the small samples they use to the unrealistic stimuli involved, to name only two.
>
> Frankly, the money spent on all of this foolish research is a waste, and, as such, a drag on marketing productivity. It may be a necessary lubricant for decision making, but it certainly is an expensive and misleading one.[12]

In January 1985, *Advertising Age* had a half-page article about the research program of New England Life Insurance Company for their cartoon ad campaign in magazines that totalled $3 million in just the first quarter of 1985 alone. What was the object of the research? To make sure that the 50 cartoon ads developed were likeable and not offensive to anyone!

The entire article contained not one single word about the advertising's effect, if any, on sales. "It's just as important that people like the ads as it is to sell the product," the article quoted the vice president for corporate communications.[13] Or (reading between the lines) even more so?

We are told that the campaign was a result of the company's reconsidering its place in the deregulated financial services industry 4 years earlier. And what was their decision? To continue their lovable cartoon series ("My insurance company? New England Life, of course. Why?") but to change the caption to read, "My financial partner?" etc.[14]

Of course it's possible that the campaign had a valid public-relations objective and could not be evaluated in terms of sales impact.

But at about the same time, in a period of only 6 years, using measured multimedia direct-response advertising, Merrill Lynch persuaded *1 million people* to invest a total of *$60 billion* in their new Cash Management Account. Doesn't it make you wonder which company was pursuing the smarter strategy?

The Potential Harm of Misguided Research

Sometimes research can actually cause harm. Anthony I. Morgan, research director of Backer & Spielvogel, tells of how close research came to killing a great campaign:

> When the Campbell Soup Company was attempting to arrest a 10-year decline in per capita consumption of their Red & White line of soups, a three-stage series of communication tasks was established: (1) tell people there is new news about soup; (2) change their perception of soup; and (3) get them to eat more soup.
>
> What happened when the initial commercial for this campaign met a standard copy-testing system? Disaster! It got the lowest scores ever for a Campbell's commercial.
>
> Fortunately, the campaign was already in its west coast test markets so there were actual, in-market research numbers to counter the copy test. In reality this commercial, plus some newspaper ads, had created an awareness level of over 50% for the "new news" about soup—exactly what it was

intended to do. The rest is history and Campbell's is today enjoying their third year of sales increases with the Soup is Good Food campaign.[15]

RCA Record Club's Interview Research and Actual Direct-Response Results

In 1981, we had a rare opportunity to compare the accuracy of predictive consumer-interview research and actual direct-response results. A total of 104 respondents were shown eight different ads for RCA Record Club, all featuring essentially the same offer to new members. The respondents were all people who had bought records or tapes within the previous 6 months, had bought something by mail in the previous 3 years, and were not totally "turned off" to record clubs.

They were asked to rank eight ad campaigns according to "uniqueness," "interest in reading further," "believability," and "interest in responding." The results of this research predicted that the winners would be the ads nicknamed "Guarantee" and "No Fine Print." According to the research, "Headphones" ran a poor fifth and "Cartoon" a miserable last.

However, when we actually ran the ads in an equal eight-way split run, "Headphones" was a clear winner. And "Cartoon," a corny but very effective cartoon ad which had consistently beaten other approaches for years, decisively outpulled the ads which the research respondents had chosen as most likely to interest and persuade them.

If RCA had relied on the predictive research, the profitability of their advertising would have been sharply reduced.

The Hazards of Flying Blind

But even faulty or inadequate research is usually better than no research at all. Out of the estimated $50 billion in national advertising expenditure in 1985, how much do you suppose was pretested or posttested, even with faulty methods?

Your guess is as good as ours. Our guess is not more than 20 percent. And hard as it is to believe, some advertising, presumably not pretested, seems to produce almost no sales at all.

In the summer of 1984, Ashton-Tate and Lotus tried to build brand awareness for their software with television advertising. Ashton-Tate spent $4 million, then pulled the plug. According to the *Advertising Age* story at the time:

Ashton-Tate's and Lotus's TV campaigns so far have had little measurable impact with retailers. "Most of us here were not really that impressed," said Jane Mosey, office manager of a ComputerLand outlet in suburban Mount Kisco, N.Y.

Ms. Mosey said the commercials did not produce any increase in sales or inquiries about the products at the store. And this is despite the fact that Ashton-Tate spent the bulk of its July spot TV money in New York. [Italics ours.][16]

And note this revealing item from *The Wall Street Journal:*

Heublein won raves from feminists for Harvey's Bristol Cream commercials in which women boldly invited men over to their apartments. "It made the brand much more visible," a Heublein spokesman says, "but I wouldn't say it had a great effect on sales."[17]

We believe this can be safely translated to mean it had no perceptible effect on sales at all.

In early 1985, the British computer Apricot launched a $7.5 million U.S. advertising campaign. The opening ad trumpeted: "January 23, 1985. The day we upset the Apple cart. Introducing Apricot." And that's all it said, except for tiny "mouse type" at the bottom of the ad: "Europe's most successful business computer company is now doing business in America. If you're Apple, you might want to take note of the date. If you're in business, you might want to take note of the company." And you might not, since this surely untested advertising told the prospect absolutely nothing about the product's advantages or benefits to consumers

A Better Way

There's got to be a better way to know if your advertising is reaching and affecting your intended target. And there is. Incorporate some form of direct response in all awareness advertising during the test phase. Then measure the difference between one advertising effort and another by comparing the number of responses received in a scientific A-B split-run test of the two efforts. (Better yet, more than two.)

You haven't solved everything: For example, you haven't precisely measured the effect of the advertising on retail sales or the long-term effect of repeated impressions. But you *have* provided a method of scientific comparison of one individual advertising effort to another. Or even, as direct marketers do so often in their direct-response advertising, comparison of just one advertising *element* to another—one headline to another, one picture to another, one price or offer or appeal to another, and so on.

Combining the winning elements into a single advertising effort, as we often do in direct-response advertising, can produce incremental improvements in effectiveness of 50 percent, 75 percent, 100 percent, and 200 percent.

Unlike brand advertisers, direct marketers never discard an old ad until a new one has been proved better. The last *Reader's Digest* mailing you received is the product of continuous evolution, the result of dozens and even hundreds of incremental improvements derived from tests over a period of years.

What about Cumulative Effect?

One telling argument made against direct-response split-run tests as a research method for all advertising is that these tests cannot necessarily measure the power of a theme which depends on massive repetition for its effectiveness.

Take, for instance, the long-running, highly successful Campbell Soup theme, "Soup is good food." As mentioned, this theme flunked a standard copy-testing system. Might it also have lost out in a direct-response split-run test against an ad with some other, more immediately compelling theme, each with the same buried offer?

Or, to put it another way, is it possible that "Soup is good food" is a very mild, innocuous claim when heard only once, but it steadily grows in power and persuasiveness the more it is repeated? If that were true, measuring comparative response to just one exposure might mislead.

Let us grant that possibility, even though over the years advertisers have wasted many, many millions of dollars on this convenient explanation. (Victor Schwab believed that "the habit of waiting for, and placing great dependence upon, cumulative effect can become simply an alibi for poor advertising." And he cited an investigation by Dr. Henry C. Link which indicated that "an advertising theme that does not have a strong effect immediately is not likely to accumulate much in effectiveness through periodic repetition over a period of months."[18])

And let us also assume that your budget is large enough to achieve this wondrous cumulative effect. (Without the expenditure of huge sums for constant repetition of your theme, your advertising is not going to have *any* cumulative effect on the public. People have too many other things to think about.)

Even so, there are still a great many ways that split testing could develop and improve the *expression* of such a theme. For example, is it better to show people or food? Does featuring one particular flavor attract more interest and, if so, which flavor? Does a human-interest story featuring a real customer increase the impact? Direct-response split testing can answer many questions like these with more precision (and usually at less cost) than any other research method.

The Promise and Problems of Electronic Testing

Until recently, the mechanical A-B split run of advertising calling for direct response by mail or phone was the only truly scientific method of copy comparison testing. (Theoretically, you can compare two ads by split-running them and including store-redeemed coupons in each. However, this process is slower and less precise, and it requires couponing, which an advertiser might not be able or willing to do.)

Now a new electronic technology is emerging which holds great promise both for brand advertisers and for direct marketers, although it is still in the developmental stage. The advent of BehaviorScan and A. C. Nielsen's rival service, ERIM, have made possible split-run advertising of brand-name package goods in a test market that measures the results at a supermarket or drugstore cash register.

By electronically metering television viewing in test households, electronically recording the purchases of the test households in their supermarkets and drugstores, and electronically correlating the two sets of data, a direct link can be established between advertising and sales. Through electronic intervention, half of or all the test households can be exposed to a test commercial instead of the network commercial all other households are receiving.

In print advertising, one advertising approach can be tested against another in the electronically monitored test markets through a device familiar to direct marketers—a newspaper insert of ad A and a newspaper insert of ad B are intermixed at the printer's before insertion. Then the actual retail sales stimulated by each approach can be accurately measured. This seems to present at last a scientific method of testing package-goods advertising and of recording the sales results at the cash register.

The method has a number of drawbacks, however. It is slow and costly. It is applicable only to package goods sold in grocery stores and drugstores equipped with scanners. It could take 6 months to a year and hundreds of thousands of dollars to determine that a new campaign or a new product is not a good idea, while the competition might be racing ahead. There is real question whether the households are sufficiently representative geographically, demographically, and psychographically, since the test markets must be "pure" smaller cities, uncontaminated by the influence of other markets. Most important, the comparison does not offer the flexibility and versatility of direct-response split-run testing, especially in publication advertising.

An eight-way split of eight ads, all with the same direct-response buried offer, can test eight benefits, eight product advantages, or eight ways to express one benefit or advantage. Such a research project, using electronic testing in test markets, is theoretically possible, but it would also be slow, cumbersome, and fearfully expensive.

Television is another story. If you are a TV advertiser of package-goods products sold in stores with Universal Product Code (UPC) scanners, then these new electronic-testing services may offer an ideal way to compare the actual sales effect of one commercial to another.

The Lonely Advocate of Response Testing

What if you are selling a product whose sales are not recordable by scanner, such as house paint or electric drills? Then it's time to take a new look at one of the oldest yet most frequently overlooked research methods, the direct-response split run.

More than half a century ago, an advertising pioneer named John Caples explained the procedure for this research. In his classic book, *Tested Advertising Methods,* now in its fourth edition, Caples showed how the question of effective advertising can be removed from the realm of opinion and decided by the actual response of the public.

But the system Caples described—which probably began with Albert Lasker's application of the simple research methods of his Lord & Thomas mail-order clients to his brand-advertising accounts around the turn of the century—gradually fell into disuse.

David Ogilvy, one of the great theorists of advertising, deserves our thanks for rekindling interest in what Caples advocated. In the foreword to the fourth edition of Caples's book, Ogilvy pays generous tribute to its value:

> On page 11 of this book, John Caples writes, "I have seen one advertisement sell $19\frac{1}{2}$ times as much goods as another." This statement dramatizes the gigantic difference between good advertisements and bad ones. . . .
>
> An earlier edition taught me most of what I know about writing advertisements. These discoveries . . . have been made by John Caples in the course of his long and distinguished career. He has been able to measure the results of every advertisement he has ever written.
>
> The average manufacturer, who sells through a complex system of distribution, is unable to do this. He cannot isolate the results of individual advertisements from the other factors in his marketing mix. He is forced to fly blind. . . .

The vast majority of people who work in agencies, and almost all their clients . . . skid helplessly about on the greasy surface of irrelevant brilliance. They waste millions on bad advertising, when good advertising could be selling 19½ times as much.

This is, without doubt, the most useful book about advertising that I have ever read. [Italics added.][19]

There are two main aspects to Caples's book: (1) the testing method and (2) the principles of effective advertising he had derived as a result of many tests. Unfortunately, the dated look and sound of the examples he provides of the latter are so foreign to sophisticated image-building requirements of today that they might cause the contemporary reader to overlook the timeless significance of the research method he used.

Almost buried in the book's wealth of practical principles of effective mail-order and direct-response advertising is a timeless but sorely neglected approach to the improvement of all advertising. This approach involves applying the testing techniques of mail-order advertising to products not sold by mail at all but rather at retail or by a salesperson.

The United States in the 1920s was bursting with eager, upwardly mobile people, many of them first- and second-generation immigrants determined to make good in the New World. Books, courses, and other methods of self-improvement were very popular and were widely sold by mail-order advertising, an ideal method of communication and distribution for that kind of product.

To accommodate these important advertisers, an increasing number of newspapers and magazines offered split-run service. The advertiser could supply two different advertisements, with the reply address in each keyed differently, and the publication would run both ads in the same issue and position. In a true A-B split, every other copy of the publication would contain ad A, and every other copy would contain ad B. This advertising research technique met the same requirements of the scientific method that Luther Burbank used in comparing the germination of two seeds under identical conditions.

Caples was apparently so eager to get on with talking about and showing what works in advertising that he did not vigorously crusade in his book for applying this research technique to awareness advertising that does not pull for an immediate order. But he did provide examples of it. "Perhaps in years to come, more advertisers will use scientific methods," mused Caples. "Perhaps more advertisers will run tested copy in tested media. In answer to the question, 'What will advertising be like 30 years hence?' a famous advertising man replied, 'It will be more exact, more scientific, and therefore more resultful.' "[20]

But, by and large, it is questionable that this has happened as indicated by the expressed doubts about copy research which we have quoted.

How the Caples Method Works

The essence of the Caples method of scientifically comparing two advertisements is to vary the advertisements—a different promise, a different price, a different method of presentation, even a different product name—but make an offer which remains identical in wording and presentation in both advertisements.

The offer—which could be a booklet, sample, savings coupon, or simply an offer to supply the nearest dealer's name—can either be featured in a reply coupon or buried in the text. (Or it can invite a phone response via an 800 number—the telecommunications breakthrough of the seventies that has added an entirely new dimension to advertising response in the eighties.) A coupon will produce more replies than a buried offer and thus lends itself to more statistically significant measurement. However, the buried offer ad will more nearly simulate what the same ad would look like without an offer.

The Caples method remains a valid way to test different appeals, product attitudes, and methods of presentation in awareness advertising today. In fact, the development of the 800 number as a response mechanism has made it even more practical.

The testing can be done in any medium where absolutely equal A-B splitting is possible. Such testing lends itself ideally to direct mail, where it is a simple matter to create any number of test cells with identical consumer characteristics. A-B tests of magazine, newspaper, and television advertising can be devised almost as easily.

Adherents of other methods of research might argue that the 1 person out of 1000 who responds to a buried offer differs from—and does not represent—the whole. And this may have some truth. But the same could be said of the consumers in a small-city test market like Pittsfield, Massachusetts, who are observed by traditional research methods. Consider also that many of the other 999 out of 1000, whose opinions and reactions are studied and observed by other methods of research, are not serious prospects and will never become serious prospects.

So the reaction of the targeted individual who is the reason for the advertising in the first place should be more significant than the reaction of a nonprospect. And the Caples method has the great virtue of being a reality-based reaction in a real advertising environment rather than an artificial laboratory experiment or observation in a theater or shopping mall.

It is fascinating to observe in Caples's book a split-run test of two different appeals for a product that is still alive and kicking today, Milk

Bones, the snack food for dogs. Both ads carried coupons offering a free gift package of Milk Bones Snacks. Both ads carried the same message that feeding your dog table scraps in the summer was dangerous, and that you should give your dog healthful Milk Bones instead. One ad used a negative appeal and the other a positive appeal:

Ad A: Don't Poison Your Dog!
Ad B: Keep Your Dog Safe This Summer!

When the coupons were counted, they found that ad B had pulled 58 percent more requests.

Do you find it hard to believe that this was a meaningful result? If you were the marketing director for Milk Bones at the time, wouldn't you have found this to be extremely useful information? Wouldn't it have been helpful in developing a sound copy platform? And wouldn't the information cost far less to develop today than dubious mall interviews or eye-movement measurements? Doesn't it defy common sense to believe that the dog owners who did respond to the offer reacted somehow differently to the two appeals than the dog owners who did not?

Can Split Testing Develop Better Television Spots?

Even if 30-second commercials don't lend themselves very well to a buried offer, wouldn't this kind of print-advertising result be helpful in planning a television commercial for the same product?

Brand advertisers who rely heavily on network television may feel that it is simply not possible to incorporate a direct-response element in a 30-second commercial. This may (or may not) be true, but there is nothing to prevent split testing, via split-cable or rotating markets, two 60-second commercials, each made up of a brand-image variable (30 seconds) and a direct-response-offer constant (30 seconds). If desired, the 30-second offer could be dropped from the commercial in the rollout (although a later chapter will argue for keeping in the offer to generate names for a prospect database).

Caples presented evidence that the advertisement which produces the most inquiries produces the most sales. However, this was not evidence about brand advertising of products sold at retail, because, until the recent development of services like BehaviorScan, accurately linking brand ad response to retail sales was impossible.

Today, however, we have that capability, even if it is still in the experimental stage. By combining the Caples method with BehaviorScan or ERIM, it should be possible to prove (or disprove) that the ad which produces the most requests for a rebate, sample, or booklet *also* produces the most sales at the drugstore or supermarket.

In *Confessions of an Advertising Man,* Ogilvy recounts using the Caples technique to develop the best promise for a Dove toilet bar. He reported that "Creams your skin while you wash" pulled 63 percent more responses than did the next best promise, "and it has been the fulcrum of every Dove advertisement that has ever run. This marvelous product made a profit at the end of its first year, a rare feat in the marketing world of today."[21]

However, if others are using the same powerful research method for package goods today, it is one of the best-kept secrets in advertising.

Why Was Buried-Offer Testing Abandoned?

If split-run testing of two or more different ads with the same buried direct-response offer is so effective, why has it fallen into such disuse today?

The answer is shrouded in the mist of advertising history. But we can hazard a guess: First, the development of radio, and then of television seemed to require—and did produce—new, more elaborate forms of copy research which came to be accepted as the state of the art.

Second, advocates of other methods of research bolstered their arguments against direct-response testing with that we believe to be a statistically fallacious argument. This argument was summarized in a scholarly book published in 1936, *Four Million Inquiries from Magazine Advertising,* by Harold J. Rudolph:

> It might be argued that replies do not constitute a representative sample of the magazine-reading population since only a small percentage of any magazine's circulation is made up of potential coupon clippers. For example, the average advertisement draws coupons from less than 1/10 of one percent of the readers to whom it is exposed. Therefore, in order to show an increase of 50 percent in replies, an advertisement need only secure responses from an additional 1/20 of one percent of the circulation. Is this a significant margin? In other words, should one advertisement be considered superior to another because it has elicited response from 1/20 of one percent more readers?[22]

Our answer is that *a 50 percent increase in response cannot be a random result explained purely by the laws of chance.** In other words, if two identical response ads are given equal exposure to two equal audiences over and over again, the total replies to each would be roughly equal (with the plus or minus variations you would get from flipping a coin). So if the responses from ad A exceed the responses from ad B by a statistically greater margin than you would get from coin flipping, ad A is statistically superior. And these are responses from real prospects in a real advertising environment, not artificially stimulated opinions and responses from human guinea pigs who may not be willing to buy your product no matter how good your advertising is.

Like all the other research methods, split-run testing of ads with an identical buried offer cannot relate each advertising exposure directly to sales. But it *can* measure and compare public reaction to the advertising message at the precise moment when it is reaching the target audience in the real media environment. By testing A against B and the winner against C and the winner of that round against D and so on, split-run testing can build incremental improvement in the proven impact and believability of your advertising.

Thus as the glaring limitations of other kinds of copy research become increasingly evident, one of the oldest forms of advertising research may become one of the newest—especially since it fits in so well with the other requirements of MaxiMarketing.

Time for a New Approach

In a series of articles in *The New Yorker* on cable television by Thomas Whiteside, video consultant Michael Dann wrote

> When Warner Brothers put a movie into the theatres, it was rolling dice; the public decided right at the box office how successful it was. Well, that's quite different from the modern marketing of consumer goods. Procter & Gamble doesn't do things that way. It doesn't roll dice. It tests markets. It picks cities, marketing areas, it test-markets variations of the product, test-markets this, test-markets that—it's done by computer.[23]

But do they know how many sales were produced by one particular advertisement in one particular publication? How many more or fewer sales were produced by a different advertisement receiving completely equal exposure? The names and addresses and brand preferences of the people who buy as a result of their advertising? (This is another benefit

---

* Unless the total number of responses were extremely small. For example, if ad A pulled 2 responses and ad B pulled 3 responses, this would not be a statistically significant difference. But if ad A pulled 2000 responses and ad B pulled 3000 responses, this *would* be a statistically significant difference.

which grows out of including a direct-response element in your advertis-
·ing.)

Achenbaum says bluntly:

> Marketers must avoid the use of unreliable, unpredictive evaluation tech-
> niques no matter how desirable they may seem. There is no sense in spend-
> ing money on research tests that don't work. Traditional market tests and
> copy research are not doing the job. *Marketers must begin to seek better ways
> of evaluating copy and marketing variables.* [Italics ours.][24]

How Response Testing Makes Advertising More Realistic

Many ads that we see in magazines and newspapers are a product of
what we call the "all you gotta do is" school of advertising. "All you gotta
do is" show the product or a striking picture with a few provocative
words. The Apricot computer ad cited earlier is a good example. Usually
the words are a clever twist on the English language that leaves it to the
reader to figure out what is going on. (The graphic element may give
you a hint, but just barely.) This approach to advertising has perverted
Bill Bernbach's creative revolution and put its practitioners in a pseudo-
creative straitjacket.

We believe that when advertisers try more than one kind of approach
and carefully tabulate and compare the responses, reality begins to in-
trude and may change the entire character of the advertising. Instead of
the advertiser telling or showing the public something it *ought* to respond
to, the public begins to tell the advertiser what it actually *does* respond to.
And all-you-gotta-do advertising begins to give way to true creativity
based on appeals, facts, information, explanation, persuasion, positioning.

However, another warning is in order. This process of incremental
improvement is possible only if the various approaches and elements
tested are distinctly and intelligently different.

Each variable tested should be an expression of a clearly stated hypothesis based on a strategic consideration, such as:

- Maybe we can reach these prospects better with a cartoon than with a
  photograph.

- Maybe we ought to provide more background information and romance about the product.

- Maybe we ought to emphasize convenience rather than economy in
  the headline.

At Rapp & Collins, we have even tested one celebrity spokesperson against another in direct-response television commercials for Save the Children, with a startling difference in results.

A brand-advertising creative team schooled and experienced in the art of developing "the" best advertising approach may find it difficult suddenly to shift gears and express the same message ten different ways. But the talent and capability are there, waiting to be used in this way.

The Bottom Line

In summary, we believe that the efficiency of almost any kind of advertising, in just about any advertising medium, can be systematically and incrementally improved by (1) incorporating a direct response element in the advertising, (2) split testing a variety of approaches, each with the same constant direct-response element, and (3) incorporating the discoveries thus made into the rollout of the campaign.

In the distance, we can hear screams of outrage at the idea of testing advertising such as "The Marlboro Man" cigarette ads, or the famous Wendy's "Where's the Beef?" commercial, or the potential impact of "Herb" on Burger King sales by adding a response element and measuring the responses.

But who can say how much more effective the Marlboro Man advertising might have been if just a tiny percentage of the hundreds of millions of dollars spent on it had been devoted to measuring various elements within the advertising itself in the actual media arena where it is meant to do its job? Besides, that leaves all the many advertisers who don't have Marlboro's or Wendy's or Burger King's megabucks to lavish on burning an indelible image into the public mind.

If you can afford an annual budget of "only" $5 million or $2 million or $1 million—or less—to convert your true prospects into customers, can you afford anything less than knowing for sure which of a number of advertising approaches will produce the most reaction from the people you most want to reach? Can you really afford not to use direct-response split-run testing to get the answer?

Split-run copy testing is so inexpensive that almost any advertiser can do it. It can add strong new muscle to your advertising, and it can provide a simple method of checking out our argument for whole-brain advertising you will read about next in Chapter 6.

6

Maximized Awareness Advertising: Appealing to the Whole Brain

The Big Picture

For almost 100 years, two warrings camps have struggled for the soul of advertising.

"Be persuasive! Present a convincing advantage or benefit!" is the battle cry of the first camp.

"Be creative! Be entertaining!" insists the second camp.

"Ridiculous!" snorts the first. "The public may be tickled to death with your advertising—but will they buy your product?"

"Well, I'd rather have them tickled to death than bored to death! You can't save souls in an empty church!"

"Bah! You're arty, that's what you are!"

"Oh yeah? Well, you're corny!"

*Today, this familiar disagreement (which has come close to caus-
ing fist fights in some advertising agencies and creative departments) is suddenly taking on new importance—because the stakes
have been raised.*

*With the proliferation of products, prospects, media, and mes-
sages, it is getting harder for your advertising to get through to and
move your prospect—and more costly if you fail. Choosing the right
way to frame your message becomes doubly important.*

*But which way is right? The truth is, both are. Each side appeals
to half of us. Together, they can appeal to all of us, although
sometimes we need more of the one kind of communication than the
other. Advertising goes wrong—often—by failing to match the
emphasis on reason or emotion with the needs of the product and the
prospect. Or sometimes by failing to nourish both sides of the brain.*

*Let's examine this historic conflict to develop a synthesis that will
give maximum sales power to your advertising approach to prospects.*

Within the last decade, the concept of *left brain* and *right brain* has
become part of pop culture, to the extent that it occasionally works its
way into comic strips. The left hemisphere of the brain controls logic
and language, and the right brain controls creativity and intuition—
right?

Well, it turns out that this isn't exactly the case. For example, a painter
named Lovis Corinth suffered right-hemisphere damage to his brain but
continued to paint—more expressively and boldly than before. (We owe
this observation to Jerre Levy, a biopsychologist who has spent most of
her career studying this phenomenon.) Apparently both halves of the
brain work together on tasks, and each half is capable of doing the
other's work, although perhaps not always as well.

Regardless of the scientific truth, the concept of left brain and right
brain is another in an ancient series of useful metaphors for the eternal
duality in the way humanity thinks and feels: Yang and yin. Logic and
intuition. Hot and cool. Dreams and reality. Art and science. Fact and
fiction. Poetry and prose. Realism and romance. Linear thinking and
lateral thinking.

This duality has frequently caused heated conflict between apostles of
one side and the other. Nowhere has this been more true than in the
world of advertising and marketing.

The Voices of Left-Brain and Right-Brain Advertising

From the beginnings of advertising theory, around the turn of the century, advocates of one side of the argument or the other have insisted that theirs is the one true path to successful communication with advertising prospects.

Some of the arguments advanced in the early days still seem valid today. And some of the points of view expressed in our own time would not have seemed out of place in 1910.

We found it entertaining and instructive to sort out and combine in a table some of the comments made through the years according to whether they expressed a left-brain or right-brain approach to advertising.

Left Brain	Right Brain
"Print the news of the store. No 'catchy headlines,' no catches, no headlines, no smartness, no brag, no 'fine writing,' no fooling, no foolery, no attempt at advertising, no anxiety to sell, no mercenary admiration. . . ."[1] —John O. Powers, advertising manager of Wanamaker's Department Store (1895)	Copy was not just the words but "that combination of text with design which produces a complete advertisement."[10] —Earnest Elmo Calkins, cofounder of Calkins & Holden (1907)
"True 'Reason-Why' copy is Logic, plus simplicity of thought, plus conviction, all woven into a certain simplicity of thought—pre-digested for the average mind, so that it is easier to *understand* than to *misunderstand.*"[2] —John E. Kennedy, who taught Albert Lasker of Lord & Thomas that "Advertising is Salesmanship in Print" (1904)	"They were almost all picture. It's the *atmosphere* in these that sells . . . the quality that gives prestige, the little imaginative sure touches that bring the thing before you."[11] —Cyrus Curtis, magazine publisher, referring to the Calkins & Holden campaigns for Arrow collars and Pierce-Arrow cars (1914)
" 'Keeping the name before the public' is wrong and 'salesmanship in print' is right."[3] —Lord & Thomas pamphlet, *The Book of Tests* (1905)	"The actual effect of modern advertising is not so much to convince as to suggest."[12] —Walter Dill Scott of Northwestern University, *The Psychology of Advertising* (1917)
"Style is a handicap. Anything that takes attention from the subject reduces the impression."[4] —Claude Hopkins, *My Life in Advertising* (1927)	"The psycho-analysts have learned this about humankind, that nearly all of the important decisions of the individual are really made *in the subconscious.*"[13] —B. L. Dunn, advertising manager, Oneida Community Silver (1918)
"Present-day advertising research has a long way to go before it reaches the level of Claude Hopkins' contribu-	Reason-why advertising consists of "a clever and semi-scientific application of the thesis that all men are fools. . . . I look upon the public as myself multiplied, and I have not yet

Left Brain

tions to efficient advertising."[5]
—Alfred Politz, psychologist and advertising research consultant (1935)[5]

"What this agency has done which is different from any other agency is to apply reason to advertising. Reason— not unconscious starvings for sex and security."[6]

"Advertising began as an art . . . and too many advertising men want it to remain that way—a never-never land where they can say, 'This is right because we feel it's right.' "[7]
—Rosser Reeves, *Reality in Advertising* (1961)

"I have never admired the *belles lettres* school of advertising. I have always thought them absurd; they did not give the reader a single *fact*."[8]
—David Ogilvy, *Confessions of an Advertising Man* (1963)

"I think people want *information*. They don't get it from advertising. Say you're buying a tape deck. Well, you're up against it—especially if you read the ads. A double-entendre headline. Nice photo. But no *real meat* in the ad. Because the people who did the ad don't think you *really* want to know. Advertising people argue that it's good to make it simple. But that's not the point. People want to know. Advertising ought to give them the information they need."[9]
—Helmut Krone, executive vice president, Doyle Dane Bernbach, a member of the Art Directors Hall of Fame (1984)

Right Brain

reached that stage of diffidence and humility which permits me to write myself down as an Ass."[14]
—Theodore F. MacManus, star copy- writer for General Motors (1932)

"It is not what is said but how it is said that influences us the most.
"Any copy in advertising is an argu- ment. It is literally throwing down a challenge to the reader . . . saying: 'Let's argue about this.' The human reaction to any statement of claim is 'Wait a minute! Who says so?' "[15]
—Pierre Martineau, research director of the *Chicago Tribune* (1957)

"We are definitely again in the age of the eye. We have less time to read, browse, meditate and muse. There is such a multiplicity of messages strik- ing us from every side . . . that it seems sometimes that only the light- ning message of a picture can strike deep and hit home when we have a moment to spare."[16]
—Margot Sherman, vice president, McCann-Erickson (1959)

"If an idea makes me laugh, that's a sure sign it's a good idea. All com- mercials should be entertaining, no exceptions made. Somebody's making the business too rational, which is wrong. Advertising is an emotional industry. . . . Everybody ought to have fun . . . if you're not having fun, then you're getting screwed."[17]
—Lou Centlivre, executive managing director—creative, Foote, Cone & Belding, Chicago (Formerly Lord & Thomas!) (1985)

". . . to move our creative effort from good to great, we add a healthy measure of our magic ingredient. We inject that absolutely necessary, posi- tively critical element—style."[18]
—Bob Fearon, chairman/creative director, Fearon/GBA Group (1985)

Fortunately, advertising, like life, is a unity of opposites. Just as the two hemispheres of the brain work together, so can the two kinds of advertising appeal work together—and sometimes they must.

Whether your advertising should stir up more activity in the prospect's left brain or right brain depends on what you are selling, to whom, and in which medium.

The following spectrum shows the correlations between left-brain and right-brain distinctions and product uniqueness, tangibility, and cost.

LEFT BRAIN ←--→ RIGHT BRAIN

UNIQUE PRODUCT ←--→ PARITY PRODUCT

HIGH-INVOLVEMENT PRODUCT ←-------------→ LOW-INVOLVEMENT PRODUCT

INTANGIBLE PRODUCT ←-------------------------------------→ TANGIBLE PRODUCT

HIGH-TICKET SALE ←--→ LOW-TICKET SALE

This diagram is intended as a thought provoker, not as an infallible guide. Even though automobiles are a high-ticket, high-involvement, differentiated product, automakers often rely heavily on right-brain communication, and they are probably right. However, makers of high-ticket computers and software have often tried lavish right-brain communication to no avail.

On the One Hand . . .

Advertising at the Left Side of the Spectrum.   One of the most successful subscriber-enrollment ads we ever did for the magazine *Psychology Today* was an all-copy ad simply headed, "The Invisible University." It was the winner hands down in a multiple split test of black-and-white page ads in *TV Guide*. Crowded into that tiny page, in 6-point type (and in a magazine published for fans of *visual* communication!), was a closely reasoned message that was deeply meaningful to the prospects.

Although one could argue that there was a message to the subconscious as well as to the conscious mind, it was principally a left-brain ad because it relied completely on the power of language. And all our tests for *Psychology Today* told us that although visual imagery could sometimes be used to reinforce the message, there was no way that "the lightning message of a picture" alone could have sold subscriptions at a comparable—or even acceptable—advertising cost per order.

Why Mail-Order Advertising Has Been So Left-Brain Oriented.   Mail-order and direct-marketing advertising has historically been skewed sharply toward left-brain communication, and our diagram shows why:

- To overcome the inertia of a prospect sitting at home, the mail-order product or service needed to be *unique*—not readily available in stores—to compel immediate action.

- The item advertised was often an *intangible* product or service, such as a home-study course, that could not easily be packaged and sold off a store shelf.

- The sale tended to be a *high-ticket* total, because mail-order selling is expensive and requires a substantial margin available for advertising and sales.

- The item involved frequently was a *high-involvement* product or service with a strong promise of life-changing benefit.

Mail-order advertising has needed copious left-brain persuasion also because the act of ordering from a distant source is a more conscious, deliberate act than the act of moving your hand 12 inches sideways in a store to pick out a bottle of Bufferin tablets rather than a bottle of Anacin tablets.

However, in recent years the smartest mail-order advertisers have been finding ways to incorporate right-brain appeal in their advertising through powerful graphics and symbolism. For instance, an outstanding mail-order catalog from Lands' End devoted the cover and first six pages simply to a beautiful photo essay, printed in rich sepia tones, on wool growing and knitting in the British Isles. Although it did have words as well as pictures, the essay conveyed in a gutty, nonverbal, nonlogical way something about the quality and craftsmanship, and distinctiveness, of Lands' End woolen garments.

. . . and on the Other Hand

At the right side of the spectrum, parity products like cigarettes, beer, and cola drinks cry out for right-brain advertising.

When J. Walter Thompson hired the noted behaviorist John B. Watson in 1927, one of his contributions was a controlled blindfold test proving that smokers could not recognize their favorite brand of cigarettes. This helped establish that such products could not be sold by rational left-brain arguments.

And it is hard to imagine a copy argument that could do as much for Players cigarettes as those all-picture ads showing a crowd of handsome male and female "yuppies" smoking and drinking and have an absolute marvelous time in a singles bar. The ads both attract the true prospects out of the mass of readers and touch a deep chord of yearning to belong, to feel at home and accepted in the "right" crowd.

Rosser Reeves Lives On— But Logic Has Its Limits

Rosser Reeves's *Reality in Advertising* (1961) was a brilliant argument for a logical, scientific approach to brand-advertising warfare (and, inferentially, for hiring his agency, Ted Bates). Much of what he said is still valid and bears rereading today.

His argument lives on that every product should use a unique selling proposition (USP) to fight for a share of mind. For instance, one recent Coors beer commercial shows a spokesperson standing in the snow of Colorado mountains explaining that the snow provides Coors with unique pure water. That is a visual and verbal USP.

Reeves would surely approve. Although he was intent on building a USP argument into all brand advertising, he certainly favored visual expression or reinforcement of the USP.

Reeves admitted that "visual symbols can stir deeply buried tides."[19] What he could not admit was that these tides run so deep that sometimes a logical USP cannot reach them. The Players ad is a good example.

Nowhere in Reeves's book does he allow for the power of the advertising tool discovered, perhaps accidentally and without full understanding at the time, by Earnest Elmo Calkins early in the century. This discovery was the power of association, beginning with Calkins's commissioning outstanding illustrators of the day to portray "The Arrow Collar Man." That was pure right-brain communication.

Reeves's idea of powerful visual reinforcement was strongly left-brain, e.g., a commercial showing a plunger driving the words *B vitamins* into a close-up of a grain of rice.

Four Ways to Advertise—Not Two

The fact of the matter is, there really are not just two ways to do advertising. There are four: *left-brain, right-brain, whole-brain,* and *no-brain.** Beginning with Earnest Elmo Calkins at the beginning of the century, most of the greatest advertising theorists and practitioners have believed in appealing to the whole brain when possible and where appropriate.

---

* About the time this was being written, Norman W. Brown, the chairman of Foote, Cone & Belding, began coincidentally to publicize his agency's "whole-brain advertising." However, Brown's use of the term is quite different from what we are espousing here. Brown is referring to a harmonious collaboration of left-brain and right-brain *people*— namely, account executives and creative people.

David Ogilvy loved facts and reasoning, but he also gave us "The Man in the Hathaway Shirt," the haughty Baron Wrangell wearing an eye patch. Running just in *The New Yorker,* the campaign was so powerful and so talked about that eventually the ads could run without any copy at all.

It is a mistaken notion to think of Bill Bernbach as being to visual advertising what Ogilvy was to verbal. "Advertising is the art of persuasion," said Bernbach, and he encouraged stunning visual impact not only to interrupt the reader's boredom but also to enhance the persuasion: "The device I use to attract the reader's attention also tells the story."[20]

Whole-brain communication is the secret ingredient which is so often missing in awareness advertising and which can do so much to increase its effectiveness.

Early Whole-Brain Advertising by Helen Resor

A pioneer in whole-brain advertising was Helen Lansdowne Resor, Stanley Resor's wife and creative director during his 40-year reign over J. Walter Thompson. Her advertising increased sales of Woodbury facial soap 1000 percent in 8 years.

Her most famous Woodbury ad was a classic of whole-brain advertising. Many brand advertisers could profitably study and emulate it today. In fact, the ad is a model of MaxiMarketing. It was dignified and tasteful but extraordinarily efficient. Just look at how many elements it had working for it:

1. A headline with a succinct USP which became part of the language of the United States: "The skin you love to touch."

2. A right-brain painting of a beautiful woman being nuzzled by a square-jawed Arrow collar type man. The illustration does far more than reinforce the headline. There is an associative message here which runs silent and deep, far below conscious reasoning.

3. Copy containing a "reason-why" explanation of how new skin forms, a preemptive claim that washing with Woodbury soap "can keep this new skin so active that it cannot help taking on the greater loveliness you have longed for," and a service message telling exactly how to do it.

4. In one lower corner, a mail-order coupon offering for 10 cents both an eight-color reproduction of the painting (by a well-known artist of the day) and a week's supply of the soap.

5. In the other corner, a picture of the product and a fine-print suggestion, "Tear out this cake as a reminder to get Woodbury's today at your druggist's or toilet counter."

Only You Can Decide Which Is Best for You (But the Public Can Help)

So, should all advertising be whole-brain? No, the puzzle and the paradox is that some purely rational, verbal persuasion, with *no* visual symbolism, has been extraordinarily successful. (The longest-running mail-order ad in history was a long-copy logical argument headed "Do You Make These Mistakes in English?") On the other hand, some purely emotional, associative, nonverbal communication (such as "the Marlboro Man" advertising in magazines) has also been extraordinarily successful.

The MaxiMarketing answer is *not* "Thou shalt include both left-brain and right-brain communication in all thy advertising." Rather Maxi-Marketing urges you to *consider* left-brain and right-brain issues in your review process.

On the one hand, are you neglecting facts and arguments and a clear, persuasive USP that might bolster your advertising's sales power? On the other hand, are you so involved in the rational argument your advertising is presenting that you are neglecting those deep, primitive, wordless wellsprings of human emotion and action that have nothing to do with logic?

Only you, the advertiser, can decide. But you can receive valuable help from the public. Let people tell you what makes them respond—not by their opinions, *but by their actual, measured responses.* (People's *opinions* about advertising, such as "I would never read that much copy," can be quite misleading.) If you split test emphasis on left brain, right brain, and whole brain, you may be amazed at what you find out.

However you accomplish it, and wherever you decide to place the emphasis, the important thing is to avoid the deadliest of advertising sins—no-brain advertising. You have seen it. We all have. No reasonable argument, at least not one that is immediately apparent. No USP. No relevant visual symbolism, demonstration, or association. And, we are tempted sadly to add, no point of view except that advertising should be "clever," "catchy," "creative," and "make me laugh."

The Wastefulness of No-Brain Advertising

The trail of advertising history is littered with the bones of campaigns that tickled the public mightily but failed to sell the product. In 1902, a new cereal called Force was launched with a series of full-page ads in Sunday newspapers. The ads introduced, with drawings and poems, a character named Jim Dumps who was "a most unfriendly man"—until he started eating Force cereal. "Since then they've called him 'Sunny Jim.' "

After a few months, Stephen Fox tells us, the campaign was assigned to Calkins and Holden. Calkins himself wrote hundreds of the jingles. Thousands more were sent in by the public. Songs, musical comedies, and vaudeville skits were written about Sunny Jim. Any cheerful fellow named James was likely to be called Sunny Jim by his friends.

Soon *Printer's Ink* proclaimed that Sunny Jim "is as well known as President [Theodore] Roosevelt or J. Pierpont Morgan." There was just one problem, and you can guess what it was. "The advertising absolutely sold 'Sunny Jim' to the public," Calkins confessed years later, "but it did not sell Force."[21]

Over half a century later, the same fate befell the creators of Bert and Harry Piel, the delightful cartoon characters who peddled Piels beer on television, with voices by those incomparable comedians Bob and Ray.

The trouble, and the temptation, is that sometimes clever advertising works. When Wendy's introduced the Clara Peller "Where's the beef?" commercial, sales went up 30 percent. But for every Clara Peller commercial, how many clever, "creative" commercials with no point of view and no impressive sales record are there? Dozens? Hundreds? (Remember Wendy's tasteless, irrelevant "Soviet Fashion Show" commercial a few years later?)

Trying to pull off a Clara Peller coup with an award-winning flight of wild fancy that has *no clear point of view* is playing high-stakes roulette with the client's money. (Actually, "Where's the beef?" contained a meaty argument within its bun of entertainment.)

Harry MacMahan did a survey to find out what happened after agency commercials won a Clio, the most prestigious award in the business (with no points given for sales success of the commercial!). Of 81 past winners, 36 of the agencies involved had either lost the account or gone out of business. This poor record could result simply from the ingratitude or boredom of clients, a not completely unknown phenomenon, but it doesn't seem likely that that is the whole explanation.

But advertising agencies don't deserve all of the blame. The advertisers must share the responsibility. We were once admonished by a prospective client, "I want a 'Where's the beef?' to beef up my sales overnight." The client is often the cause of silly and irrelevant advertising produced by an agency.

No-Brain Copy—The Decline of Print-Advertising Skill

There is some excuse, however slim, for excesses in television, where we are still investigating the mysteries of a new kind of visually dominant communication and a new generation that grew up with it.

In print advertising, however, there is no excuse. Especially when it is so simple to call for and compare responses. And yet we see millions of dollars frittered away on advertising which does not effectively speak to and persuade the left brain, the right brain, or the whole brain.

Part of the problem is that creating print advertising isn't as much fun as creating a commercial. You don't get to mingle with show business folks. You don't get to go on location to unusual places. As Alvin Achenbaum, the J. Walter Thompson veteran, put it, "Let's face it, print is boring to create, evaluate, and service. Television is exciting; it's the movies. Moreover, it takes a lot fewer television than print units to spend a million dollars in the media."[22] So television has tended to command the most attention and the best brains, whereas print advertising comes off second-best.

But the glamor of television is not the whole answer. Bad advertising can come from good people in all kinds of agencies, large and small, with or without television accounts. It also can and often does come from the orders of misguided clients, over the agency's dead body. The common denominator is absence of a point of view other than that advertising should be catchy, punchy, and funny to break through the clutter. What an ad says or does after it gets noticed often seems to be a minor consideration.

"Merely to let your imagination run riot, to dream unrelated dreams, to indulge in graphic acrobatics and verbal gymnastics is *not* being creative," argued Bill Bernbach, the guiding genius of Doyle Dane Bernbach, in a company pamphlet. "The creative person has harnessed his imagination. He has disciplined it so that every thought, every idea, every word he puts down, every line he draws, every light and shadow in every photograph he takes, makes more vivid, more believable, more persuasive the original theme or product advantage he has decided he must convey."

Some Depressing Examples

Often we have personally taken part in the struggle for an advertising idea. We are painfully familiar with, and sympathetic to, what creative people must go through daily. Because of this awareness in our careers, we have largely refrained from speaking critically in public of the advertising efforts of others.

But in writing this book, when we started looking at the huge amounts of money being wasted on advertising lacking a sound and clear point of view, we decided that we had to be specific—with examples of what we see as wastefulness as well as effectiveness.

Glancing through recent publication advertising, we found the following examples of advertising which failed to appeal to either hemisphere of the brain. Instead they relied on the "catchiness" which John O. Powers resolutely avoided in his advertising for Wanamaker's nearly a century ago.

> *"Okay, Summa . . . Mac my day."* This is the headline of an ad for "a serious digitizer" for the Apple MacIntosh computer; it accompanies an illustration of a hand holding a stylus pointing straight at the camera so that it faintly resembles a gun.

> *"The First Supper for a good solid start."* This is obviously the ad person's clever takeoff on da Vinci's *The Last Supper,* selling Mead Johnson's Pablum baby cereal. Instead of 12 disciples, there are 12 babies in high chairs. And no body copy. The advertiser or the agency could not or would not consider what might be said about the product that would be of great interest to new parents.

> *"And now a word from Sony."* This appeared as the headline of an ad in *The Wall Street Journal* for a Sony word processor. (Get it?)

> *"Great offices begin with Modern Mode."* A small all-caps headline in white letters against a two-page color photograph of empty, undecorated office space with two modern chairs in it. No copy. Just an empty claim and an empty photograph. (Think what a field day Ogilvy would have had telling the reader what the advertiser brings to furnishing an office.)

> *"Our cows are up with the Times."* Headline of a Brown Cow yogurt newspaper ad in which the copy explains that newspapers in the Northeast have given them rave reviews and offers to send copies to the reader. But who would have guessed from the headline? And why should I bother to read the ad unless I'm raising cows?

> *"We're giving the other guys fits."* This ad for Vivitar lenses appears in a photography magazine; the ad implies that Vivitar drives the competition crazy by making such good optics. Buried in the body copy is some hard information that would have been of great interest to camera owners if they had the patience to get past the puffery—namely, that Vivitar has "the world's first truly inter-

changeable auto focus lens, the only auto focus that doesn't require a special camera body."

Perhaps these are extreme examples (although two of them were cited as examples of outstanding advertising by a trade publication). But if ads like this account for only 1 percent of all advertising today, we are talking about the wasteful expenditure of *$1 billion*. The real amount is probably much higher.

No-Brain Art Direction Can Defeat Whole-Brain Copy

Sometimes good right-brain copy is betrayed by no-brain art direction—and the advertising trade publications often egg them on with praise. In the May 1983 issue of *Art Direction/The Magazine of Visual Communication*, the editors proclaimed:

> Body copy—it comes in all shapes and sizes. But many art directors consider copy a nuisance and try to shunt it off into some obscure corner. But, hard as it may be to believe, body text can not only decorate but [be] an integral part of the design. Type, a very flexible variable, can be molded into nearly any form. Sure, lots of art directors choose to wrap it around product shots, but in some respects that's merely an example of accommodating the visual. Why not make the copy a visual? *Art Direction* has come across many ads that do just that, ads that make the copy an extension of the design. . . .[23]

Alongside this essay appeared the first example provided, an ad for Zyderm Collagen cream, a facial treatment offered only through dermatologists and plastic surgeons. The photographic illustration (a cropped photograph of the head of a statue of Aphrodite) and the body copy below it had been "molded" into a kind of backward S-shaped swath running down through a sea of white space.

The copy has *no paragraphing*, obviously because it would interfere with making the body text "not only decorate but [be] an integral part of the design."

To the left of the swath, floating in the white space, is a small headline, "Aging Beautifully." On the right side is a subhead which is actually in smaller type than the body copy, "A new kind of program for aging skin that only a doctor can provide."

How the copywriter must have wept to see the USP, the rather carefully constructed, informative argument, and the offer of more information—all so artfully concealed behind a wall of pure design!

One of the most common ways in which whole-brain copy is defeated by no-brain design is the indulgent practice of white lettering—not just for headlines, but for body copy—on color half-tones or a black background. Ogilvy writes of a fund-raising organization whose entire ad was set in "reverse"—white letters on black. When he suggested they test the identical copy using black letters on white, they *doubled* their results.

If copy is not meant to be read, why bother to include it in the ad? If it *is* meant to be read, why not make it legible? Yet take a look through a few magazines. See how unreadable or uninviting a great deal of advertising text is. And never ever let anybody massacre your message again!

Today's Special Need for Left-Brain Communication

Perhaps because we live in the age of breathtaking video imagery, left-brain persuasion is not admired and honored as it once was. After the age of video was in full swing, Pierre Martineau declared that we were "wrong in considering copy, or logic, sacred. Words more often than not play a minor role in what is actually happening."[24]

What Martineau overlooked was the question of what is being sold and to whom. Were you ever sold an insurance policy by an agent using pictures only?

Actually, the need for skills in purely verbal persuasion was never greater. Why? Because introduction of new kinds of services and high-tech products demands words—skilled words.

As we move deeper into the information age and the service economy, many of the flood of new products are not products in the usual kick-the-tires sense; rather, they are packages of information and service. In less than a decade, lawn-care *services* like Chemlawn wiped out 40 percent of the sales of lawn-care *products*. In the knowledge industry, The Electronic University had 15,000 students taking university courses at home via two-way computer communication in 1985. Over 1700 colleges and universities were participating and offering credit. The founder hoped to have 50,000 enrolled by the end of 1986.

Until such products and services are fully established in the public mind, their advertisers must provide prospective customers with information, facts, explanation, rational and emotional persuasion—left-brain communication.

This seems an obvious point. But it is often not realized for a long time. In the computer software field, to take one example, the torrent of new products descended on an advertising community woefully un-schooled in—or unfavorably disposed toward—left-brain advertising. The result has been in far too many cases a huge spill of advertising dollars. The following is just one of many sad examples, from September 19, 1985, *The Wall Street Journal:*

> Ashton-Tate Inc.'s television debut during last year's Summer Olympics was well, unusual. It was also a flop.
>
> The software company hired a big-name Madison Avenue agency to produce a campaign for "Framework," a new business computer program. The result featured a group of people gathered around a large, glowing mock-up of the software's logo. Avoiding any discussion of the program's abilities, the announcer heralded Framework as software "for thinkers." Says Penny Grote, Ashton-Tate's advertising manager: "It was almost magical . . . like a 'Close Encounters' type experience."
>
> But the commercial failed to produce many close encounters between consumers and software dealers, and the $695 program didn't become the hoped-for hit. Last week, Ashton-Tate unveiled a new and improved Framework II—without TV ads. The company now plans to concentrate its messages in computer and business publications and stick to specifics about its products' strengths. . . .
>
> Many hardware and software companies now agree with Ashton-Tate that vague image-building ads won't sell computers.[25]

"Software is the new disaster area of American advertising," declared Robert Bailey, senior vice president and director of marketing services of BBDO/Chicago. Too many advertisers, he pointed out, have turned to one of two extremes: the "technical spec sheet ad" or the "creative fluff puff ad."[26]

By 1985, there were between 5000 and 7000 software publishers. Most stores are unwilling or unable to carry more than a few hundred items of software. Many of the publishers are doomed to fail. The ones that succeed will not do so by creating a brand image (did you ever go to a bookstore and ask merely for something from Simon & Schuster?) but by painfully rediscovering scientific reason-why advertising.

Because of the plentifulness of product and scarcity of retailer shelf space, software companies are being forced into direct marketing. The publisher of *PC World* magazine, with 200 pages of advertising per issue, noted in 1985 that 24 percent of the advertising was now mail order. But much of it is amateurish mail order, even if crudely effective, because the advertisers and their creative aids are reinventing the wheel. Too often, we still see them trying to apply right-brain or no-brain creativity to a marketing problem that calls for careful crafting of an irresistible left-brain argument.

The same mistake occurs in the marketing of high-tech hard goods. When Commodore introduced its Amiga, according to experts a really remarkable computer, it launched it with what it said would be a $40 million advertising campaign, most of it to be spent on television. And what did the first commercials show? A distinguished middle-aged man dressed like a high priest ascending to a stone altar where sat the Amiga computer emitting an eerie glow. Almost magical, you might say—a real *Close Encounters* type experience. As he begins to type (a letter to his mother?) the voice-over says something about a computer for those who want the "creative edge."

What is noteworthy—and significant—about the commercial is that *it could easily have been created by people who didn't know anything about computers and didn't know anything about the Amiga.* And indeed that may have been the case.

How much more effective it would have been, from our point of view, to have used that precious television time to sift out and inform and persuade the true prospect—by offering a smashing brochure on the Amiga or an enthralling videocassette demonstration! To heck with the image, tell us about the computer. Members of the new information society want more than images and symbols to guide them in an important buying decision.

Apple's Whole-Brain Triumph

A striking contrast was provided by the way in which Apple skillfully used both right-brain and left-brain advertising to introduce the MacIntosh computer. The corporation may have been experiencing a good deal of turmoil and difficulty in recent times because of growing pains, the excesses of success, saturation of the market, and the difficulty of slugging it out with IBM, but these difficulties should not be allowed to detract from the brilliance of the MacIntosh marketing.

On New Year's Day, 1984, Apple fired a blast of pure right-brain communication with its famous "George Orwell" commercial on the telecast of the Super Bowl game. One million smackers to produce the commercial, it was said, and another million to air it—once.

That may or may not have been a profitable expenditure. Advertising observers have been debating it ever since. A case could be made that although very few viewers understood it, remembered it, and rushed out to buy a MacIntosh computer because of it, the publicity value was worth more than the advertising cost. It was an outstanding example of the new event marketing that benefits as much from the public relations as from its direct impact.

But Apple didn't stop there. They ran a 30-page ad in *Newsweek*. This ad did everything that critics who had complained about computer l-vertising had begged for. It accomplished what that wise direct-marketing pioneer, Victor Schwab, used to advocate as "taking you by the hand

and leading you from where you are to where the advertiser wants you to be." With words and pictures that were models of simplicity, clarity, and completeness, the ad told people who didn't know anything about computers just about everything they needed to know about the MacIntosh computer. Pure—and brilliant—left-brain advertising.

Emulating Apple's Left-Brain Blockbuster for a Fraction of Their Cost. Okay, so you can't afford to buy out an issue of *Newsweek*. But there is nothing that Apple did in *Newsweek* that a niche marketer with a smaller budget cannot profitably emulate for a fraction of the cost.

How? Prepare a brochure that is just as complete, just as detailed, just as clear, just as long (if necessary), and mail it to rented lists of clearly identified prime prospects. Or mail a brochure to your own list of prospects compiled by inviting inquiries from interested readers in your regular magazine advertising.

There Are More Readers Than You Think, Even in the Television Generation

You may be concerned—and well-meaning experts may tell you—that in this video age, with its short attention span, "Nobody will read long copy any more." However, it is the paradox of the video age that along with impressive growth of the television business since 1950 has come an equally impressive growth in the book-publishing business—from a few-hundred-million dollars then to over $6 billion today.

It is true that large general magazines like the old *Life, Look,* and *The Saturday Evening Post* were wiped out by television, but a surprising fact is that the total number of titles of magazines published and copies per issue is far greater today than a generation ago.

And do you know who the biggest readers are? The answer may astonish you. According to a report published by the Book Industry Study Group, the heaviest readers are in the 25 to 34 age group: 59 percent of these people, as against 50 percent of the entire adult population, read at least one book in a given 6-month period.

The number of bookstores in the United States has grown from roughly 5000 in the mid-1960s to around 20,000 today. All this is not so surprising when you consider the raised level of average education. Between 1950 and 1980, the number of Americans with at least 1 to 3 years of college rose from a little over 6 million to nearly 21 million.

Somebody out there still can read. And does read. And *will* read your copy about the product or service you are advertising. Far more copy than you may realize. As long as you are providing the clear information the prospect needs and wants to know—and you understand and empathize with the prospect's deepest hopes and fears.

Herbert D. Maneloveg is a consultant who has held top media and marketing positions with several famous agencies. Not long ago, in the trade press, he wrote a commentary on this question which can only be described as profound. We wish we had room to reprint it all. He wrote, in part:

> We are presently in a promotionally oriented marketing mode, where a more knowledgeable, more discerning public will wisely, calmly wait out a purchase until the marketer puts it on sale or offers a "deal." What we're seeing is the slow, inexorable erosion of brand loyalty for many product categories, the public now selecting from the numerous product lines it senses as all similar, with price break being the sole determining factor. Thus a growing number of product managers, faced with sales below planned objectives, are turning to a series of short-term promotional flights that indeed move product but at a much lower profit margin: a kind of Catch-22 situation that perpetuates the dilemma rather than solving it.
>
> Unfortunately, much of today's advertising communication (and the ad *community*) has become an unplanned culprit in this situation, perhaps a larger part of the problem than we'd wish to admit. Why? Because many are just not reading our public correctly; they're not facing up to the fact that *today's upscale, more educated consumer wants to learn more about a product rather than less.*
>
> . . . take the untold hundreds of millions spent on soft-drink and fast-food advertising. How much of a marked difference in market share has there been from one year to the next? You name the category—coffee, beer, shampoo, liquor, cigarettes—and try to count on the fingers of both hands those product campaigns that truly educate and convince rather than merely remind and entertain.
>
> Accordingly, the public watches this $90 billion annual avalanche of national advertising, elects not to be loyal to almost anything because few marketers have offered any communications reason to be loyal. The consumers wait to buy when they're ready, not when the marketer would like them to purchase; and the magic of advertising just doesn't work today.
>
> Yet it can work. . . . We must learn to adroitly blend short-message impact with compelling reasons, longer-length copy and expanded ideas to sell in the current marketplace; to make out people brand-loyal again.[27]

Chapter 7 discusses other ways to deal with the phenomenon of brand-franchise erosion because of too much promotion and too little persuasion. However, the point we want to make here is simply to shout "Hallelujah!" to Maneloveg's plea for, in effect, more left-brain advertising and more left-brain content in advertising.

The New Generation Is Not That Different

All right, so the new generation is different. But it's not *that* different. In *Ogilvy on Advertising,* the author says that shortly before Bill Bernbach died, he was asked what changes he expected in advertising in the eighties. He replied:

> Human nature hasn't changed for a billion years. It won't even vary in the next billion years. Only the superficial things have changed. It is fashionable to talk about *changing* man. A communicator must be concerned with *unchanging* man—what compulsions drive him, what instincts dominate his every action. . . . For if you know these things about a man, you can touch him at the core of his being.[28]

"A gentleman with brains," commented Ogilvy admiringly.

More than that, we would say—a gentleman with a whole brain, a brain with unusually well developed left and right hemispheres. And though he was one of a kind, you too can use both sides of *your* brain to communicate with both sides of your prospect's brain.

Then you will be fully engaged in MaxiMarketing communication.

The Bottom Line

Whether your advertising should be predominantly left-brain, right-brain, or whole-brain depends on what you are selling, to whom, and how. Each kind of advertising has its uses, and responses to your advertising from the public can help you determine the right mix for you. Responses may also help you avoid the deadly sin of no-brain advertising—messages that are merely clever and bad art direction which obscures good messages.

Today, the proliferation of amazing new high-tech products and entirely new kinds of services has created a special need for highly skillful left-brain and whole-brain communication. And don't let them tell you, "Nobody will read all that copy." There are more readers today than ever before, and they often want to read and know more than many advertisers are willing to provide them.

Your advertising need not—and often cannot—tell your whole story upfront. But it must break through the clutter to a true prospect and leave a meaningful impression of an advantage or benefit promised by the product or service you are advertising or by the additional information you are offering.

In planning or reviewing the creative strategy and execution of your company's advertising, here are some questions to ask:

■ *Will it attract and communicate with the prospect we are trying to reach?*

■ *Does what we are selling call for left-brain, right-brain, or whole-brain communication?*

■ *Should we—and is there some way we can—add whole-brain appeal to this proposed left-brain or right-brain advertising?*

■ *Will the body copy in this print advertising be clearly legible and inviting to read? Does the graphic element reinforce the message in the words? Does the headline reveal or conceal the promise being made to true prospects?*

Whatever your responsibility in the advertising management chain—from product manager to corporate advertising director—you can make a difference in the effectiveness of your company's advertising by asking pointed questions about left-brain and right-brain orientation. There's too much at stake not to do so.

7

Maximized Activation: Better Sales Promotion and More Inquiry Advertising

The Big Picture

So what happens after your prospect is made aware of what you are advertising and (you hope) wants it? In far too many cases, nothing at all happens. And the advertiser does nothing to make something happen.

Sales promotion is the art and science of making something happen. As William A. Robinson, president of the sales promotion agency bearing his name, has put it, "Advertising creates an acceptable environment and we push the products through the pipeline. I know it sounds corny, but promotions ring the cash register."

For the phrase making something happen, *we have used the broader term* activation *in our MaxiMarketing diagram. Activation includes sales promotion and inquiry advertising—in which you invite the prospect to call or write for more information.*

Today's sales promotion is the child of the demassified market. Product proliferation has inevitably led to intensified competition and intensified sales promotion. But today's sales promotion can be a problem child: greedy, costly to feed, sometimes bad-mannered, sometimes downright destructive—and still, a necessary member of the family, handy to have around when needed and, at times, a brilliant performer.

We believe that by demanding of all activation advertising the same accountability that we urged for awareness advertising and by using the same tools of accountability, the usefulness and profitability of sales promotion can be maximized.

But, in the long run, sales promotion is no substitute for persuasion—more persuasion than you are able to present within the limits of your up-front advertising. So along with improved sales promotion should come an intelligent plan for inviting inquiries in your advertising and for giving your follow-up material just as much careful attention as you give your up-front advertising.

Sales promotion is big business. According to a recent Donnelley Marketing survey of national advertisers, promotional budgets accounted for 64.4 percent of total marketing expenditures, and advertising accounted for only 35.6 percent. Estimates of current promotional expenditure have ranged as high as $80 billion. (Of course much of that is trade deals.)

And yet, for package-goods manufacturers, the results are astonishingly unrewarding. Studies have shown again and again that an expensive promotional campaign will produce a spectacular short-term gain in share of market. Then, as the effects of the promotion die away, the brand share returns to its previous level—*or lower*.

Over the long term, excessive promotion has been shown to erode and even destroy brand share. Tryers attracted by special promotions are often brand hoppers who shop for the best price, not the best brand. And regular users become accustomed to getting a direct or disguised discount and refuse to buy when the brand returns to its regular price.

How Excessive Promotion
Can Erode Profits

Professor Roger Strang of the University of Southern California has suggested that long-term sales begin a decline when the ratio of advertising to promotion falls below a certain "threshold"—probably 60 to 40. He cited a study by R. J. Weber to show what happens when brands get sucked into a promotional war.[1]

The product manager of company A, the leader in its category, began cutting back on television advertising and pouring money into promotion. The next two nearest competitors followed suit.

All three just about doubled their total advertising and marketing expenditure, but the percentage devoted to advertising dropped dramatically.

After 3 years, the market share of each brand was about the same or less. But the profit contribution per case shipped had sharply declined. And the higher the promotion-to-advertising ratio, the greater the profit decline! Thus company A, whose percentage of expenditure devoted to brand advertising declined from 64 percent to 32 percent, experienced a drop in per-case profits from $3.36 to $2.33. But company C, whose brand advertising dropped to just 9 percent of its marketing total, saw its profits per case drop from $2.58 down to just 74 cents.

So Why Do They Do It?

So why do package-goods manufacturers spend so much on promotion, often more than on brand-image advertising? Apparently there are a number of reasons, some valid, some questionable.

1. A new product launch needs all the help it can get, including agressive promotion. Promotion can help entice curious consumers into a trial and can pressure retailers for shelf space.

2. The product-manager system tends to favor short-term gains. Spectacular increases in share points due to heavy promotion can make the product manager look like a hero in the short term. And in the long term, when normal share of market and profits per case may have declined because of overpromotion, the product manager may not be there to receive the blame because he or she has moved on to a better job!

3. Top management may be under pressure to demonstrate sales gains to Wall Street in a quarterly or annual statement and may succumb to the temptation to artificially inflate sales by means of promotion.

4. Retailers may have come to expect it and demand it even though it may accomplish very little in the long run.

5. It's hard to resist engaging in defensive couponing when the competition is out there giving away the store—even though, as Schultz and Robinson wryly observe in their book *Sales Promotion Management,* "No one wins a sales promotion war."[2]

6. The company simply may not have done the kind of long-term hard-nose analysis needed to determine what overpromotion is doing to its brand share and case profit over the long pull.

"Trying to Get Out of the Discounting Box."   This subject of an *Adweek* cover story has become a very important concern of package-goods advertisers. In *Adweek's* story, a vice president of General Foods bluntly described the problem as "widespread and heading toward the edge of the cliff."[3]

If you are involved at some level of decision making in package-goods advertising and promotion, your long-range planning should include exploration of ways to lessen your dependency on sales promotion which is mere price cutting and which may erode your brand franchise. As you strengthen your communications and relationships with your best customers, in ways suggested in this book, you may find you have less need for a promotional "fix."

Meanwhile there are a number of possibilities for making your package-goods sales promotion more *productive* and more *accountable.* And if you are involved in management or marketing *outside of* package goods, in a field in which sales promotion is underutilized and your promotion is less likely to be neutralized by a competitor's counter-promotion, your opportunities to realize the benefits of carefully conceived sales promotion can be far greater.

Sometimes It "Can't Get No Respect."   Often part of the problem with sales promotion is that it is viewed as the useful, necessary, hard-working scullery maid rather than one of the favored members of the marketing family. And so it fails to command the intense attention and interest inside the company and the advertising agency that the production of a dazzling new television commercial does. It is viewed as a separate activity rather than an integral part of the creative strategy.

Even the language sometimes used is revealing. Awareness advertising is "above the line." Sales promotion is "below the line"—that is, everything that happens after the bottom-line expenditure for image advertising. But the expression says more than is intended.

Achenbaum has summed up the problem with relentless frankness:

Despite the large sums spent on merchandising and sales promotion, they
have continued to be treated by most marketers as a secondary factor—not
totally integrated into the marketing program; not consistent with its strategic thrust; and usually not properly evaluated as to their real effect on
annual sales. . . .

Merchandising and sales promotion activities are viewed as discreet proj-
ects which are assigned on an individual basis and put out for bid. As a
consequence, the companies who prepare the material often lack the
knowledge and experience to understand the strategic foundation underly-
ing the activity. Nor do they feel, for competitive reasons, that they can
afford to oversee a project from the strategic point of view. They are,
therefore, prone to look for so-called "big ideas" rather than what is necessary for implementing the strategy in an integrated fashion consistent with
the rest of the marketing mix.[4]

The first step in maximizing the effectiveness of sales promotion is to
treat it with utmost respect—to put it not "below the line" but alongside
awareness advertising as an equal and equally respected partner in marketing.

The Need for More and
Better Testing

Substantial improvements can be made in sales promotion efficiency and
profitability through more and better testing.

Schultz and Robinson say that if you mention testing to a group of
sales promotion managers, you'll probably get a nod of agreement and a
comment something like, "We know we need to do it but we don't have
the time, money, people or (you fill in the blank) to do it."[5]

Roger Strang surveyed 55 of the largest package-goods manufacturers and found that 20 percent budgeted no money at all for sales promotion research. We discussed in Chapter 2 how direct response makes the
various parts of the MaxiMarketing process work together. In the case of
sales promotion, coupling it with direct response can accomplish several
valuable objectives:

1. *Comparative measurement.* Measuring the number of direct responses from each of your sales promotion efforts in each of your
   media cannot tell you the overall sales and profit effect of promotion.
   But it *can* allow you to compare precisely the *comparative* efficiency
   of one promotional effort or media source to another. The cumulative effect of a series of tests, each set of findings building on the
   previous set, should result in distinct and measurable progress toward the campaign objectives.

2. *Quick and inexpensive.*   Compared to other forms of advertising and market research, direct-response testing can be comparatively quick and inexpensive.

3. *Reality based.*   Direct-response testing happens in the real world, not in a questionable simulation.

4. *Potential secrecy.*   And if you choose, it can be done privately (via direct mail) so you won't tip off your competition, upset your retailers, or confuse the public.

5. *Database-building.*   Finally, capturing the names and addresses of prospects and customers through sales promotion can feed the customer database, the value of which we will discuss in Chapter 10.

As we examined the practices, problems, and opportunities in each of the principle kinds of sales promotion advertised in media—couponing, premiums, sampling, and sweepstakes—we saw how the above approach might have prevented or salvaged some doubtful promotions and made some good ones even better. Let's take a look together . . . .

Couponing

Couponing is a good place to start because it consumes (some would say burns up) so many dollars.

In examining the current state of couponing, it is hard to avoid being struck by a paradox: use of couponing continues to increase along with doubts about its value. From the brand marketer's point of view, it bears an uncomfortable number of points of resemblance to dope addiction.

It's expensive. It makes you feel good for a while, but then you need some more. You don't really want to do it, but the other fellows are doing it and you don't want to fall behind. You know it's not good for your health in the long run, but you're too busy worrying about your next fix to worry about the long run.

Coupons began to zoom in popularity in the 1970s with manufacturers, retailers, and consumers. Manufacturers liked them as a way to force the proliferation of new products through the pipeline and get the dealer to stock and display them. Retailers liked them as a way to build store traffic. And consumers began to clip and hoard them because they offered a way to fight back against inflation and recession.

Coupon use rose from 58 percent of households in 1970 to 76 percent in 1980.

By 1985, manufacturers were distributing over 180 billion coupons a year, over 2000 pieces per household, an increase of 10 percent over the year before. Coupon redemptions rose to nearly 7 billion, up 75 percent over 4 years earlier. The number of manufacturers using coupons has doubled to 2000 companies in the last decade, according to Nielsen.

That's a lot of activity—but how much of it is desirable activity?

The Doubts about Couponing

Here's what the doubters have been saying: Don Schultz, marketing consultant and professor of advertising at Northwestern University:

> One of the great hazards is that you will generate a group of consumers that are deal-conscious and that you will destroy the price structure of your product. A lot of the information that is coming out of the scanner studies looks like you have a large number of people who buy only when there is some kind of featured price or when there is some kind of promotional activity.
>
> Look at the soft drink business. The greatest volume of soft drinks is sold in the weekends in supermarkets when there is a feature. By emphasizing promotions, marketers are building a market of people who don't care if it is Dr. Pepper, 7UP, or Coke. All they care about is that it's $1.09. You end up destroying the brand franchise that way.[6]

Robert Evans, director of promotional services, Gilette Company, and chairman of the Promotion Marketing Association of America (PMAA):

> One of the things that is starting to become a problem is that media costs are skyrocketing and are starting to knock out the smaller brands and causing those brands to devote almost their entire marketing budget to promotional expenditures. As a result, they are not building the brand identity that they might have in the past, and the question being raised frequently is, *"Does the consumer really know who you are or are they buying the brand that is being promoted this week?"* [Italics added.][7]

Len Daykin, editor of *Brand Management Report*:

> When coupons were just growing, they were used selectively by the manufacturer. Now it's almost automatic—if there's a promotion pushing into the warehouse, there's usually a coupon device to pull it out. And that has a negative effect, because in any given week, a consumer with a sharp eye can find coupons in almost any product group. *I think what's being created is a very large group of consumers who are loyal to coupons, not brand.* [Italics added.][8]

Alvin Achenbaum:

> An impediment to marketing productivity that I have found most peculiar is the growing emphasis marketers are placing on price-off promotions, often at the expense of brand franchise building advertising and irrespective of the evidence that this form of price competition has had little overall sales effect.

It seems to elude many marketers that coupons, premiums, and twofers, to name a few of the tactics used, are nothing more than short-term price reductions. Since most off-price promotions are usually matched either immediately or shortly thereafter, the ultimate result is usually a sales standoff. *Nielsen people have shown time and time again that most brands rarely gain market position as a result of these promotions.*

Yet it is now estimated that more money is spent today on these price-off promotions than on franchise building advertising. To some degree, I attribute this interest to the short-run thinking of the product group system, whereby the brand manager is less concerned with the long-run health of the brand and more interested in the immediate sales goal. [Italics added][9]

Manufacturers are said to be unhappy with the 4 percent to 5 percent redemption rate. But that percentage would be terrific if it meant getting that many people to try the product. The trouble is, so many of the coupon redeemers are existing customers and cheaters. And nobody even knows how many. (Of course, couponing to present users has some value in preventing defection to a competing brand.)

"You can measure how many coupons are redeemed," points out Robert Blatternberg, a University of Chicago professor who has developed a computer model to evaluate sales promotions. "But it's very hard to analyze what real impact you've had. You don't know if the coupons have led to increased sales or just deferred sales. You don't know if you are getting purchases from an existing user or a new user."[10] Or from a cheater.

The Case of the Cheating Consumer. Most of the expressed concern about misredemption has been focused on large-scale fraud by gangs who buy and clip from bundles of newspapers, or even reproduce coupons, and redeem through larcenous retailers. But one research group, Management Decision Systems, uncovered in 1982–1983 strong evidence that one coupon out of every three submitted was being improperly redeemed not by organized crime but by consumers themselves, costing marketers more than $500 million a year.

The company said it stumbled across this information by accident: "We were trying to see if people switched brands as a result of a coupon or if they bought their normal brand or nothing."[11] But they found that about a third were using the coupon to buy a competing brand (with the collusion of store personnel, obviously).

Their conclusion roughly coincides with the findings of a study by K. C. Blair. This study showed that consumer misredemption of coupons ranged from a high of 54 percent to a low of 14 percent, with an average of 33 percent.

At Least Sixty Percent of Coupons Redeemed by Present Users? There are no meaningful figures on how many coupons are redeemed by loyal existing customers, because that would vary by the product's share of market. But it is reasonable to assume that the larger the share, the larger the percentage of redeemed coupons that are coming from existing users.

According to Irene Park, "the competition's users with an historic pattern of 'other brand use' can be lured away only with the highest level coupons. However, *even at the highest coupon values, current users account for more than 60% of the coupon redeemers.*"[12] [Italics ours.] If that were true, and if it were also true that 30 percent of the redemptions were coming from cheaters who use the coupons to buy a different brand, a pathetic 10 percent of the redemptions would be coming from thrifty brand hoppers and genuinely interested tryers.

In short, by the time you add up the existing users who just want a discount, the cheaters who intend to remain loyal to some other brand, and the bargain hunters who don't give a hoot about brands, it seems to leave mass couponing with little if any long-range value to the brand. It may cost only half a cent to distribute a coupon, but the true cost of distributing a coupon to a nonuser who redeems it and thereby becomes a regular user may be several hundred times as much. It raises a serious question whether that money couldn't be better spent in direct communication with the desired prospect.

The Popularity—and Wastefulness—of Couponing in fsi's

And yet, despite the problems inherent in couponing today, brand advertisers seem trapped in the system—not unlike the way the United States and the Soviet Union find themselves trapped in a costly arms race nobody wants. Brand advertisers continue to increase their couponing activity. And not only that, they give most of the increase to a comparatively wasteful and inefficient method of coupon distribution, Sunday newspaper free-standing inserts (fsi's)—up to 42.7 percent of all coupons in 1984, compared to 36.6 percent in 1983 (A. C. Nielsen clearinghouse). They give almost no increase to direct mail (up from 4.3 to 4.4 percent) even though it offers much greater targeting capability.

Couponing fsi's seems especially wasteful and inefficient, because it offers no opportunity to screen out existing users or treat them differently—and little opportunity to be heard with a meaningful advertising message in the midst of the much-deplored clutter of coupons. (Some Sunday papers carry as many as four fsi's, each more than 20 pages.)

Electronic Couponing—A Step in the Wrong Direction

Recent marketing experiments have been conducted that lead couponing off in an even worse direction—in-store video couponing. Several companies have been installing coupon-dispensing kiosks in stores—you push the button, or touch a picture of the desired product on the screen, and the machine prints out and ejects coupons.

Why a worse direction? Because such tactics are bound to increase redemption by present users. It reminds us of the old joke about the store that proclaimed, "We lose on every sale, but we make it up in volume!" One of the video coupon companies actually boasts, "Our machines only dispense coupons that the customer wants, so our redemption rate will be very high." What can this mean but that consumers are using the machines to get price cuts on brands they intended to buy anyway?

Indeed, one company's machine has a sign on it saying, "Free valuable coupons for your favorite products here. Save money on products you know and trust." It seems a blatant admission that the coupons dispensed by the machine will be most attractive to—and most used by—present users of the featured brands. (Although one company has been market testing a system which provides coupons printed by the cash register and avoids couponing buyers of the couponed brand, it is a long way from costly national rollout.)

In all fairness, it must be said that although getting along with couponing is pretty bad, trying to get along without it would be pretty bad too. As we suggested, it's like nuclear defense—you feel you can't disarm unless and until the other guys agree to do it too. Except that in brand warfare you can't even discuss it with the other guys—the government would accuse you of price fixing.

Not only are the manufacturers addicted to couponing, so are the retailers:

> According to the A. C. Nielsen "Reporter," the trade is more likely to accept a deal when a coupon is part of the plan. Of 137 new items studied, 34.4 percent were accepted, but the acceptance rate increased to 57.8 percent when a coupon was included, and when the distribution methods for the coupons were part of the presentation, the take rate increased by 75 percent.[13]

The Road Back to Sanity

We have examined the problems of couponing with you in some detail because we believe it's time for advertisers to reconsider this marketing practice, as indeed some brand advertisers are doing. As in network television advertising, clutter and waste are valid concerns. These concerns lend added weight to the importance of looking at alternative ways to maximize sales such as those discussed in other parts of this book.

Meanwhile couponing is not going to go away overnight. And if your company is a brand advertiser involved in couponing, it is distinctly worthwhile to consider ways that your couponing can be made more efficient.

We have three MaxiMarketing recommendations; not all are original with us, and some overlap. As with every other method of improving advertising effectiveness, if everybody adopted them right away, they would tend to cancel each other out. But we don't flatter ourselves that this will happen. And those who jump in first could score a significant advantage—as always.

1. Develop "Super CFB" Couponing.   Robert M. Prentice, an advertising and marketing consultant of Cos Cob, Connecticut, has developed a method of sales promotion analysis which divides it into two kinds— consumer franchise building (CFB) activities and non-CFB activities.

The first kind—CFB activities—effectively registers the brand's unique advantages or attributes in the consumer's mind, which, according to Prentice, "rules out much of the couponing being done today via freestanding inserts." It would include brand-image advertising, store demonstrations, recipes in service-magazine ads, and sampling.

> Non-CFB couponing, according to Prentice, . . . simply accelerates the buying decision by reducing the price temporarily, or by adding extraneous value (such as a premium or opportunities to win a sweepstakes prize), or by obtaining trade support with a trade deal or allowance. . . . These are important and necessary functions. But . . . they do not register, by themselves, any ideas about a brand's unique attributes or advantages. . . . Much, but not all, fsi couponing is a non-CFB promotion.[14]

Note that Prentice is describing not two kinds of advertising but rather two kinds of "activity." Thus a single advertisement could contain a 50-50 or a 90-10 or a 10-90 mix of CFB activity and non-CFB activity.

If a cents-off coupon were added to the lower-right corner of a brand-building advertisement, that could be fairly described as 80 percent CFB and 20 percent non-CFB. But a "trade coupon" for the brand by a retailer, unaccompanied by any selling message, would be 100 percent non-CFB.

Prentice analyzed 43 case histories, relating CFB and non-CFB expenditures to sales and profits over periods up to 15 years. He found that "successful profitable brands follow a CFB/non-CBF pattern that is exactly the opposite of the pattern followed by unsuccessful brands." His conclusion was: "When a brand's CFB ratio drops below the 50-55 per cent level, profits will almost always decline, either immediately or within the next year or two."[15]

To Prentice's approach, we propose adding an extra whammy based on our long experience in direct-response advertising. Let's call it "Super CFB sales promotion advertising." The need for our proposed method of developing Super CFB is rooted in the limitations of advertising research discussed earlier.

Because advertising research has no convenient, scientific way to compare the actual effect of two, three, or more different ways to express a product positioning or copy platform, there has been little opportunity to test one approach directly against another in "live" media. Consequently, both the creative team and the client tend to look for *the* ad or *the* series which will be the ultimate expression of the agreed-on creative strategy.

But in direct-response advertising we have no such testing limitation. We can create and test as many as eight completely different ads and rank their differing appeals in order of sales effect rather precisely— and, compared to many other forms of advertising research, quite economically. Furthermore, we have learned from this experience that, in an eight-way split, although the strongest ad may not perform 19.5 times better than the weakest (the multiple from John Caples cited approvingly by David Ogilvy), it quite commonly will perform as much as 2 or 3 times better.

Finally, we have learned that no experts, including ourselves, and no research system can predict the winner and the rankings in advance. From time to time in our field, someone will announce a breakthrough in predictive research that will supposedly permit us to skip all that multiple-split testing. But then it never seems to pan out, and soon is never heard about again.

Actually, in direct-response advertising, our multiple-split run-buys *are* our predictive research. Combined with performance records of various media, they enable us to predict fairly well how a winning test ad will perform when rolled out.

The obvious question arises: In view of the frequently admitted limitations of advertising research, why couldn't direct-response advertising's method of predictive research be used to strengthen the CFB advertising designed to accompany cents-off coupons?

The result would be: Super CFB! Advertising which would do a proven, unusually strong job of making the reader want not just the coupon, but the brand.

How would that work? Well, suppose for test purposes that eight creative approaches to the coupon advertising were prepared and approved, all within the framework of the agreed-upon copy platform.

One ad might feature benefits; another testimonials; another, laboratory tests; another, persuasive, reason-why long copy; another, a powerful graphic element and no copy; and so on.

Each of these ads would be printed on a single card-stock sheet as an fsi stand-alone. Then the eight sheets would be uniformly intermixed by the printer to guarantee equal exposure of each and scheduled in enough newspaper circulation to provide a statistically significant result. (These various approaches could also be split-tested in direct mail as self-mailers.)

Although the coupons could be designed for store redemption and tracked through the clearinghouse, we would prefer otherwise. Tracking store redemptions is a slow and comparatively erratic process.

Instead, each of our research ads would have a mail-order reply coupon and/or toll-free 800 number merely offering—for test purposes only, to stimulate response—a high-value coupon to those who respond. (High-value because to the consumer it's too much trouble to send away for a 20-cent coupon but it's worth the trouble to send for a $1 or $2 coupon.)

If the ads ran on a Sunday, we could project the total responses to each by the following Thursday. And all our experience in direct-response advertising for direct marketers tells us that there would be a clear variation in response from one ad to another.

If that proved to be the case—and if the offer stayed constant and only the ad approach varied—wouldn't that mean that the ad which was pulling more requests (whether from present users or curious nonusers) was saying something which makes those consumers want the product more? Not just any product in that category, but that *particular* product, *that* brand?

Then if the winning ad were rolled out with a usual-value coupon, it should mean that the coupon was being supported by Super CFB advertising—again, advertising which can do a proven job of making the consumer want not only the coupon but also the brand.

2. Target Nonusers. There is now a way to skip current product users when couponing. It has two limitations: It costs more than fsis. It can't reach as many people. But when you consider the hidden cost of a high percentage of fsi coupon redemptions by users, this other way begins to look not only attractive but also cost-effective.

It is what *Marketing Communications* has dubbed "undercover marketing." Or what Gary Blau of Select & Save chooses to call "guerilla marketing—before the competition figures out what's going on, it's too late and we've already communicated with their hard-core users."[16]

Chapter 3 pointed out how service companies like Select & Save, CSI TeleMarketing, and JFY circulate by mail or phone a detailed questionnaire on buying habits and purchases by category and brand name to about 50 million households. The replies are entered in a database by name, address, demographic information, and other identification characteristics, and they form a powerful marketing tool. They make it possible, at last, to send samples by mail, or coupons in a co-op mailing, to consumers known to use a different brand in your product's category. And, if you wish, to skip households known to be using your brand already.

It's not the complete answer. But it's certainly a step in the right direction. Even for a new brand with no share, or an existing brand with a small share, at least it gets the coupons into the hands of users of that product or service category, i.e., coffee coupons to coffee drinkers, hair-coloring coupons to hair-coloring users, or health-spa coupons for fitness fans.

As we saw in the Ecotrin pain tablets case history in Chapter 3, although the cost per distribution in this kind of direct mail may seem high, the cost per redemption can be at least as low as that of coupons in fsi's. And by building in a direct-response element and relating the tabulated responses to known characteristics of the responders, you can gain priceless marketing information about your best prospects. (Such as, quite possibly, that households with personal computers are interested in headache remedies!)

3. Try Min-Max Marketing.   But what if you believe that couponing your present customers as well as nonusers is a valuable part of your sales promotion activity? In a variation of targeting to nonusers, you can mail to users as well as nonusers, but send the former a lower-value coupon. This can have dramatic results in controlling the overall cost of the program.

Oscar Mayer provided a striking example of this method in a direct-mail test through JFY. The audience was divided into three cells: Oscar Mayer users, competitive product users, and nonusers of that category. Each cell received a different letter and a coupon with a different value. Although the report in *Marketing Communications* does not make it completely clear, the strong implication and reasonable assumption is that the users got the lowest value coupon, the competitive product users got a higher value, and the nonusers received a full-value certificate, in effect redeemable for a free sample.

The letter to current users thanked them for buying the product and expressed the hope that they would continue to buy it. (After all, existing customers are important too! Indeed, they are your most valuable asset.)

The letter to users of a competitive product sought to define the attributes and benefits of the Oscar Mayer product compared to other brands. And the letter to nonbuyers in that category introduced them to the product and invited them to try it at no cost.

The greatest number of redemptions occurred in the groups at either end, the Oscar Mayer users and the nonusers who got certificate good for a free package, both with redemption rates of 55 percent. Understandably, the competitive product users were the most difficult to penetrate and came in with a redemption rate of 14 percent to 15 percent.

Oscar Mayer's campaign provides a nice example of the power of segmentation and targeting in couponing: The users were encouraged to remain loyal but were not wastefully overrewarded. The nonusers were tempted to taste Oscar Mayer at no charge, and almost 15 percent accepted. And perhaps through the use of Super CFB (tested copy about the brand), the percentage of redemptions by the competitive product users and the nonusers could have been raised even higher.

This is really a new kind of advertising—"private advertising." You talk to consumers privately, and what you say depends on what you know about them. And even if your competitors find out what you are doing, it will probably be too late for them to neutralize your promotion with countercampaigns.

Couponing by Other Kinds of Advertisers

Of course, couponing is certainly not limited to package-goods manufacturers and fast-food chains. Almost any kind of selling by or through retailers can use couponing and rebate offers—usually without the saturation problem that has neutralized the value of couponing for established competitive package-goods brands.

Says Professor Thomas Nagle of The University of Chicago:

> The industries that are using (sales promotion tactics) most intensely now realize that they have gone overboard and are trying to cut back. But that is going to be more than made up for by the expansion of sales promotion techniques into industries that have never used them before, like financial services, the airline industry, and alcoholic beverages.[17]

Waldenbooks opened a new bookstore on Manhattan's Lexington Avenue in the spring of 1985. They blasted it off the launch pad with a full-page ad in *The New York Times* containing not one, not two, not three, but *five* coupons:

1. Thirty-five percent off book purchases (same day only).

2. "Free Membership in Waldenbooks Romance Book Club—for Romance Book lovers—a bi-monthly newsletter, free books and special offers."

3. "Free Membership in Waldenbooks Otherworlds Club. For SF/Fantasy buffs—a newsletter, exclusive offers and a huge selection of books."

4. "Free Membership in Waldenbooks Happy Birthday Club. For kids 14 and under—a birthday card and a birthday bonus."

5. "Free" (picture of cup of coffee).

Note that although not every retailer may be able to afford a full-page ad in *The New York Times,* there is nothing in this vigorous promotion that could not be emulated *in principle* by any retailer, no matter how small.

High-Ticket Couponing. In advertising a high-ticket purchase, it is possible to offer a coupon with a dramatically large face value (although if it is too large, it runs some risk of losing credibility).

Holiday Inn ran a powerhouse promotion in *Reader's Digest* with five $10 coupons bound in, accompanied by a backup page explaining and promoting the deal.

During the rebate craze that swept Detroit a few years ago, all the manufacturers were offering rebates, and just as in the packaged-goods field, they tended to cancel each other out and leave everybody in the same place. But in 1985, after the rebate mania had faded into the past, one company came tip-toeing back in with a cleverly disguised rebate which the company insisted was not a rebate.

Chrysler sent an elegant direct-mail piece, gold-embossed and printed on heavy stock, and bearing a message from company chairman Lee Iacocca, to nearly 4 million people. In appreciation for their having enough faith in Chrysler products to have bought one during the company's dark days, they were presented in the mailing with a "Thank You, America" certificate good for $500 on any 1985 Chrysler vehicle.

A company spokesperson said the promotion was "eminently successful." Within a few months, year-to-date sales of domestic cars were up 30 percent over 1984 figures. More than 2 percent of the certificates had been redeemed at dealerships, and the sale of 130,000 cars and trucks was attributed directly to the program.

Thus, one of the lessons of couponing seems to be: It's hard to squeeze permanent gains out of it if all your competitors are doing it, but it can work to beat the band when you can catch your competitors off guard.

First Interstate Bank, which has 1100 branches in 15 states, has run coupon ads addressed to people who have just moved into a new home. The ads offer them a coupon book with discount coupons worth up to $4000 in exchange for opening an account with the bank—and more coupons just for sending in the reply coupon. An outstanding promotion, with rifle-shot targeting to that prime bank prospect, the new resident.

Harley Street Private Physicians, Ltd. (even the name makes you feel better!) has run ads with a coupon good for $100 toward the cost of a complete medical evaluation. Even doctors are doing it!

A universal law of merchandising is that the better a promotion concept works, the greater the likelihood of ultimate saturation usage by an entire category. As a MaxiMarketer, you need to look at where couponing stands in your category. Is it just beginning to come into favor or is it at a mature or saturated level? Choose the couponing strategy that fits your product or service at this time.

Sampling

Sampling, when done properly, can be so effective that it's surprising it's not used more often. Even if your company has had its own positive experiences with sampling, it's worth taking a fresh look at a tool you may take for granted.

Aaron Cohen Marketing Services of Scarsdale, New York, did a study to determine how a user of a particular brand would react after receiving a sample and/or redemption coupon of a brand he or she did not use.

The sales impact of ten products in John Blair Marketing's sample pack was studied. The sampled brands experienced market share increases ranging from 5 percent for a brand with over half the volume in its category to a high of 3533 percent for a new product that started with a very low base.

Schultz and Robinson describe an impressive marketing experiment with sampling conducted in 1978 by TRIM Tele-Marketing Research Movement, Inc. (TRIM). The customers of test supermarkets were treated three different ways. The customers of the "A" group of supermarkets got no special promotion. Most of the customers of the "B" group of supermarkets were mailed a cents-off coupon for the product. Most of the customers of the supermarkets designated "C" received a cents-off coupon plus a sample of the product.

The "B" stores produced sales of the product that were 250 percent better than the "A" or control stores. But the "C" stores produced sales that were more than 300 percent better.

The significant aspect of this result, in our opinion, is that the additional increment of better than 50 percent *had to be an expression of increased desire for the product engendered by the free sample.* In contrast to promotion, which merely motivates brand hoppers to enjoy a saving or existing customers to load up, those additional sales due to the sampling in this case cannot be explained except in terms of attitudinal effect.

Of course you need to have a good product. But if you're launching a new product or trying to revive an old one, it had better be good. And if the public is disappointed or indifferent, sampling is a quick way to find out.

Also, needless to say, it's not possible to mail out samples of a perishable or refrigerated product like butter. But the equivalent of a sample (although an expensive full-sized sample) can be provided by a full-value coupon.

But, you may be thinking, sampling is costly. Yet if the cost is evaluated the way direct marketers would—weighing the advertising cost *per new customer acquired* rather than the cost per advertising impression—we believe that sampling comes out as one of the most economic forms of advertising, not one of the costliest.

And as the ability to target prime prospects via direct mail continues to improve, the cost-effectiveness of sampling becomes even more attractive. With today's vast databases of households accurately audited for individual interests, habits, and current brand usage, you can distribute your samples precisely where they will do you the most good.

"Cold" Distribution versus Requested Samples

Should you *mail* unsolicited free samples directly to targeted prospects or merely *offer* samples in sales promotion advertising? The advantage of the first way is that you can reach greater numbers of people. The advantage of the second way is that you will end up sending samples only to seriously interested prospects, and a greater percentage of them are likely to be converted to regular users.

Which way would come out better on the bottom line for your product could only be determined by a comparative test, but if merely offering a sample showed promise, our experience in direct marketing tells us that the response rate could then be improved as much as 200 percent to 300 percent by multiple testing of different expressions of the offer. And the arithmetic would be helped by eliminating the cost of sending samples to people who aren't interested or won't consider switching from their present brand.

One Spectacular Sampling Success

Surely one of the most spectacular sampling successes of all time was the introduction of Finesse shampoo and conditioner.

Helene Curtis spent $10.5 million to mail out 70 million little blue packets to middle- and upper-income women (backed by $18 million in television awareness advertising). Within 6 months, Finesse conditioner was number 1 in its category with a 12.2 percent market share, and Finesse shampoo had captured a 4.2 percent market share. And these percentages were expected to increase, because the company had not yet been able to get enough product into the stores to meet the demand.

What do you think would have happened if Curtis had spent all $28 million on television and skipped the sampling? Not nearly as much, our guess would be. Often $20 million, $30 million, or more is spent on television advertising for a brand with little to show for it in terms of improvement of market share.

Sampling in Other Fields

With imagination, sampling can be applied to fields where you wouldn't expect it.

Bantam Books has offered readers a preview of five top summer titles with 200,000 copies of a sampler of excerpts given away in bookstores.

And now sampling has been applied to the promotion of magazine subscriptions: Even though an army of experts could have been assembled to persuade Italian publisher Franco Maria Ricci that it couldn't and shouldn't be done, he decided to launch the U. S. edition of *FMR: the Magazine of Franco Maria Ricci* by mailing out 8 million copies to affluent readers—not of a real 160-page magazine, but rather a 16-page or 32-page sampler.

The cost was $5 million, but within a few months he had 100,000 subscriptions at $48 a year, which would mean a gross of very close to $5 million. And most magazine publishers who invest in new-subscriber promotion are happy to get back enough dollars just to cover that investment.

Some enterprising computer software manufacturers got the idea of offering diskettes loaded with samples of their programs. A co-op service called Computer Buys listed eight trial disks offered free or (mostly) for a service charge of around $10. One leading software publisher even bound a demonstration disk right into a computer magazine.

Sampling in the form of Scentstrip is revolutionizing the fragrance business. (The Scentstrip releases a fragrance when the prospect lifts a folded flap as directed.) Between 40 and 50 million Scentstrips were produced in 1984 for use in magazines, store catalogs, and direct mail.

Giorgio of Beverly Hills, the sensation of the fragrance industry, was a retail shop that began to go national with its house fragrance, using the Scentstrip for sampling. By 1983 they were mailing out 4 million a year and including them in mail-order advertisements in some 40 regional and national magazines. By 1984 their sales were estimated to reach nearly $70 million from a modest beginning just a few years earlier.

The Scentstrip "may forever change sampling as we know it today," said Annette Green, executive director of the Fragrance Foundation. "Everyone is getting involved. But it was Giorgio that started it all."[18]

Imagine a single retailer in one community revolutionizing an entire category because it found a better way to sample its product and could prove it was right with direct-response advertising. Giorgio is another example of the new breed of MaxiMarketer that dares to take a familiar technique (in this case, sampling) and use it in a whole new way to conquer the market. (Of course you must also have a product the public likes and wants, and Giorgio managed to accomplish that as well.)

Now the successor of the Scentstrip is here—the cosmetic color strip, paper strips of different shades of rub-off, rub-on eye shadow and other makeup preparations. Working women too busy for department-store browsing can experiment with different shades at home. At last report, the future of color strips was somewhat clouded by a U. S. Postal Service rate ruling that, unlike Scentstrips, color strips are product samples, and magazines carrying them would have to be mailed at the third-class postal rate instead of the lower second-class rates. But even if the ruling stands, one supplier still expects to see 1.5 billion color strips distributed by the end of 1987.

How You Might Be Able to Make Your Free-Sample Advertising Pay for Itself

By charging a nominal sum for postage and handling or for service, and by doing multiple split-run tests to find the best way to maximize response, you might be able to do free-sample advertising which will come close to being self-amortizing.

For instance, we once had a film-processing client who made a small fortune offering free color film. It was a foreign film that, in the beginning, most photofinishers were not set up to process, so it had to be returned to our client for developing and printing. We were legitimately able to say "free film—just send 25 cents to help cover the cost of postage and handling." The ads, mostly black-and-white half-pages in *TV Guide*, were so wildly successful that the advertising cost per response averaged as low as 25 cents. So the quarters that came in were paying for the advertising!

The cost of manufacturing many products is relatively small compared to the ultimate selling price. This means you may be able to charge a nominal sum for your sample which will be equal to your actual cost of providing it. It's also possible that you may do even better. By careful split testing of different creative approaches and different prices, you may eventually be able to develop a direct-response sample offer with the right copy and the right price which will bring back enough dollars to cover *both* the cost of the sample and the cost of the advertising. Or, if not, you can at least come close, stretching your advertising dollars far beyond your expectations.

How Not to Do Sampling

If you're not as careful and painstaking with your follow-up as you are with your up-front advertising, the full impact of your sampling may fall short of its potential.

Celestial Seasonings—which sells herb teas—had an interesting idea for self-amortizing sampling, but it fulfilled the orders in such a mediocre manner that the promotion may have done more harm than good.

Here is a company with romantic origins, a product that shook up the established giants in its field, and a wonderful product and company story to tell. Their packaging alone makes delightful reading at the kitchen table. For instance, printed on their carton of chamomile tea bags are not only a couple of the parables and inspirational quotations for which they are famous but also this captivating background copy about the product:

> Chamomile has been recognized and used by many different cultures for centuries. In the middle ages it was a stewing herb, and the Spaniards have long used it in making their finest sherries. In a bath it is said to be a moisturizer and blondes have often used it to highlight their hair. Try a cup of chamomile tea with some honey or perhaps a dash of freshly ground ginger. Chamomile has a soothing quality and makes a beautiful golden tea.

Someone had a bright idea—in fact, a brilliant, bold idea. Why not do a 2-minute direct-marketing television commercial on cable offering a sampler pack of a variety of Celestial Seasonings tea bags for $10 (high enough to help pay for the advertising), with the founder Mo Siegel as the spokesperson? And they did it. Who knows? Maybe they even got a PI deal (payment to the medium per inquiry received), so they couldn't lose.

But then the payoff of a great idea was sabotaged by the way they delivered the sample. The fulfillment package had no letter, no booklet, no inspirational sayings (except one on each of the canisters), none of the charm and romance of the Celestial Seasonings Tea story to heighten the perceived value of the samples.

The package contained three bags of each of six kinds of tea, two enameled oblong metal tea canisters, and four 25-cent coupons with a cool little thank-you note. It certainly did not seem like $10 worth. It may have won some new customers (along with annoying some prospects) but not nearly as many as a stronger resell and a better merchandise value would surely have done.

Direct-Response Advertising without Direct-Response Skill

In looking at much of today's free-sample-offer advertising and premium advertising, we are forcibly reminded once again that many of these advertisers have stumbled into direct-response advertising without benefit of the direct-response advertising skills and discoveries which direct-marketing professionals have inherited or accumulated over the years.

Bigelow herb teas, for example, recently ran a magazine ad with copy at the top urging previously disappointed herb tea tasters to try Bigelow. (But it didn't say *why* they should try it.) This was followed by full color photographs of six different kinds of its tea.

Centered at the bottom of the page was a mail-order coupon for ordering two bags of each of the six teas plus a 25-cent coupon, all for $1. But the copy at the top didn't mention the offer or the coupon!

The ad was weak in terms of both consumer franchise building and maximizing response. Surely there was a creative solution to the problem of accomplishing both objectives. Multiple split-run testing could have uncovered such a solution.

Hanes Hosiery's magazine ad for Winteralls hosiery had a large picture of the package in pale blue on poorly rendered snow or something that looked like snow. Plastered across it in large red italic letters with a white outline is the headline: "Low cost heating!" Clever, clever, but is it clear, clear? The mail-order coupon does have a smaller display line with the offer: "Save 55 percent! This time only!" But the promotion cries out for multiple testing to improve its effectiveness.

A Theragran vitamins sample-offer ad we looked at has a headline of three curving lines of white Gothic caps superimposed on a full-color half-tone showing a close-up of a surprised jogger, with television's grin-

ning "Theragram" messenger leaning over his shoulder and pushing a
bottle of Theragran-Z vitamins against his ear.

Once again, the body copy doesn't even mention the offer of a free 30-
day supply featured in the reply coupon. So the advertisement ends up
with neither a strong brand-building message nor a strong activation
element.

We could go on—but see for yourself. Page through a service magazine as a consumer. Note how often the ads that offer a free sample
maximize neither the brand image nor your desire to send for the
sample.

Sampling the Right Way

However, we do see some advertisers doing it the right way.

Benson and Hedges ran a three-page bleed insert that shows only the
product on a gold-tooled table-top and an invitation envelope with
"R. S. V. P." peeping out. No body copy, true, but how much is there to
say about a parity product like a cigarette anyway? The display copy
simply says, "Benson & Hedges. You are invited to enjoy two complimentary packages of Deluxe Ultra Lights. Only 6 mg. yet rich enough to
be called deluxe. Regular and Menthol."

And the best part is a bound-in postpaid reply card with reply copy in
elegant wedding-script type.

We don't know whether the ad is the best possible sales pitch for the
brand—we're not experts on cigarette advertising. But the handling of
the sample offer is very clear, professional, appropriate, and supportive
of the brand positioning. Best of all, the bound-in reply card should
have increased response by 5 to 10 times over what the same ad would
have done with only an on-page reply coupon.

Alberto-Culver's FDS feminine deodorant has run outstanding free-
trial advertising for its spray. It was a rare and impressive demonstration
that a free sample can be offered in a way that is dignified, tasteful, and
persuasive, strengthening the image of the brand and staking out a
unique selling proposition: "Because your body changes every day, you
need the protection of FDS every day."

The illustration has three silhouettes of a ballet student in white leo-
tards and a picture of the product, all superimposed on a calendar.
Below that are 114 words of persuasive copy in readable type and a reply
coupon.

For the following reasons, this is the kind of outstanding Super CFB
advertising we would expect to emerge from a testing program such as
we advocated earlier:

1. It strengthens the brand image.

2. It heightens interest in sending for the sample.

3. It will heighten the *perceived value* of the sample when it is actually tried.

The FDS ad is also an example of how a reply coupon can be easily added to existing brand advertising, making it possible to start a relationship with interested prospects by mail and/or phone without detracting anything from the dignity, taste, or brand-building power of the advertising.

If effect, what Alberto-Culver has done here is to gain no-cost advertising space for its free-sample promotion. Its agency's art director has stolen just one-eighth of the page to add the reply coupon, space which would otherwise probably have been used simply as additional spacing for all the other elements with no visible gain in impact or effectiveness.

We believe response could have been increased even more, without harming the CFB activity of the ad, by adding a little copy about the offer. Better yet, if the headline had been followed by a subhead, "Send for a free sample and prove it to yourself," it would have further increased response at no harm to the overall appearance and dignity of the ad.

And if Alberto-Culver thinks we're wrong, just consider how easy it would be to find out—with a split-run test of the changes we suggested. And if we're right, the result might be an increase of 50 percent in the number of responses at no increase in media cost.

The MaxiMarketing Approach to Sample Offers

Our Super CFB approach to free-sample advertising calls for preparing six or eight different advertisements, printing each on light card stock with a detachable business reply card on the flap, intermixing all six or eight uniformly at the printing plant or bindery, and running them in a representative selection of target-market publications.

Then we would roll out the winning ad. And we would also enclose a reprint of it not only in the free-sample carton (along with a warm, friendly resell letter) but in *all* cartons of the products (if it uses a carton), for maximum resell of the product at the point of use.

Test Sampling on Television?

And why not experiment with the same add-on technique in television advertising? The public is now thoroughly familiar with, and comfortable with, use of the toll-free 800 number. By purchase of an additional

15 or 30 seconds, you could add an offer of a trial coupon or sample to an existing commercial and invite response via an 800 number. This would provide a running index to the efficiency of your television advertising—the more effective commercials and the more efficient buys would produce more responses.

The names and addresses of respondents could be fed into your database. The phone operators could be trained to screen the calls and separate present users from nonusers. Each cents-off coupon mailed out could be imprinted by computer with the name and address of the respondent, and comparison of the redeemed coupons to the database would reveal who was using the coupons. Thus you could begin to target and motivate prospects with a far greater degree of precision and control.

Too expensive? Don't forget you can partially or totally liquidate the cost of your sampling with a modest service charge.

Slow Delivery of Requested Samples Hurts

Like most trial offers, the Winteralls ad warns "allow 6 to 8 weeks for delivery." Part of the reason is a valid economic consideration—the use of cheap bulk-mail postage rates for delivery.

But we know from experience with some of our direct-marketing clients that slow delivery mars the effectiveness of follow-up. When correspondence schools offering free information about their courses tested mailing out the first booklet by first-class mail versus the much slower third-class, conversion to sales of the inquiries answered by first-class mail were always far higher.

One of our mail-order clients once examined the total sales to test cells of customers whose first shipment had been sent within 24 hours of receipt of the order, within 2 days, within 3 days, and so on. He found that eventual sales to each test cell were in inverse proportion to how long the customers had to wait for their first order. First impressions count.

When requested samples arrive 6 weeks later, the recipients have forgotten all about the offer and their original enthusiasm for it.

Perhaps bulk-mail delivery is absolutely necessary because of the economics of the promotion. But we would like to see some market research comparing consumer reactions to the two kinds of delivery, measured not only in terms of intermediate reaction but also in terms of later purchases.

The Advertising-Enhanced Sample

There is another frontier of sampling, and that is the distribution of a free sample accompanied by advertising which enhances its perceived value. To explain what we mean, we must digress briefly.

Banana Republic sells off-beat casual clothing via unique mail-order catalogs filled with clever, wildly romantic descriptions and illustrations. For instance:

> 100% COTTON GURKHA SHORTS. It was 1814. A young British lieutenant led his Indian troops against Nepal. In one skirmish, the fierce Nepalese so frightened the soldiers that they fled. Not the young officer. "I've not come so far in order to run away," he told his Nepalese captors. They replied, "We could serve under an officer like you," and thus Britain inherited the famed Gurkhas. For them, British tailors developed these classic wide-legged shorts, still without peer in sticky situations.

Banana Republic now also has a chain of (extremely popular) retail shops carrying the same merchandise as the catalog. If you saw these Gurkha shorts in one of their stores, without having read the description, they might seem like just a nice pair of shorts. But the catalog description and illustration bestow on each garment a vastly greater *perceived value*. In your mind, the item takes on an extra quality not visible to the naked eye or apparent when handled or worn.

Just as good advertising increases the perceived value of Banana Republic clothing, we believe good accompanying advertising can also increase the perceived value of a product sample. And the more valuable the sample seems to the recipient, the more often the recipient will purchase a full-sized product. It will be a much more effective form of sampling than the common practice of simply sending out a sample with little or no accompanying advertising.

But you don't have to take our word for it. You can easily test this enhancement of a free sample via accompanying advertising and prove or disprove our thesis. And if it is proved, then the way is cleared for improving the enhancement. That is, you can split test the control enhancement advertising approach against other creative approaches until the results show you have found even more effective advertising enhancement.

It is highly probable that these will be some of the new sampling techniques used by package-goods advertisers in the 1990s. Those with the vision to seize on them before then will, in our opinion, gain a significant advantage over their competitors.

Premiums

Premium promotion often suffers from many of the same ills as the other main categories of sales promotion—sometimes even more.

It seems obvious—but apparently it is not—that good premium promotion should:

1. Strengthen the image of the brand's unique benefit or positioning or personality

2. Encourage continued use of the brand

3. Stimulate the widest possible response from the public, but most especially from real prospects

How Not to Do Premium Promotion

The marketplace abounds with examples of advertisers who did—and did not—observe these reasonable guidelines. We looked, for example, at a four-color bleed page from *Woman's Day*, which may have come into being largely because the merchandising managers from two companies struck a swell deal:

The makers of
MOP & GLO WILL SEND YOU
THE PERSONAL TOUCH RAZOR
FREE when you buy Mop & Glo

The ad does nothing for the product except remind consumers of its existence with a big product picture and the copy line: "Get a beautiful shine on your regular or no-wax floor." The body copy is almost entirely devoted to the deal.

The premium has no logical connection to the product except that many women use both—at very different times, and for very different reasons.

There are two coupons at the bottom, a cents-off coupon for Mop & Glo floor-care products and a mail-order coupon for ordering the razor. To get the razor, you must send proof of purchase (part of the label *and* cash-register receipt) *plus* 50 cents for postage and handling, *and* spend another 22 cents for the stamp on your outside envelope! Note how much the consumer has to go through to get this very mundane, unrelated, uninteresting little premium.

We don't mean to single out this particular ad for special criticism—we selected it at random as just one example of a common practice of treating the consumer thoughtlessly or indifferently in costly premium promotion.

The cartoonist Borth, creator of the long-running series "There Ought to Be a Law!", effectively satirized this odd way of winning the hearts and minds of prospects in a cartoon reprinted in *Advertising Age.* It shows the manufacturer conferring with his marketing advisor.

> MANUFACTURER: How can we get more people to buy our product?
>
> ADVISOR: Easy! Offer them a $1.00 refund coupon with each purchase of a large bottle.
>
> MANUFACTURER: That could cost us a million dollars if a million people used those coupons!
>
> ADVISOR: So we tell them they have to send along the label which is glued on the bottle . . .
>
> . . . which means they have to remember not to throw out the bottle after it's empty . . .
>
> . . . then soaking off the label in one piece and drying it. Then we tell them to include the cash register tape which they probably lost . . .
>
> . . . then use their own envelope, put a 20 cent stamp on it and mail it, then wait eight weeks. Who's going to do all that for 80 cents?
>
> MANUFACTURER: Okay . . . but make sure they can only have one refund per family![19]

Sounds exaggerated for humorous effect, doesn't it? But the obstacle course proposed in the cartoon bears an uncanny resemblance to many premium offers we see that seem to have as their goal the discouraging of responses.

Failure to promote the brand in an ad with a premium offer could be forgiven if the ad did a powerful enough job of promoting a relevant premium and if the advertising literature packed with the premium contained strong brand-building advertising. But a very common error we encounter in premium ads pulling for response is that they ignore the basic principles of maximizing response.

Carnation's Come 'N Get It dog food, for instance, ran a premium-offer ad which we found lacking in this respect. The ad included a 50-cent coupon and a reply coupon for requesting (with proof of purchase) the premium, a free copy of a paperback edition of the best-selling book, *No Bad Dogs the Woodhouse Way,* by Barbara Woodhouse. So far, so good—a soundly conceived, relevant premium.

The ad shows a dog with the book in his mouth, and the "cute" head-line, "Take it from me, FREE!" But nowhere in the ad is there *any* selling copy about either the dog food or the book! The "all you gotta do is . . ." school of advertising strikes again.

Yet all our direct-response advertising experience tells us that intelligent, specific, interesting, persuasive selling copy about the book could have doubled or tripled the response from dog lovers.

Anacin ran a baffling coupon and premium ad headed "Save $100!" The opportunity was to send the mail-order coupon with 50 cents and proof of purchase for a "new 32-page book packed with coupons, discounts, and rebates to save you money, plus exciting articles that can make your life easier, healthier, and more fun."

But there was no explanation—none—about either the editorial content of the booklet or the value coupons. Were the coupons good for 3 nights in a modest Florida hotel? For a 10-year supply of Anacin tablets? The reader is left to guess.

This is a prime example of what Achenbaum calls "marketing strategy erosion":

> This is the situation where the strategy of a market communication is eroded in its execution because of faulty and incompetent oversight. Although it exists in advertising, it is most prevalent in the merchandising and sales promotion areas.
>
> Despite the large sums spent on merchandising and sales promotion, they have continued to be treated by most marketers as a secondary factor—not totally integrated into the marketing program; not consistent with its strategic thrust; and usually not properly evaluated as to their real effect on annual sales.[20]

And now for some good news. Along with disappointing examples like these, we have observed cases of excellent premium promotion that meet at least some of the guidelines we listed.

The Philip Morris Magic

Philip Morris has done an outstanding job of promoting Virginia Slims cigarettes since 1968. Today its brand share is about double that of all other women's cigarette brands combined. It, like the Benson & Hedges ad we cited approvingly, is an example of what has been called the "Philip Morris magic."

"The Philip Morris magic formula is no secret," says Ellen Merlo, group director of brand management for Virginia Slims cigarettes. "It's the same for all of our brands—Marlboro, Benson & Hedges, Merit. You create a clearly defined brand image with advertising. You vigorously support that image with every other element of the marketing mix."[21]

An integral element in the Virginia Slims marketing mix has been the use of self-liquidating premiums which support the consistent advertising theme, "You've come a long way, baby." These have included such previously all-male prerogatives as a little black book for telephone numbers, a jogging suit, a rugby shirt, and boxing shorts and robe.

But the promotional mainstay since 1970 has been the Book of Days. It is an entertaining hardcover daily appointment calendar that reinforces the brand's "then and now" theme every day of the year with illustrations, quotations, and anecdotes.

One million copies of the Book of Days are attached to 1 million Virginia Slims cartons in late November or early December. They are usually distributed and sold within 2 weeks. Some stores report that their supply is wiped out in 2 days.

The book is also featured earlier in the season in mail-order ads which offer to send a copy in exchange for $1 plus two end labels from any pack or box of Virginia Slims. These advertisements perform double duty (a desirable function examined later in this book): They catch women who don't buy by the carton (or might miss the opportunity in stores), and they build up the demand for the premium at the retail level.

The caring about your customer advocated in *In Search of Excellence* even extends to the fine print setting forth the usual offer limitations. It concludes: "Please note: We want to make sure you're completely satisfied with your order—and that you get it on time. But sometimes things go wrong. If they do, be sure to let us know. Write: Virginia Slims Book of Days, 120 Park Avenue, New York, New York 10017."

In striking contrast to the careless, unintegrated kind of sales promotion deplored by Achenbaum, the Book of Days is treated as a major creative effort, which of course it is. The book is prepared by the brand's advertising agency, Leo Burnett, and creative planning for the book starts more than a year in advance.

Is the Proof-of-Purchase Requirement Always a Good Idea?

A booklet offer always extends a sensible opportunity to encourage product usage and promote brand reinforcement. But limiting its distribution unduly may be self-defeating.

Kellogg's, for instance, has run a hard-working little mail-order ad offering their Bran Idea Book for $1 plus two proof-of-purchase seals from one of four featured bran cereals. The respondents also receive cents-off coupons.

Kellogg's deserves a gold star for a good promotion. The headline is clear and communicates a strong promise: "Get delicious new ideas for adding fiber to your life!" For an ad which is only a fraction of a page, it has fairly good selling copy about the booklet.

At the same time, however, the ad is confined by the boundaries of traditional marketing thinking. It may be traditional to force customers to get or find boxes of Kellogg's with the required seals before permitting them to order the book. But is it really desirable or necessary?

What if the requirement for seals were eliminated? All our direct-marketing experience tells us that the easier it is to order something, the more responses you receive. Without the seals requirement, Kellogg's, a leading provider of bran fiber products, would get perhaps two or three times as many copies of the book, and trial coupons, into the hands of prospects and customers highly interested in incorporating more fiber into their diet. Doesn't it seem reasonable that they would sell more bran cereal that way?

Saco buttermilk powder did it the right way in their fractional-page ad. They combined a brand-building headline—"Some of my best recipes call for buttermilk, and . . . Saco cultured Buttermilk Powder is always in my pantry when I need it!"—with a mail-order coupon offering five buttermilk-recipe card sets for 50 cents each. No proof of purchase required.

We might quibble about details, e.g., the offer is not mentioned anywhere except in the coupon, and there is no mouth-watering mention or description of any of the recipes. But it still seems likely that the Saco approach is reaching and influencing more prospects for their product than the Kellogg's approach.

How Can Powerful Premiums Be Developed?

An underutilized tool of premium promotion is pretesting. *Not* through asking consumer panels for their opinions—a course that is filled with booby traps and will not furnish any quantitative measurements—but rather through mail-order testing of a number of promising possibilities.

You can do this publicly, by direct-response tests in selected magazines or newspapers, or privately, via direct mail. The test can be performed in either of two ways:

1. A multiple split run that split-tests a number of different advertisements, each one offering a different premium with the required proof of purchase and payment

2. A self-contained single test in which a number of premium possibilities are listed and described in the same advertisement and the respondent is invited to choose one

In either case, the public will inform you by its responses which is the most appealing premium for you to offer in future ads.

Sounds like it's too much trouble? Take a moment to check out how many advertising dollars your company is devoting to direct-response premium advertising this year. Then calculate what it would mean in dollars if prior split-run testing of premium possibilities had resulted in doubling or tripling the responses you are getting. It would be like getting two or three times as much premium-offer advertising for the same money.

Direct-marketing companies often do a "dry run" test, in which a possible product such as a set of books is tested in direct-response advertising without actually creating the product, This technique could be adapted to quick, inexpensive pretesting of premium ideas while they are still in the concept stage.

What More Price Testing of Premiums Could Accomplish.   Testing of different price points for a self-liquidating premium via direct response might strike gold. You might find that you could charge enough to cover the premium *and* the advertising that offers it. *Then you could run, in effect, "free" advertising for your premium!*

Must Successful Premium Promotions Never Be Repeated?   The first people to tire of an advertising campaign are often not members of the public but the advertisers themselves.

And since premium promotion has usually not been operated under the same laws as direct marketing (in which a proven promotion may run for years), many successful premium promotions are probably abandoned simply because a new year has rolled around. Strictly controlled and measured direct-response testing of premiums could tell you when an attractive image-reinforcing premium might be profitably continued or revived.

Schenley Industries, in 1976–1977, offered for $3.95, as a self-liquidating premium, a cruet set which enabled you to reuse your empty minibottles of Mateus wine as salt, pepper, oil, and vinegar servers. There is nothing particularly dated about the idea, and simple retesting in a few publications would instantly reveal whether the promotion might be successfully revived 10 years later.

Continuity Premium Programs.   One lodestone region that few have mined is the ongoing program of premiums to be earned partially or entirely by continued purchase of the product or family of products.

Brown & Williamson Tobacco Corporation's in-pack coupon promotion is an outstanding example. Since 1932, well over 50 billion Raleigh (and, later, Belair) cigarette coupons have been distributed in-pack, and 77 percent have been redeemed for merchandise in their catalog. This is surely some kind of premium promotion record.

In 1984, Brown & Williamson Tobacco mailed 3.5 million copies of the premium merchandise catalog to in-house lists and to people who had requested the catalog. And, for the first time, they provided a cash option, allowing smokers to speed up the coupon redemption process by paying for part of their order with cash. This, plus the promotion of the catalog in print advertising, resulted in 128 percent more orders than the previous year. Early market tests also indicated an increase in market share.

The part-cash option made it possible to spice up the catalog with big-ticket items, such as a Disneyland vacation for two, which would require, if not accompanied by cash, more than 30,000 coupons!

General Mills's on-pack offer of Oneida Community stainless table-ware is another long-time premium continuity program. A fractional page mail-order ad offers a monogrammed Oneida stainless letter opener for $4.50 with no proof of purchase required and no mention of tableware.

We responded to the offer, and the letter opener arrived all by itself in an otherwise empty mailing carton. This was followed shortly by the fulfillment mailing containing the catalog of continuity premiums, such as china and stainless flatware, that could be obtained with a combination of cash and on-pack Betty Crocker coupons.

The fulfillment mailing was adequate but not outstanding—for instance, the accompanying letter was set in printer's type instead of type-writer type, a glaring direct-mail no-no. But the most serious and puzzling flaw was that while the mailing referred several times to the fact that Betty Crocker coupons could be found on "over 200 of your favorite General Mills products," nowhere were the 200 products listed! The mailing merely mentioned a dozen or so examples.

Is this a once-great program that a new generation of management at General Mills is merely routinely continuing? Enthusiastic umbrella promotion in responsive and appropriate media—making clear which 200 General Mills products carry coupons, for instance—might give the program powerful new life. And why wait until customers respond? What if General Mills tested putting a premium catalog or minicatalog inside every feasible package? We think they would move more premiums and sell more package goods.

Sweepstakes

By this time, the power of a well-planned sweepstakes is legendary, and the appetite of the U.S. public for sweepstakes opportunities appears to be insatiable. But many sweepstakes promotions seem perfunctory and unrealistic in their expectations of what millions of prospects will be willing to go through at the store to find out if they are winners.

Some Problems

Remember that barely 20 percent of the population has ever sent in a contest or sweepstakes entry. Of those who do, over 75 percent accompany their entries with facsimiles rather than proof of purchase. And many are professional entrants.

Then when you also consider that many of the proof-of-purchase entries will be from present customers who would buy your product anyway, you may be left with a tiny percentage of entrants who were persuaded by your sweepstakes to try your product.

One final problem: You can't test a million-dollar sweepstakes in Peoria and then abandon it if the sales results are disappointing. Not unless you want to make the residents of Peoria $1 million richer. So running a big national sweepstakes takes some skilled high-risk seat-of-the-pants flying.

When Are Sweepstakes Most Justified?

Sweepstakes make the most sense when applied to a comparatively high-ticket or high-mark-up sale. If you are using a sweepstakes to sell a 59 cent can of pineapple which returns a manufacturer's gross profit of 10 percent on each sale—and if all the analysis indicates that the sweepstakes merely inflates sales temporarily without increasing long-term share points—then maybe you ought to wonder if you should do it at all.

But let's say you are selling something with a higher price tag or greater mark-up. Maybe it's an exercise machine for $300. Maybe it's a magazine subscription for $15, and you know you have a 50 percent chance of getting a renewal a year later. Maybe it's 1 or 2 nights' room rental in a motel for $40 or $80. In cases like these, if the sweepstakes gets enough additional people to engage in *just one transaction,* it may do more than pay for itself regardless of the additional value of any follow-up sales.

The Best Sweepstakes Promotion

A sweepstakes has to be imaginative, fun, appropriate, and brand reinforcing.

Philip Morris does the Benson & Hedges 100 sweepstakes—more of that "Philip Morris magic"—and it is an outstanding example of a good promotion. Almost every year since 1971, when the sweepstakes was begun to promote the first 100 millimeter cigarette, the advertiser has offered 100 opportunities to win 1 of 100 different whimsical, topical, sometimes nonsensical prizes. These prizes have included such gems as

100 pairs of argyle knee socks, 100 assorted T-shirts, 100 singing tele-
grams, and 100 pounds of spicy meatballs. (The winner of the last opted
for $200 in cash instead.) In 1982, when the brand was repositioned
upscale as Deluxe Ultra Lights, the prizes were made more deluxe also,
including such offerings as 100 inches of mink coat, 100 bottles of
French champagne, and 100 pieces of sushi from Tokyo.

The company doesn't know how many people enter the sweepstakes,
since anyone can try for prizes in more than one category, with or
without proof of purchase. But in the 1982–1983 promotion, more than
5 million entries were received. Although it would be difficult to prove
how much the promotion contributes to the Deluxe Ultra Lights market
share, Philip Morris is obviously well satisfied that the contribution is
substantial.

The Self-Prize Sweepstakes

This sweepstakes sometimes offers a way to get a lot of mileage out of a
modest prize structure. Your prizes are . . . the products you are selling. Thus you attract as entrants the people who are most interested in
what you have to sell, and the possibility of winning can cause them to
study and dream about your product's outstanding features.

Lanier Business Machines asked our agency to develop a direct-mail
campaign to business firms which would increase the quantity of sales
leads for their pocket dictating machines without decreasing the quality
of the leads. To have offered a typical nonrelated extravaganza of prizes
to a business audience could have been harmful to Lanier's image as a
manufacturer of quality business machines. But by conducting a tasteful
sweepstakes in which the prizes were the Lanier dictating machines the
sales reps hoped to sell, we were able to double their flow of leads with
no deterioration in lead quality.

Dodge ran a direct-mail sweepstakes which offered prospects a chance
to win a Caravan minivan, an Aries wagon, Ram wagon, Ramcharger, or
imported Colt Vista minivan. Each of five brochures depicted a U.S.
family and their transportation needs, then described one of the five
Dodge wagons and how it was designed to solve each family's driving
problems. Prospects picked the vehicle that suited their family's needs
and sent in the sweepstakes entry entitling them to win that vehicle.
About 7 percent of the 400,000 recipients of the mailing returned the
coupons, and it seems reasonable enough to assume that many of those
who didn't win couldn't stop dreaming about their choice and decided to
buy it.

Creating Store Traffic

A sweepstakes or other promotion to create store traffic pays off best when the advertiser or franchisers own the store.

Wendy's, in the latter half of 1984, spent $30 million on combining a revival of the much-publicized Clara Peller "Where's the Beef?" campaign with a Monday Night Football game. Beginning in August, 13.5 million game cards listing the names of National Football League teams were distributed each week to nearly every Wendy's restaurant in the United States.

Customers scratched off the blanks to see if their cards bore the names of the two teams scheduled to play the next Monday night. If so, they could mail their cards to Wendy's and thereby become eligible for a sweepstakes drawing held during the Monday Night Football game. Out of the 13.5 million game cards, the odds were that about 900,000 would have the names of the two teams. About 25 percent of these were mailed in.

Bruce Ley, vice president of national marketing, said he "couldn't even begin to guess" how much of a 26 percent sales increase in 1984 sales to $2.42 billion could be attributed to the promotion.[22] But it, along with Clara Peller, obviously played an important part.

Lest more modest advertisers be staggered and intimidated by these astronomical sums, it is worth pointing out more than once that many promotional successes achieved with millions of dollars can be emulated with budgets of only thousands or even hundreds. It is not at all hard to imagine a local merchant working up a very successful game of this sort involving city or state high school football or basketball play-offs.

In fact, we can't think of a promotional device used by giant companies that could not be successfully adapted by the tiniest of businesses. An appropriate and brand-reinforcing premium? Sure—how about a T-shirt with the name of your product or store? A free sample? The most modest delicatessen can put a sign in the window, "Stop in for a free taste of my fantastic potato salad." And so on.

If you have a small business, try collecting sales promotion advertisements by national advertisers and playing "What if?" with the promotion techniques and devices in them. You may be surprised at the profitable ideas you come up with.

"Send for More Information"

As indicated at the beginning of this chapter, sales promotion is part of the broader function of activation—getting your advertising's audience to take some immediate, specific action. The other principal means of activation in advertising is stimulating inquiries—inviting requests for more information.

This device costs so little (nothing, actually, if it is skillfully built into your advertising without subtracting from your sales message), and it can accomplish so much. Running *any* advertising without offering the public an opportunity to ask for more information seems almost a crime. Especially in this day and age of the toll-free 800 number, which makes it even easier for the consumer to contact you.

Use of this device can (1) monitor the comparative effectiveness of your latest advertising copy, (2) rank and rate the value of each advertising medium you use, (3) give you a chance to expose the people who are potentially your best customers to two or three times as much advertising (in your follow-up) without doubling or tripling your cost, and (4) start an in-house database of solid gold prospects whom you can continue to cultivate.

But it is not enough *merely* to invite requests for more information. Unless a sound follow-up advertising strategy is conceived and executed by someone in your company who "loves the prospect and loves the product," as we discuss in Chapter 9, you may discourage prospects rather than encourage them.

However, once you have developed an excellent conversion program, you can make a stronger up-front offer of more information—which will lead to more inquiries received, which will lead to more sales, which will lead to more income to spend on more advertising in a delightful feedback loop!

The Bottom Line

If you are aiming to make a high-ticket sale or series of sales with tens or hundreds of dollars of margin available for promotion and profit—and you are not selling a parity product in an overpromoted field—thoughtful, well-integrated sales promotion can turn consumer awareness into blazing action. And the tools of direct marketing and direct-response advertising can start you in the right direction and verify that you're on the right track.

If you're slugging it out in the package-goods field—up against similar products and similar promotion, working with promotional pennies per sale instead of dollars—running a good promotion is a little tougher. Sales promotion often produces an illusion of success and a zero or negative effect on profits.

But opportunities are problems in disguise. The tougher the race, the bigger the hero you will be if you win it. There are ways to make big sales promotion improvements in package-goods marketing. By strengthening the brand-image content of your promotion. By targeting your promotion more sharply. By conducting split-run direct-response tests to get the best brand-image message, the best premium, or the best way to showcase and enhance your free sample. Through careful testing of appeals and prices, you might even develop a premium or sampling offer which is self-amortizing, giving you, in effect, free advertising.

In addition to making a sales promotion offer, you can turn passive prospects into active customers by inviting inquiries—offering more information, and then following up with powerful resell advertising, as you will read about in Chapter 9.

And if you have a small business, even a tiny one, you can use the same secrets as the biggest "kids on the block" to make something happen that you can see and count and profit from.

8

Maximized Synergy: Double-Duty Advertising

The Big Picture

There is a way to maximize the power and synergy of your advertising which may not add a cent to your advertising budget. The secret is the extra value that can be extracted by arranging for a single advertising effort to accomplish two (or more) different jobs.

Single-duty advertising may be the most costly mistake you can make in advertising today, given the current high cost of media space and time. It is often astonishingly easy to create multifunctional advertising that works two or more ways to reduce costs and increase sales and profits.

Here are ten ways you can maximize the synergistic effect of

planning your advertising and marketing for two or more pur-
poses.

The beauty of double-duty advertising is that the second function it
performs often costs you nothing or almost nothing. It gets a free ride.

Actually, many examples of double-duty advertising are scattered
through this book, but we thought it would be useful to summarize in
one place the many ways that advertising can perform a second or third
function and often enhance the original intent at the same time.

1. Combine Awareness and Sales Promotion

Is it necessary or desirable to do one campaign for brand reinforcement
and another campaign to promote a premium or distribute a coupon?
By careful planning of the use of space in print advertising, one ad often
can accomplish both jobs, to the benefit of both. Although it may be
more economical or productive to do "naked" sales promotion, advertising devoid of brand-building copy, the Robert Prentice study cited in
Chapter 7 suggests that too much of this creates a danger of brand
franchise erosion.

2. Promote Two Channels of Distribution

The graveyard of computer companies is littered with the bones of
software promoters who were terrified of alienating retailers they didn't
have and couldn't get. So they refrained from selling their product
directly to the public and meanwhile couldn't get shelf space in computer stores.

What they failed to realize is that the extra sales which result from
inviting ordering *either* from their retailer *or* directly from themselves
repay the cost of the advertising. This makes it possible to afford more
advertising. And the additional advertising stimulates additional demand at the retail level.

Borland International is a software company that was started in 1982
with $20,000 scraped together by a French mathematician named Phi-
lippe Kahn. But Kahn's products, notably Sidekick, a program that
could perform desk-top functions while another program was running
on the computer, were priced at only $50, and other companies were
selling comparable software for $150 to $600. Software distributors

refused to handle the products because they felt there wasn't enough profit margin for themselves and their retailers.

So Borland began to run double-duty ads in computer magazines. The ads invited direct orders with a mail-telephone order coupon distinctively shaped like a computer disk. The top of the coupon was printed with "Available at better dealers nation-wide. Call 800-556-2283 for the dealer nearest you."

The result was the best of both worlds for Borland. They got enough mail orders to afford more mail-order advertising. The expanded mail-order advertising created a retail demand as well. The adventurous cadre of early tryers spread the news about the product through cost-free word-of-mouth advertising. Before long, dealers were confronted with hordes of customers demanding the Sidekick program. Suddenly it was a best seller both by mail and in stores, selling 175,000 copies in its first year. And Borland was able to chalk up $12 million in sales in 1984.

An added advantage of this double-duty approach is that the discipline imposed by getting and counting direct orders tends to make advertising more efficient, no-nonsense, and hard-working. The result is more effect at the retail level than might be achieved by some blue-sky image advertising expressive of "creativity" run riot.

Never forget that some people prefer to order directly and some prefer to come into a store and "kick the tires." By promoting both channels of distribution simultaneously, your advertising reaches and moves more people.

3. Do Well by Doing Good

Advertising in which your brand name is associated with a worthy cause can often "do well by doing good." You can tie your corporate contributions to a cause through donations based on the number of sales of your product, or you can simply lend corporate support to the cause for the public relations value.

The icing on the cake is that everybody wins. The public feels good about painlessly supporting a worthy cause. The cause feels good about getting additional support. And you, the advertiser, get to feel good about both increased sales and social usefulness.

American Express has been a leader in this kind of promotion. Their widely advertised program for making sales-related donations for restoration of the Statue of Liberty—a penny for each charge-card transaction and $1 for each new card issued—raised $1.7 million for Miss Liberty. It also generated a 30 percent increase in charge-card activity and a 15 percent jump in membership applications. Since then, everybody has been getting into the act.

Nabisco offered to mail packages of its Almost Home cookies to members of the armed forces in return for three proof-of-purchase seals from the family at home.

American Cyanamid Company made a tie-in deal with the Easter Seal Society that boosted coupon redemption for such products as Pine-Sol cleaner by more than 15 percent.

Coors beer set up a $500,000 scholarship program for children of soldiers who died in combat in Vietnam. The commercials advertising it were like a corporate tribute to the dead soldiers, and the program tastefully did not tie the fund to sales of the beer. The results, while hard to measure, must have done wonders for Coors's public image, which had suffered some hard knocks.

American Express's cause-related marketing operation has shown how such programs can be brought down to Main Street. By linking consumer use of American Express products and services to the company's donation to their Hometown American program, they expected to raise and distribute about $3 million in one year to help local groups "tackle human problems at the grass-roots level." In the preceding 5 years, American Express had donated nearly $6 million to 58 causes in this way.

4. Sell an Event While Selling a Product

Event marketing, like cause-related marketing, is another way to sell a product through favorable association and free publicity. Claude Hopkins made Cotosuet shortening a big success by going from city to city and running advertising announcing the baking of the largest cake in the world. In Chicago, during 1 week, 105,000 people climbed four flights of stairs to see such a cake. Announcements of such events can easily be given a "free ride" in advertising largely devoted to brand promotion.

Smithsonian Institution sent out a membership solicitation mailing which showed how the unique capability of direct mail can customize such announcements regionally. The computer-personalized outer envelope carried on the back an announcement of a Smithsonian traveling exhibition and the local address and date.

This direct-mail personalization technique could be nicely combined with cause-related marketing to tie a company's generosity to the sales and philanthropy needs of specific market areas. The computer could print on the outside of the envelope, "If you respond to the enclosed membership invitation within the next 60 days, we'll donate $1 to the United Way of (computer fills in city of addressee)."

5. Share the Advertising (and Its Cost) with Another Advertiser

A common form of promotion involves two related products, such as a brand of coffee and an artifical sweetener, that do a joint promotion and split the cost. Thus the advertising sells two different products simultaneously.

It's worth mentioning, because if you try a "force fit," you may come up with a surprising new combination. For instance, suppose you own a bookstore next door to a restaurant. The two of you could do a joint promotion in which a purchase at one place entitles you to a discount at the other. Even without paid advertising, such joint promotion could generate business simply by each business's displaying the offer next to its cash register.

Publishers Clearing House did a recent sweepstakes mailing which displayed impressive synergy. It combined sharing the cost, doing well by doing good, and supporting one medium with another. The mailing included an envelope of store coupons worth $8.50 from Procter & Gamble. For each coupon redeemed, Procter & Gamble promised to donate 10 cents, up to $750,000 total, to support local Special Olympics events for the mentally retarded. And Procter & Gamble ran television commericals calling attention to the sweepstakes mailing, their coupons in it, and their support of Special Olympics.

Thus Publishers Clearing House got help from another advertiser, whether in direct payment per thousand mailings or simply in additional television support advertising or both. Procter & Gamble got economical coupon distribution in a mailing that was highly likely to be opened. And both Procter & Gamble and Special Olympics benefited from the donations offer. Everybody won!

As mentioned in Chapter 4, companies with catalogs, like *Bloomingdale's by Mail, Nieman-Marcus,* and *The Sharper Image,* are partially defraying the cost of printing and mailing their catalogs by accepting paid advertising for products like Chevrolet and Ford cars. Combining this revenue with co-op ad money from manufacturers whose brandname products are featured in the catalog makes it hard for them to lose!

6. Support One Medium
While Advertising in Another

You can steal a little space or time from your advertisement to call the public's attention to another advertising effort elsewhere. For instance, national advertisers have had difficulty figuring out how to use cable television effectively. Most network television advertisers have considered the audience share for any one cable network too small to bother with. But if you are selling electric power tools, and you used just an inch or two of your advertising pages in *Popular Mechanics* and *Popular Science* to announce the networks and times for your home workshop program on cable, you could build up an audience for a 30-minute infomerical. And the audience would be solid-gold prospects, so that the percentage of the total television audience watching your program becomes a far less important question.

Using this technique in direct mail would be even more effective, because you could customize each mailing by computer to tell each addressee the exact local time and channel of the program in that area. The direct mail could do triple duty by (1) selling the products, (2) promoting the cable television infomercial, and (3) delivering a rebate coupon or other stimulant to encourage the recipient to act after seeing the television programming.

7. Promote Your Brand While
Promoting a Separate
Profit Center

You can use your brand advertising to support a new profit center—and then use your new profit center to support your brand.

Jack Daniel Distillery operates the Lynchburg Hardware General Store and Catalog as a separate profit center. The catalog is filled with country-style items, all chosen for their value in enhancing the image of Jack Daniel's whisky. Items include a pair of red long johns, a field tester cap, blue denim "hog washer" overalls, a front-porch rocker for sippin' and whittlin', and even a Tennessee redbone coon hound. Over the years, the catalog circulation has risen to 2.5 million, and in 1984 its sales volume crested $5 million.

There really is a Lynchburg Hardware and General Store, situated on the Lynchburg, Tennessee public square. The retail store accounts for about 20 percent of the operation's total revenue. Each year about 300,000 tourists go out of their way to visit it, driving down the two-lane highway from Mulberry or Tullahoma.

This is a classic example of MaxiMarketing dynamics. The brand advertising adds interest to the catalog. The catalog ambiance adds interest to the brand. The brand and the catalog build store traffic for the General Store, which in turn adds interest to the brand and the catalog.

So Brown-Forman Corporation, the parent company, enjoys a nice little profit center which meanwhile does a powerful job of building and reinforcing lifetime loyalty to Jack Daniel's whisky.

Brown-Forman uses a similar strategy to promote another of its well-known brands. *Southern Comfort* is promoted via *The Paddle Wheel Shop*, a mail-order catalog of Victorian lamps, plantation hats, wicker rockers, etc. Three mailings a year reach 1 million targeted Southern Comfort liquor customers and prospects. Only about a dozen of the catalog items bear the Southern Comfort name. But there is additional soft sell in the Comfort editorial message: "As you examine the selections, you may notice that some items bear the name of a unique liquor of Southern origin. It, too, is part of a venerable tradition, dating back more than a century." The brand manager has acknowledged that the catalog's prime purpose is to enhance consumers' attitudes toward the brand and that a study showed that this objective has been met.

Coca-Cola has provided a spectacular example of MaxiMarketing synergism with its Coca-Cola clothes by Murjani, sold in its own futuristic Fizzazz boutiques. A great many of the techniques discussed in this book are combined in a single operation:

1. The brand name supports the profit center, and the profit center supports the brand name. The logo boldly displayed on many of the garments provides free advertising for the brand, and the huge investment in the brand name and logo give instant recognition value and trendiness to the clothes.

2. The in-store touch-screen video catalog sells the clothing through an exciting, enjoyable new medium.

3. Customer names are entered in a database, and good customers are followed up by mail with a videotape catalog and printed order form. Catalog recipients may order by mail or phone, 24 hours a day, 7 days a week, and the toll-free 800 number is displayed frequently throughout the video.

4. The video catalog is more than just a catalog—the mundane item-by-item plugs are sandwiched between two sensational music videos with high entertainment value. This increases the chance that recipients of the videotape will want to show or lend it to their friends, many of whom will thus be persuaded to order from the catalog or visit the store.

5. The mail-order videotape catalog subtly promotes drinking Coca-Cola soft drink with a quick shot of people drinking a dark-brown liquid which the viewer is not likely to think is Pepsi soft drink.

6. The videotape catalog also supports the retail store with shots of the store and filmed interviews with ecstatic customers.

Sorry, Pepsi. While you were looking the other way, we think Coca-Cola stole a base on you. Time will tell.

8. Build a Database While You Build Your Brand

This recommendation lies at the heart of MaxiMarketing. The millions your company may spend on building a brand image for your products or service can serve an additional purpose at little additional cost. By inviting and encouraging response from the public and capturing the names and addresses and other data about your customers and best prospects, you can obtain not one but two important company assets: (1) your consumer brand franchise and (2) your in-house database.

Chapter 3 mentioned the L'Oréal ad with an offer to users of the chief competitive product, Loving Care hair color. This is a fine example of triple-duty advertising. (1) It builds the brand image. (2) It makes a powerful sales promotion offer targeted narrowly to prospects who are users in the category but nonusers of L'Oréal. (3) It gets the name of a prime prospect for possible follow-up through an in-house database.

9. Use Your Brand Name to Sell Your Premium and Your Premium to Sell Your Brand Name

A premium need not be just a trinket. It can be a powerful, permanent part of your entire marketing program, with a life of its own. Then when you use your advertising to promote both your brand name and your premium, you are really setting in motion a chain reaction which leads to more premium sales—and more brand product sales—and more premium sales.

Glenmore Distilleries has built up a richly synergistic campaign of this sort around its *Mr. Boston Official Bartender's Guide.* Just look at how all the pieces work together.

In 1935, Mr. Boston Distiller published the original guide. It became the accepted standard for professional bartenders and interested members of the public. Over 10 million copies have been sold in 62 editions.

The guide is now available as videocassette, book, and computer software. Packed with each is a four-color, eight-page brochure describing all the versions and providing separate order forms for each. The videotape is sold in liquor stores in states where this is permitted. In addition, bottle hang-tags promote mail-order sales in states where the video can't be sold in liquor stores.

Each Glenmore product ad invites requests for a recipe booklet. *Glenmore receives 800,000 requests a year*—an astounding number. Now the booklets are accompanied by the eight-page brochure and order form, plus an 800 number for ordering by phone.

The videotape is also sold in video stores, bookstores, department stores, gift shops, and liquor stores. The computer disk is sold in computer stores and mail-order catalogs. In addition to the recipes for all 1200 drinks, the disk allows users to search for a drink recipe by various criteria or to print out a recipe for a friend.

And all this activity keeps promoting the Mr. Boston name and creating a favorable environment around it, in a way that must largely or entirely pay for itself and more. It's a far cry from the passive poster ads for liquor of the past, such as those simply showing a gentleman in a top hat bowling and declaring "It's always a pleasure." The Mr. Boston program actively involves the public in the process of building brand-name recognition.

10. Advertise the Brand While You Advertise the Distribution Channel

We're talking here about retailers and catalogers using available co-op ad money and about brand manufacturers doing a better job of making it available. Both parties get more advertising for their money.

Armstrong Floors researched just how their co-op advertising actually affected sales. They selected at random the accounts of 200 retailers who were qualified for co-op ad money and divided them into two groups, those who actually used the money and those who didn't. They found that the accounts that had used the co-op money *had grown 340 per cent more than the other group*.

So you'd think that co-op ad programs would get 100 percent cooperation from retailers, wouldn't you? But you'd think wrong. *"More than $15 billion was available for cooperative advertising in 1984, and less* *than half of it was utilized by dealers.*"[1] That was the estimate of Charles Benard of Benard/Resnick & Company, one of the companies that specializes in designing and implementing co-op programs.

But the brand manufacturers must share the blame for this failure to utilize available dollars. Pinpoint Marketing, another company specializing in advising and auditing co-op programs, commissioned a market research firm to find out retailers' biggest gripes about co-op deals. Here's what retailers said they want and often don't get:

1. *Fewer restrictions.* Some programs have such numerous and complicated requirements that they drive the retailer crazy.

2. *Pay quickly.* This means a lot to a hard-pressed retailer.

3. *Pay fairly.* Don't quibble over pennies which have little meaning in the overall relationship between the buyer and the seller.

4. *Communicate.* Keep your retailers well-informed on your national advertising plans and how much co-op money will be available.

5. *Provide good tie-in materials.* The retailers said they appreciate and use good display materials and repro material, but some advertisers fail to supply anything.

The Bottom Line

The maximized synergy of double-duty advertising enables you to get twice as much advertising for your money. Take a moment to stop and think how each of the techniques described in this chapter might be adapted to your advertising for the product or service you are selling.

Can you tie in with an appropriate local or national cause or charity?

Can your brand-awareness advertising also be used to produce inquiries or sales for your own mail-order profit center?

Can your mail-order catalog also boost sales in your stores by including the addresses of store locations or carry paid advertising to help defray your costs?

Can you add a sales promotion offer to your brand-image advertisements?

Can you steal a little space from your ads or direct mail to announce a sponsored event or cable program?

Is there some way your awareness advertising can also scoop up extra sales to consumers who can't or won't purchase your product through your retailers?

Can you create a brand-reinforcing product that can hitchhike a free ride in your brand-awareness advertising and also stand alone as a retail product which reinforces your brand?

If you are a brand advertiser, do you have a co-op ad program that is clear, simple, fair, and helpful? If you are a retailer or catalog merchant, are you letting valuable co-op ad dollars slip between your fingers?

Try adding a little "hamburger extender" to your advertising! You may find that it is a delicious, nutritious, and satisfying way to make your advertising dollars go further.

9

Maximized Linkage: Encouraging Interested Prospects

The Big Picture

In today's increasingly demassified marketplace, the role of mass advertising is destined to change. Instead of influencing "everybody" in the media audience, a more proper function for it may be to attract, interest, sift out, identify, gather together, and communicate with the comparative few who are the immediate prospects for what is being advertised.

Then what happens next becomes as important as what has gone before. The curiosity of this minority is converted into a firm buying intention by additional advertising and promotion of equal quality, sent directly to the home of the interested prospect.

We call this form of advertising "linkage." It links the up-front advertising to the sale with additional arguments and benefits which the up-front advertising didn't have space or time to include.

Giving this follow-up process more serious attention and funding must—and will—become an important part of the marketing strategy of the smartest companies.

Of course, we realize the idea of inviting an inquiry, and sending out follow-up literature in response to it, is almost as old as advertising itself. But until now, this part of advertising has rarely been taken very seriously—except in direct marketing, of course, and sometimes in lead-generating advertising for a personal sales force.

Both the offer of more information and the follow-up material that is provided have been treated by most advertisers who bother with it at all as a kind of casual after-thought. It seemed to be viewed as an incidental service rather than as the vital function of building a bridge between the up-front advertising and the sale— despite the fact that a great deal of awareness advertising leaves the consumer not entirely clear about the product and bewildered about what to do next or where to buy.

We checked this out recently by answering a number of ads. There was seldom any evidence that the same kind of thought and care and creativity that went into the up-front advertising had been devoted to planning and preparing the follow-up material.

In the MaxiMarketing model, this scorned Cinderella of advertising is invited to step up and share the throne.

We want to pass along some of our observations of how advertisers are failing to bridge the gap between the advertising and the sale, how linkage can remedy this omission, and how you can focus more of your advertising on those people in the total media audience who are potentially your best customers.

As mentioned in Chapter 2, mail-order selling involves essentially the same process as that of brand advertisers selling through retailers, but direct marketing compresses it into a kind of one-stop shopping. Why-you-should-have-it, why-you-should-get-it-now, and here-it-is are all contained in the same advertisement. The store is right there in your hand or on your television screen.

The skillful mail-order advertiser tries to maintain the flow of the process in a single continuous uninterrupted stream, from attracting the prospect's attention to putting an order form in his or her hand. As the late Victor Schwab frequently reminded apprentices in direct-response advertising, "You must take the reader by the hand, and lead him (her) from where he (she) is to where you want him (her) to go."

When the marketing process is viewed in this light, a costly fault is exposed in the procedures of many advertisers who distribute their products through retail channels: They fail to bridge the gap between the advertising and the sale.

When awareness advertising seeks to drive the prospect to the retail point of sale, it is confronted by an enormous gap of time and physical distance, like a broad river, between the advertising impression and the cash register. Instead of constructing a bridge, and leading the reader or viewer by the hand across the bridge, many advertising campaigns simply point the prospect in the general direction of the river and hope for the best. No wonder many interested prospects wander away and never make it to the other side.

Nobody Is in Charge of Loving the Prospect

Why has this happened so often? We think it can partly be explained by fascination with advertising creativity as an end in itself.

Week after week, the advertising trade journals fill their pages with critical acclaim for the latest breathtaking flights of fancy in print and broadcast advertising. Whether the advertising successfully led enough consumers across the river to purchase the product is hardly ever mentioned. To put it another way—the advertiser's management insists on being able to love the advertising but neglects to put anybody in charge of loving the prospect.

Do you remember the classic Peter Arno cartoon in *The New Yorker* many years ago? A salacious old gentleman in a restaurant is pinching a pretty waitress passing by, and she turns to protest, "Please, sir, it's not my table!"

This is one possible explanation for why many advertisers fail to lead prospects all the way to the cash register: It's nobody's table.

As companies grow large, they get compartmentalized and departmentalized. Responsibilities are divvied up and parceled out. The chief executive is busy running the company and managing its assets. The marketing director is busy allocating and approving budgets and seeking that breakthrough new product. The product managers are busy building up their advertising recall scores and getting their dealers to stock up and provide a good display. The sales promotion manager is busy distributing cents-off coupons, making deals with retailers, and promoting novelties from Hong Kong as premiums or trips to Hong Kong as sweepstakes prizes.

But—or so it would seem—nobody is busy worrying about the prospect and about building a bridge that will help the prospect travel from the advertising to the sale.

Mind you, we are not merely talking about the need for a good customer service department. We're talking about the need for a continuous, planned marketing process from the moment of attracting a prospect's interest to the moment of completing the sale.

The Case of the Unbuyable Dress

A reporter in *The Wall Street Journal* told of a maddening experience which, although somewhat extreme, dramatizes and typifies the problem:

> Two weeks ago, *The New York Times Magazine* carried an ad for an off-the-shoulder black-and-white formal that some women readers thought they might die for. One of them, this reporter, naively assumed the dress could be bought, and set out to buy it.
>
> The first stop was Bloomingdale's in the Short Hills Mall in New Jersey. Although the sales help there breathlessly admired the picture of the dress, they said they didn't have it. Nor did the B. Altman & Co. or Abraham and Strauss department stores there.
>
> The next day, this now suspicious reporter went to Macy's at Herald Square. The saleswoman was not amused. "If one more person shows me that picture . . ." she said peevishly. "We don't have it, never had it and aren't going to get it," she continued, very, very calmly.
>
> The next day, a call went out to the manufacturer, Leslie Fay Co. The dress had been ordered by Saks Fifth Avenue in New York and Marshall Field in Chicago, they said.
>
> At Saks, the subject of the dress brought weariness to the voice of the saleswoman. "I know the dress, but we don't have it—never did," she said.[1]

And so on—we'll spare you the painful additional details. Finally, when the reporter learned that she absolutely positively could not buy the dress, she called and asked a spokesperson for the company what the point of the advertising was. "It wasn't really an ad," he said. "It just showed products that Leslie Fay makes." In other words—it's not my table!

. . . The Wordless Word Processor

A similar tale of consumer frustration was unfolded in a letter to the editor in *Advertising Age,* written by Jack Maxson of Maxson Creative.

> Some time ago, NEC unveiled the new APC III word processor. They ran daily ads in the *Boston Globe* to announce it, along with an attractive package deal, and said the sale was for a limited time. I was interested enough to drive 60 miles to visit a dealer listed in the ad. He demonstrated the machine and threw all the usual "compugook" at me—RAM, ROM, kilobytes and all. Nice job.
>
> Since I do not regard computers costing $3,000 or more as impulse items, I asked for literature at the end of the visit. The dealer had none—had not even been told, in fact, about the newspaper campaign. He took my name and address and said he would send me literature when it came in. That was Oct. 6. Nothing.
>
> I got impatient about a week later and wrote NEC's area headquarters and asked for any information they could send me.
>
> I've heard nothing from anyone. The newspaper campaign has disappeared. . . .
>
> What went wrong? Haven't they produced the literature yet for a product that's been on the shelves for two months or more? Should I have sent them a stamped self-addressed envelope?[2]

Meanwhile, as the letter's writer pointed out, NEC was spending millions airing a commercial showing people climbing a wall, conveying that NEC was gaining on the biggest computer companies.

Wouldn't it have made more sense to devote some of that advertising and promotion budget to capturing this prospect's name and address, "taking him by the hand," and leading him to the moment of buying decision?

Friendly, informative, complete, reassuring direct-mail follow-up could answer questions, remove doubts, instill confidence, and stimulate immediate action with a tempting reward. (In fact, direct-mail follow-up doesn't even have to be direct mail any more. With high-ticket high-tech purchases, you'll soon be seeing many videocassette demonstrations doing a bang-up job of converting undecided prospects.)

We wish the two stories above were isolated examples, but you know they are not. Stop and think of your own personal experiences in becoming interested in a product or service through advertising and then being disappointed, frustrated, or confused by your efforts to learn or do more about it.

Page through your favorite magazine. See for yourself how often the advertising calls attention to itself with its blatant cleverness. And then, just when you may begin to get interested, it stops abruptly or trails off. You, the reader, are left high and dry—the victim of the *discontinuity* of so much of today's advertising.

Who's in Charge of Loving Your Product?

Another thing that often seems missing in corporate marketing structure is someone who loves the *product*. In the sales department, yes. In the course of personally persuading customers to love the product, the sales personnel have found that they must first love it themselves.

In mail-order selling—which is really the last outpost of the "salesmanship in print" espoused as the purpose of advertising by the legendary copywriter Claude Hopkins at the beginning of the century—the love of the product shines through because it is absolutely essential to company survival. It must be fully conveyed right then and there on the page or the video screen—or the prospect will never make it to the reply form or telephone.

But in marketing the endless cascade of products sold through retailers, it is very easy for all the people in the chain of command to become cynical and indifferent about the product itself. And it often shows in the carelessness and mediocrity of the follow-up communications sent to interested prospects. The advertiser often has nothing much more to say about the product in a "bridge communication," because nobody in management is in charge of loving the product and conveying that love to the public.

Five Structural Components in Building a Good Bridge

What is the ideal bridge that will lead your prospect from your awareness advertising to the completion of the sale? It really involves the same components as those in a successful direct-marketing effort.

1. Activation. The first step must be to engage the prospect in *dialogue*—in two-way communication. You've got to provide in your advertising some reason for the interested prospect to respond—an offer of where-to-find-it, of more information, a sample, a premium, a rebate, etc.

And the invitation to respond should not be a casual afterthought, something "we might as well" add to the advertising, but an integral part of the marketing and advertising planning.

Once this premise is accepted, logic dictates that thought should be given not only to how to invite and encourage response, but also to how to maximize it.

2. Information.   Warm, friendly, persuasive, detailed information about the product—all the things that you'd like to tell your prospect but didn't have room or time for in a 30-second commercial or one-page ad with a big photograph.

And don't listen to those voices of the right brain whispering in your ear that "nobody will read all that copy." Think of "all that copy" as smorgasbörd, a feast of information spread out before the prospects, from which they will take what they need or want. Some, who are hungry for information, will take it all. Others will take just the smoked fish, still others just the deviled eggs.

3. Persuasion.   Information alone is not enough. Ideally you should "take the reader by the hand" and lead him or her emotionally from present problem to ultimate benefit.

4. Propulsion.   Direct marketers have learned the hard way that one of the greatest enemies of sales success is the human tendency toward inertia and procrastination. "Oh, yes," says the prospect, "that sounds like a very nice idea. I must do something about that sometime." And the impulse slips away, often never to be revived.

To turn that "sometime" into right now, direct marketers use what they call the "hot potato"—they put something in your hand that propels you to act. A deadline. An early-bird discount. A gift for acting at once. In other words, the direct marketer's own kind of sales promotion.

We would like to see more brand-awareness advertisers try this way of using sales promotion—sales promotion not as a means of *starting* a process with the consumer but as a means of *completing* it.

You have obtained the name and address of an interested prospect. You have given more education and persuasion to the prospect. And now you use the tools of sales promotion to activate the prospect, to get her or him to visit the dealer right now.

And, of course, you can provide a list of all your dealers—or, better yet, a computer printout of the names and addresses and phone numbers of the dealers nearest to the prospect's zip zone.

5. Consummation.   In direct marketing, we try to make it as easy as possible to order. Great care is exercised in designing a clear, simple, inviting, friendly order form. The retail equivalent is a sales clerk who understands what the promotion has made the customer want and who is prepared to provide it.

This, alas, is not completely in your control as the advertiser. But planning for it and controlling it as well as you can is also part of the marketing process, of loving the product and the prospect. Failure to do so can result in "disadvertising"—advertising which creates enemies, not customers—as the Leslie Fay and NEC experiences just cited suggest.

Obviously the urgency of the need for bridge building varies in direct proportion to the price and availability of the product. Bridge building may be neither practical nor necessary for a 39-cent product which is on sale right next to every cash register in the country. It can be crucially important for a product or service that is selling for $30, $300, $3000, or $30,000 at just a few locations in each area and perhaps is attempting to succeed on a comparatively limited advertising and marketing budget.

Four Common Failings in Follow-up Literature

To monitor the bridge-building performance of advertisers, from time to time we answer ads which invite a request for more information by toll-free phone call, letter, or coupon. More often than not, the fulfillment package we receive is a disgrace to the name and reputation of the company that sent it to us. It makes us wonder who is in charge of creating such a poor impression of a company that has just spent $10 million in advertising to get our interest. The following are the most common failures to love the prospect or the product that we have encountered.

1. No Letter or a Poor Letter.   This would have to be placed at the top of our list of complaints about company communication with prospects and customers.

In direct mail that has to pay its own way, no one bothers any more to test a direct-mail package without a letter enclosed. The importance of the letter has already been proven conclusively. It is simply the most important component when it comes to generating a response.

But material sent out by an indirect marketer quite commonly has no letter at all. You wanted a booklet? Okay, here's the booklet. You asked for a cents-off coupon? Okay, here's the coupon.

If there is a letter, it is likely to be short, blunt, amateurish business correspondence; often it has no salutation and is typeset in forbidding printer's type instead of friendly, personal typewriter type.

A common error is to think that if the enclosed booklet tells the whole story, there is nothing more for a letter to say. But direct marketers know that a letter gives you a priceless opportunity to tell your story a second time—in warm, human, personal terms.

People have been known to read and respond to a letter that is 8, 10, or even 15 pages long—but only if it is a compelling piece by a master of the art, a skilled professional who loves the prospect and loves the product. "Ah, but my problem is different," you may say. "I can imagine an interesting letter about a Caribbean cruise or an exercise machine. But who wants to read a letter about toilet tissue?"

Sounds like a tough problem, doesn't it? That's because it is. But if slice-of-life commericals can present consumers talking with warmth and genuine interest about their favorite brand of toilet tissue (as they have done), then surely a creative copywriter who loves the prospect and loves the product can compose a pleasant, persuasive note to accompany a cents-off coupon for such a product.

2. Hard-to-Read Typography. This may seem like an odd item to place on this list. But it very much belongs in any consideration of loving the product and loving the prospect. We have received brochures with a bad case of "art-director-itis" in which long stretches of text type are set in unreadable white letters on a black background. Or worse, on full-color half-tones with great variations in tone, so that sometimes the reader must even struggle through white letters printed on a background of white clouds!

Other common typographic sins are (1) type too small to be read, surrounded by acres of artistic white space; (2) type that is set in a measure that is too short or too long; (3) pale, thin sans-serif type; and (4) type that curves around the visual element with such flair and style that it is impossible to read.

Take a look at an article in *Reader's Digest* or *Newsweek* and notice how effortlessly the eye glides into and through the text. Then look at your company's product literature and see if it presents the same ease in reading.

3. Slow Response. Says *Boardroom Reports:* "Recent industrial advertising monitoring shows only 44 percent of advertisers respond within 60 days to inquiries prompted by ads or publicity releases. About 30 percent of the remaining 56 percent fail to respond even within 16 weeks. Result: potential customers are turned away by lack of interest in their needs."[3]

The same situation and the same consequence prevails in consumer advertising. Some companies we contacted did pretty well in promptness of response, especially advertisers of high-ticket items. Others were miserably and inexcusably slow, so slow that most inquirers would have forgotten having inquired.

A case can be made for the economic need to use slow third-class mail instead of fast (well, fairly fast) first-class mail in sending out a low-value coupon on a low-price package-good product. But is it a *good* case?

The cost of just one prime-time commerical airing, if rechanneled, could buy an awful lot of stamps. And a reply in the prospect's mailbox just 4 or 5 days after a request was sent in would be a wonderful way to say to that person, "We respect you! We take you seriously! We care about you! We want you! We love you!" Especially if it were accompanied by a warm, chatty letter.

4. Unclear or Inadequate Purchasing Alternatives.   Some companies do pretty well about enclosing a list of dealers. Few go so far as to set up a complete program in which the computer prints out the name of the nearest dealer for the inquirer and sends the name of the inquirer to the nearest dealer.

And then there are those two magic, seldom-used words, *either* and *or*. The prospect can either obtain the product at the nearby dealer listed *or* can order direct. The incremental business obtainable this way—not merely tolerated, but positively encouraged with clear ordering instructions, order form, money-back guarantee, incentive, etc.—can produce extra income which can pay for more advertising, which can stimulate still more direct and retail purchases. Everybody wins.

There was a time when companies fretted that their dealers would boycott them if they accepted direct orders, even quietly and privately. Today—forget it. There is too much happening, on too many fronts, for busy store-merchandise buyers to keep up with and worry about hypothetical threats of competition from their own suppliers. (We will examine this question in more detail in Chapter 11.)

Some Examples

Come along and look over our shoulders as we examine some of the follow-up material we sent away for.

We are going to skip the two extremes. At one end there is the lonely, naked cents-off coupon in an envelope all by itself or with a curt note. This practice is inexcusable but so common and standardized that further examination of it would be repetitious.

At the other extreme is literature from companies whose survival depends on follow-up, like long-distance phone services and financial services, and whose mailings can be expected to—and do—exhibit a high degree of professionalism.

Instead we're going to look at advertisers somewhere between these two extremes. These examples were chosen more or less at random, and we are not singling out the advertisers for special criticism. Whatever limitations we found are common ones.

United Airlines Hawaii Promotion

We answered a full-color ad in *Vogue* about wonderful Hawaii, "The Big Island," with a coupon offering more information. The information arrived 6 weeks later, a self-mailer booklet. No letter.

The booklet is comprised of six color spreads, each headed by a one-word theme: "Beautiful!" "Spectacular!" In each spread, both text copy and insert photographs are superimposed on a bleed-spread photograph. Some of the text copy is black letters on a dappled rough-textured snow and defies reading. Other spreads offer acres of text printed in white type on blue water or blue sky with white clouds.

In each spread, one brief combination caption attempts to describe both the bleed photo and the three or four inset photos, leaving the reader to match up the information with each photo.

The last spread is a calender of events and a map of the Island of Hawaii.

Buried in the copy are interesting, colorful details that some copywriter slaved over, but they are almost completely inaccessible to the reader. And there is just nothing in the mailing to complete the building of the bridge between the advertising and the sale.

One has no sense that somebody back there loved the product (except maybe the poor betrayed copywriter) and loved the prospect, and passionately wanted to see the two get together.

How David Ogilvy would groan over those captionless photographs and that inaccessible copy. And what an irresistible booklet he would have prepared on "Surprising Hawaii."

Mercedes-Benz

This was an exciting idea and a handsome, muddled presentation. It must be a successful program, since the brochure said that 100,000 Americans had already chosen it. If so, it is a triumph of product over presentation.

It is the Mercedes-Benz European Delivery Program. "You can bring down the cost of Europe when you bring back a new Mercedes-Benz," promised the ad we answered. "Pick it up at the Stuttgart Delivery Center and enjoy a driving vacation unmatched for comfort, convenience and freedom. Avoid costly car rentals while saving on the price of your new Mercedes-Benz."

The brochure, which was promptly mailed first class ($1.07 postage), was as handsome as you would expect from Mercedes-Benz, with the title gold-embossed on a misty painting of Europe on the cover. Inside there is well-written copy about the program, set in readable type and well illustrated.

There is a letter of sorts. But it is really a brief acknowledgment letter, not a sales letter. And nowhere does the mailing "take the reader by the hand" and spell out, in dollars and cents, the advantages of taking delivery of your car in Europe, driving it around on a European vacation, and then having it shipped to your dealer back home.

It's a big idea—but the copy never seems to come to grips with the big idea in the way a direct marketer would.

A noted direct-marketing copywriter named Ed McLean once wrote a famous letter that sold out 1500 Mercedes-Benz 190D diesel sedans— more sales than had been achieved by all the company's previous efforts combined. His letter, signed by the president, offered to buy all the new owner's gas and oil for a year.

To accompany this beautiful but inert brochure on the European Delivery Program, Ed could have written a letter that would "take you by the hand" and whisk you out the door. You would be running to catch the next plane to Europe.

Honda

We answered a Honda ad headed "It Comes with a Conscience." The ad explained:

> Honda has always made good cars. People love them. But with any loved one, things can sometimes get very emotional.
>
> Honda understands. And on our own we have set up a third-party arbitration program with the Better Business Bureau, to give you an extra voice, if you need it.
>
> But please talk with your dealer first. And follow the problem-solving procedure described in your manual.
>
> Our new program will help to resolve product-related questions about your Honda. This program is free. Just ask any Honda dealer for a booklet containing more information.
>
> Or call 800-521-1613. You see, Honda wants you and your Honda to have a long and happy relationship. It's only right.

It was not clear whether this ad was aimed at present or prospective Honda owners. But it sounded great, like "Hey, we really care about your complete satisfaction."

We called the number and asked for the booklet, which arrived fairly promptly. It turned out to be a publication of the Better Business Bureau (BBB), explaining their national program for mediating disputes between auto owners and manufacturers. It sounded less like a program that Honda had "set up" with the BBB than a program with which they and other manufacturers were cooperating.

With the booklet was a slip of paper from Honda with no signature and no logo. It told us that if we had a problem, we should first talk to our Honda dealer, then to the Honda Zone Customer Service Office, and then, if we were still not satisfied, to call Autoline, the arbitration service of the BBB.

It is not clear what Honda hoped to accomplish by this advertising and follow-up. To us, it came across as disadvertising.

The implied message we got was, "You may have trouble with your Honda that your dealer will refuse to do anything about, and you may have to go to the Better Business Bureau to get satisfaction." That's sending the prospect off in the wrong direction—away from the bridge.

Royal Copenhagen Porcelain, Georg Jensen Silversmiths

We answered an ad headed "Come Dine with Kings," which showed Royal Copenhagen Blue Line porcelain dinnerware, a Jensen candlestick, Gotham flatware, Holme Gaard glassware, and several Georg Jensen patterns. The ad invited, "Send $1 for the complete color folio."

We received two 4-page color folders and a price list which had been copied on an office machine—you could see where the staples and binder holes had been.

The two folders showed all the pieces in the Blue Fluted Plain and the Blue Fluted Full Lace patterns of Royal Copenhagen porcelain dinnerware. There was a brief blurb in three languages on the back page of each folder. The price list covered *only* the Blue Fluted Plain Border line.

There was no letter.

There was *nothing* about Gotham flatware *or* Georg Jensen silverplate *or* Holme Gaard glassware.

We'd like our dollar back. Apparently the purpose of the $1 charge was not really to defray the cost of the follow-up but rather to discourage response.

Horror stories like those we've described may not be the universal condition. But they are certainly common enough to give every company a good reason to stop and reexamine its own advertising follow-up practices and procedures.

Whatever position you hold in your company, dig out your most recent advertising and take a look at it. If it has an offer for more information, play consumer and answer the ad. You may get the shock of your life when you see what comes in the mail and how long it took to arrive.

Today, in the face of sharply escalated media costs, paying more attention to your communications with interested prospects is more than just desirable. It is rapidly becoming a marketing necessity. For if the object of marketing becomes to sharply define and specifically appeal to targeted prospects, then giving those prospects all the information and help they need becomes critical.

A new day is dawning, in which offers and information available by phone or coupon request will not be a casual afterthought added to upfront advertising efforts but rather an integral part of the total marketing mix.

And the advertising material sent in response to requests will not be a hastily assembled grab bag of whatever literature happens to be available or can be improvised. It will be conceived and executed with the same care and professional skill as the up-front advertising and will be considered a vitally important link in the marketing process—a bridge between the advertising and the sale.

Cuisinart Food Processor

It was fascinating and heartening to observe one national advertiser moving in this direction during the months in which this book was being written. Cuisinarts began its adventure in bridge building by offering in its magazine advertising "a free three-month membership in the Cuisinart Cooking Club, with benefits including monthly collections of recipes, techniques and tips that enable you to use your food processor to its fullest." And the ad concluded: "For recipes, as well as more information about our food processors, cookware, and our magazine, 'The Pleasures of Cooking,' write. . . ." It also appended a toll-free number to call for the nearest dealer.

Our inquiry was answered promptly, by first-class mail (cost, 56 cents). Apparently the advertising appeared before the planned follow-up had been developed, and we received a grab bag of poorly coordinated literature which did not fulfill the promise in the ads. There were no recipes. There was no further explanation of the Cuisinart Cooking Club. There was no literature on the various Cuisinart food processor models, just a black-and-white folder on accessories.

A month or so later, we answered another Cuisinart ad. This time the follow-up was better but still left much to be desired. A professional letter sold Cooking Club memberships, but the letter was addressed to "Dear Owner," not correct for prospects answering the ad. There were

still no photographs of the different Cuisinart food processor models
and copy about what they could do.

Still later, we answered a Cuisinart ad for the third time. This time, the
follow-up was enormously improved. It was almost a model of what
could be accomplished in bridging the gap between the advertising and
the sale. The contents included:

1. A warm, personal, enthusiastic letter from the president, Carl G.
   Sontheimer, about the club, addressed "Dear Friend and Fellow Food
   Lover"

2. An order form for enrolling in the club

3. A full-color folder headed "Which Cuisinart Food Processor Is For
   You?" comparing the features of the various models

4. A full-color folder headed, "They Really Are That Much Better,"
   showing and explaining the various accessories

5. A full-color folder headed "It Really Is That Much Better," showing
   and describing the Cuisinart lines of stainless steel cookware

6. A full-color sheet headed, "How to Get the Most Out of Any Food
   Processor," showing, describing, and offering six food-processor
   cookbooks

7. A full-color sheet on their superb magazine, *The Pleasures of Cooking,* with a sample page of recipes on the back

8. An order form for the magazine

We could quibble about improvements still needed—for example, the
literature still doesn't quite "take the reader by the hand" and say, in
effect, "Well, so you're thinking of buying a Cuisinart food processor.
Let me point out to you . . . ." We would also like to see a little propulsion toward the dealer of the kind we mentioned earlier in this chapter.
And better promotion of their spectacular magazine, *The Pleasures of
Cooking,* would inevitably sell more Cuisinart food processors.

But overall the last follow-up we looked at was so greatly improved,
and so much better than the mediocre miscellany we received from
many other advertisers, that we salute Cuisinarts for its progress toward
becoming an exemplary MaxiMarketer.

Linkage—Critical in
Demassified Marketing

We believe this kind of bridge-building promotion is destined to become
such an integral and vital part of the marketing of tomorrow that it
deserves a special name. We have chosen to call it "linkage."

Linkage is born of demassification.

It reduces the wastefulness of massive advertising expenditure lavished on prospects and nonprospects alike.

It permits you to divert some of that expenditure to coddling, cultivating, and converting your prime prospects who have taken the trouble to tell you, "Here I am. Help me." (See Figure 8.)

Magazine Advertising That Costs One Million Dollars or More— Yours for Only a Fraction of That Amount

Linkage permits you to break out of the severe length limitations imposed on your advertising message by the high cost of media: In 1985, it cost about $50,000 to reach the roughly 3 million readers of *Newsweek* with a black-and-white page.

But suppose you have a wonderful story to tell and yearn for lots of room to tell it. And suppose your fairy godmother granted your wish. Suppose, instead of being confined to a single page, you were allowed to fill 12 pages, or 16 pages, or even 32 pages, with powerful photographs, details of laboratory tests, favorable press comment, customer raves, dealer listings, etc. And this additional advertising would *not* cost the $500,000 or $1 million that such an insertion might cost in *Newsweek*. It would amount to only a fraction of the cost of your single black-and white page.

There's just one catch, not a very serious one. Your 32-page advertisement will not be read by all 3 million readers of *Newsweek*, but by only the comparative few—1 percent?—who are keenly interested in what you are offering, eager to read about it, ready to buy.

This is the magic of linkage. Instead of running your 32-page advertisement in *Newsweek*, you *mail* it to readers who devoured your 1-page advertisement and then by coupon or phone call said to you, "Tell me more!"

Instead of having to shout your wares at every house as your peddler wagon rolls down the street, you are invited to enter the homes of really interested prospects, sit down in the living room, and carry on a leisurely, persuasive conversation. This metaphor is useful in more ways than one. Let us examine it more closely.

When Is Linkage Appropriate?

Perhaps some products and services don't deserve such lavish attention. Perhaps busy prospects wouldn't be interested in sitting down with you to discuss paper towels or candy bars for half an hour. And perhaps you, the advertisers, don't really have enough to say to fill up the time anyway.

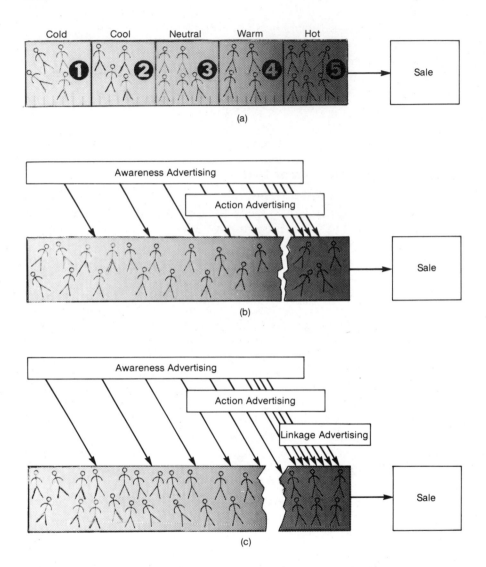

FIGURE 8.   Linkage: The MaxiMarketing Approach to Upper-Ticket, Upper-Involvement Sales.

(a) For any product or service, in any mass medium, the total audience is spread out over a spectrum of interest. (b) The "hottest" advertising cannot move the coldest prospects. (c) The linkage process identifies prime prospects by name and address through making an offer calling for a response and then seeks to develop the sale *and the relationship* by sending additional information (customized, if possible), persuasion, promotion, and purchasing assistance.

But wait! Even in cases like that, you might be surprised. What if, as is so often the case these days, your paper towels are just one of dozens of products your company puts out? Then you would have much more to talk about once you got "inside" your prospective customer's home— and you might be able to think of ways to interest the prospect in buying many of or all your products.

However, we admit that linkage still may not be practical and desirable in marketing *all* the thousands and thousands of advertised products and services. What we do say is that it is far more applicable than is yet widely realized.

The Linkage Assessment Grid

To help you determine whether you should be using the power of link-age in what you are selling, we have constructed a grid (Figure 9). The grid's horizontal poles represent high-ticket and low-ticket sales, the vertical poles, high involvement and low involvement.

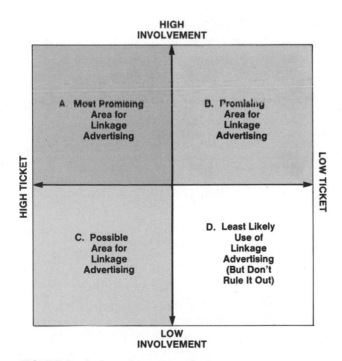

FIGURE 9.   Linkage Assessment Grid.

Buying an automobile or a stereo is obviously a high-ticket, high-involvement purchase. You not only weigh your purchase carefully but may brag about your choice to your friends.

Paper towels are probably a low-ticket, low-involvement item. Surely no one sits around the kitchen table over a cup of coffee and debates the merits of competing towels the way "Rosie" does in the commercials for Bounty. People may each have distinct preferences, but more important things in life demand their time and attention.

Gourmet cheeses or fine wines could be low-ticket, high-involvement purchases. That is, they involve only a few dollars of expenditure, but to the true prospects they are subjects of great interest and well worth half an hour of informed conversation.

An example of high-ticket, low-involvement items might be hard goods in a mature industry, such as a standard no-frills portable TV or a videocassette recorder (VCR). You need it, you want it, and they all seem very similar, so price becomes the most important consideration.

So it could be said that the application of the principle of linkage would be:

Most desirable in the high-ticket, high-involvement quadrant (A)

Also desirable, with careful financial analysis, in the low-ticket, high-involvement quadrant (B)

Possible but less likely in the high-ticket, low-involvement quadrant (C)

Least likely in the low-ticket, low-involvement quadrant (D) with the possible exception of advertisers who sell a number of related products (e.g., the Betty Crocker catalog of Oneida Stainless and other tableware premiums provides some linkage between the advertising and the sale of more than 200 low-ticket, low-involvement General Mills products, although the potential seems poorly realized)

More Than Old Wine in New Bottles

Advertising veterans will scoff at linkage as simply old wine in new bottles. And indeed, in a sense it is. For decades—in fact, for just about as long as advertising has existed—many advertisers (especially direct marketers seeking a high-ticket sale) have mailed large amounts of information and persuasion to those who requested it. Sometimes the mailing is done skillfully—sometimes, as we have seen, with appalling carelessness.

What is different about linkage is that it proposes this old method as a new strategy, a new way to plan advertising and to allocate resources for a much wider variety of products and services.

Thanks to the computer, a brand new element has been added—the capability to enter not only name and address but additional bits of information about the respondent in a prospect database. These additional bits of information about each prospect make it possible to mail out a customized communication or series of communications to each prospect. The computer file also enables you to track sales results and to analyze the payback over time of your investment in linkage advertising.

You are not limited to the use of mail, of course. In the age of the toll-free phone, a telephone dialogue between seller and buyer can help provide successful linkage. You are not limited in the mail to literature, either. You can send an audio or videocassette. Soloflex achieved spectacular sales of its exercise machine by mailing out a demonstration videocassette to inquirers who had VCRs.

In fact, direct mail follow-up doesn't even have to be mailed. If you have a demonstration video of a high ticket, high-involvement product or service, you can amaze your prospect by delivering it via 1-day air express. Or additional information for computer owners can be sent through telephone lines from your computer to theirs.

Creative Requirements of Linkage

Effective linkage might seem impossible even when it *is* possible. A whole new television generation of creative people (and their supervisors) have sprung up. Many of them have *never been required to think of a great many interesting things to say about the products and services they are selling and may find it hard to start*. But they can rapidly learn under pressure of necessity. As usual, the innovative companies will lead the way—and others will scramble to acquire the skills necessary to follow them.

Linkage offers a partial answer to brand advertisers caught in the television squeeze of rising rates and declining audience and the no-win defensive couponing war. In a budget of say, $30 million, a mere $3 million diverted to linkage can, we believe, produce far more impact on sales than the same number of dollars lavished on additional up-front mass advertising. But linkage will sometimes require a change in the creative strategy of the up-front advertising, putting less emphasis on conditioning *all* prospects to choose your brand "some day" and more emphasis on hearing from and talking with your *immediate* prospects.

Armstrong ran an ad for their floor-covering products in home-service magazines which illustrates what we are talking about. The ratio of space devoted to the brand image and space devoted to the offer was about 80/20.

The ad was headed "6 Reasons Why an Armstrong Floor Is the Perfect Choice for the Do-It-Yourselfer." There was a simple little color sketch and a caption for each of the reasons, which were things like "Armstrong quality," "affordability," and so on. The sixth reason was the "free project planning pack," accompanied by a toll-free number and coupon for ordering it. It was a decent, pleasant ad. But in terms of the linkage approach, the creative strategy left room for improvement.

The real target audience for this ad is people who are planning to redo their floors soon—very soon. Not a big percentage of the total readership of the magazine. Surely not more than 1 or 2 percent.

Sure, people who are going to redo their floors 1 or 2 years from now are *theoretically* prospects. But are they really going to carry in their heads for all that time that Armstrong means quality, affordability, easy installation, and the fail-safe guarantee? Most readers wouldn't be able to recall the ad the next *day*. In fact, would people who are not preoccupied with redoing their floors right now bother to read the ad at all?

But the real prospects, the prime prospects, the hot prospects, the *ready* prospects, are keenly interested. They are the only ones likely to order the project planning pack—to read and study it avidly—and to act on it.

Let's say that on an interest scale of 1 to 5, the 5s are the ones who *did* order the planning pack. The 1s are not interested in floors, or not interested in do-it-yourself floors, or already have lifetime floors, or whatever. So what more could the ad have done to reach beyond the 5s and also deeply influence the 4s and maybe the 3s?

Once you get the right question, the right answer often steps up and hits you over the head: Wouldn't a better creative and marketing strategy have reversed the image-to-offer ratio to something more like 20/80?

Such a strategy would have produced an ad headed something like, "If You Are Planning to Install a New Floor, Send for Our Free Armstrong Floor Project Planning Pack." Also included would be photos, captions, feature call-outs, etc. selling the "sizzle" of the pack.

The "6 Reasons Why" would still be listed, and there would have been plenty of room in the follow-up—the linkage—to discuss the six reasons with the readers who count most, the prime prospects.

The advertising would have located, identified, communicated with, and provided massive persuasion to two or three times as many interested prospects. Our experience in direct-response advertising tells us that such an advertising approach might have doubled or tripled the response.

So the strategy of linkage has three components: (1) Ask for a response in the up-front advertising. (2) Maximize the number of responses through the attractiveness of the offer and the ease of response. (3) Maximize the effectiveness of the linkage or follow-up advertising furnished to respondents.

As a postscript, Armstrong earns a gold star for the way their operator answered our call. The ad instructed us to "ask for Dept. 56GWD." We did so, but the operator did not thereupon transfer us to "Dept. 56GWD." She merely took our name and address, told us the information would be sent to us, and thanked us for calling.

Obviously the department number told her both the source ("WD" was *Woman's Day*) and the offer, so she was able to save her time and mine and complete the call in about 20 seconds. If only all 800-number transactions were so efficient!

You're Never Too Small to Use Linkage

We have a friend who is a struggling young videocassette producer. She wanted to offer her services to advertisers interested in using videocassettes as an advertising medium, but she didn't know whom to contact and how to get through. We suggested the use of two MaxiMarketing principles: (1) fish for the prospect (see Chapter 3), and (2) build a bridge between the advertising and the sale.

Translating this into action, we recommended that she (1) run a 1-inch ad describing her services in *The Wall Street Journal,* and (2) end the copy with, "Write or call for more information." She would then be able to send interested prospects enough information about her services and qualifications to fill a whole page of *The Wall Street Journal*—at an advertising cost of only a few hundred dollars and a follow-up cost of no more than a dollar to two per prospect.

She might get only a handful of replies—but they would be truly interested prospects. She would need to convert only one with her bridge-building follow-up material to repay the cost of the promotion many times over.

The Power of Linkage— Two Outstanding Examples

The Lincoln-Mercury Story. Many Lincoln-Mercury advertisements contain an 800 number that interested readers can call for more information. In 1984, they received more than 62,000 calls and sent out literature to each caller.

The advertising manager estimated, based on dealer feedback, that approximately *25 percent* of these inquirers turned into buyers. Assuming an average sale of around $20,000, over $300 million in sales would thus be traceable to a phone number that cost nothing to add to the advertisements and a direct-mail follow-up program which could not cost more than a few hundred thousand dollars.

Of course, many of these people *might* have bought a Lincoln or Mercury anyway. But many might have wandered away, to Cadillac or Mercedes-Benz, if it had not been for the carefully constructed bridge leading them from the advertising to the sale.

South Carolina Division of Tourism.   Buried in the annals of the *Journal of Advertising Research* are the results of a fascinating study by Dr. Arch G. Woodside, professor of marketing at the University of South Carolina, and William H. Motes, then a candidate for a Ph.D. in marketing at the same university.[4]

What interested us about their study was that it proved something more than they intended. Although it was not their purpose, hidden in their data was a startling revelation of the power of linkage and more— *the power and profitability of designing the up-front advertising to support the linkage follow-up material rather than the other way around!*

The study's stated purpose was to compare inquirers who responded to image advertising (with the invitation to respond an incidental feature) to those who responded to overtly direct-response advertising. They had reviewed the files of an impressive number of trade and business publications going back 15 years and had found "few published attempts to determine whether or not there are significant differences in the consumer profile of direct-response and image-advertisement inquirers."

They decided to undertake such a study, and they found the ideal data at their doorstep—the print advertising campaign of the South Carolina Division of Tourism. The promotional program they analyzed involved placing advertisements promoting South Carolina as a wonderful place to vacation in 41 magazines and newspapers.

The image ads were four-color spreads highlighting Charleston and South Carolina beaches. The action ads were fractional black-and-whites, and, although they sold the "product" in the headline, were mostly devoted to the offer of a free South Carolina trip kit and a reply coupon. The four-color ads also offered the kit and also included a reply coupon.

They found that the advertising cost per inquiry (CPI) from the direct-response advertising was only $3.19 and the CPI from the image advertising was $14.31. They also found, from a random-sample investigation, that the two groups averaged about the same expenditure per party when they visited the state.

So the net-net was that the return on investment (ROI) produced by each dollar of the direct-response advertising was $56.53, and the ROI produced by the image advertising was only $11.80! By extrapolation, we estimated that if all the advertising money had been spent on the direct-response advertising, it would have yielded about $28 million in traceable tourist revenue instead of about $19 million.

There is a missing piece in the research for our purposes. What sales effect did the image advertising have on people who saw the advertising but did *not* respond? Obviously at least some of them were influenced by the advertising and did travel to South Carolina and did spend money there as a result.

However, it seems unmistakable that the direct-response advertising scooped up most of the best, most interested prospects and exposed them to a great deal of additional advertising—including literature with the same beautiful color photographs of Charleston and the South Carolina beaches found in the image advertising. And that this was a wiser expenditure of advertising money.

What is revealed here, in addition to the stated purpose of the research, is an important truth about marketing strategy: Advertising a high-price, high-involvement product should focus first on getting a response from prime prospects rather than on creating an image and then on converting that response to a sale by providing powerful linkage.

This does not mean foreswearing image-making! There can and should be image-making up-front and plenty of image-making in the linkage. But the desire to create an image should not stand in the way of building a bridge between the advertising and the sale and giving your best prospects a firm push in the direction of the bridge.

The North Carolina story took place in the early 1970s. Around that time, the average state or territory travel promotion budget was $853,000. Ten years later, the average had risen to over $2.5 million. Forty-seven states reported that their tourism advertising was designed to generate inquiries. In 1981, almost 9.5 million inquiries were produced by state travel campaigns. Forty-six of the states attempt to measure the effectiveness of their direct-response advertising through conversion studies of varying degrees of sophistication.

Obviously the state tourism bureaus have learned the power of linkage in advertising, and are using it to the hilt in the fierce competition for the estimated $140 billion spent by Americans on nonbusiness travel in the United States. But hampered by budget restraints imposed by state legislatures and/or by lack of advanced marketing sophistication, few have advanced beyond this to building a permanent prospect database and doing customized marketing to segments of it. Nevertheless, what the states have learned and are doing contains a valuable lesson to any company or institution charged with marketing a high-ticket, high-involvement product or service.

A Revealing Comparison of the Tourism Advertising of Two States

As we have indicated, a logical consequence of recognizing the power of linkage is to rethink the creative strategy of the up-front advertising. Is the best use of up-front advertising to create a favorable image—and then, incidentally, to invite response from interested prospects? Or is it better merely to start creating a favorable image while *maximizing* response—and then to continue the building of the image in follow-up advertising sent to a greater number of interested prospects? A fascinating comparison of the two approaches was provided by advertisements for California tourism and Alaska tourism in the same issue of *Travel & Leisure*.

The California ad was a two-page full-color spread with insert card. The headline was, "Some People Need a Lot of Vacations." The insert card was headlined, "Californias, Here I Come." The ad had a short copy block about the joys of California—no reference to the offer—and a number of colorful pictures and captions. There was also a coupon in the ad with a picture of the "free pocket guide."

The Alaska ad was a single full-color page and card. Against an atmospheric bleed photo of mountain scenery was superimposed the headline, "100 Pages of Free Advice for Anyone Wishing to Experience the Vacation of a Lifetime." The reply card was boldly headlined, "Send for Your Free Official State of Alaska Vacation Planner." The only copy in the ad was entirely devoted to selling the booklet, with a picture of it alongside.

Of course, comparing California and Alaska is comparing the old metaphorical apples and oranges. And it could be argued that California did a better job of awareness advertising for the casual reader who did not bother to send away the reply card but is still a prospect. But what was most striking was the obvious difference in creative strategy.

Our direct-response experience tells us that for *one-half* of the cost of California's two pages (exclusive of the cost of the insert card), the Alaska single pages was likely to have produced, other things being equal, up to *double* the number of requests for more information.

If that were true, the response efficiency or advertising cost-per-inquiry of the Alaska ad could be up to *four times* as good as that of the

California ad. That means that per dollar of up-front advertising expenditure, up to four times as many of the best prospects would be exposed to more information and persuasion.

There are striking parallels here with the two kinds of advertising run by the South Carolina Department of Tourism. And we know what the results of those two different approaches were.

So the Alaska ad models the new MaxiMarketing strategy of linkage. Not only does it expose people who respond to your up-front advertising to powerful additional advertising, it also changes the up-front advertising creative strategy to maximize the number of prospects who will receive this additional advertising.

The Bottom Line

The new marketing will frequently expose the more interested prospects to additional follow-up advertising and promotion after inviting their responses and capturing their names and addresses. The need for this follow-up varies according to what extent your product is a high-ticket, high-involvement item, but there is always some possibility of application no matter what you are selling.

The strategy of linkage between your up-front awareness advertising and the ringing up of the sale requires that someone in your company's management be responsible for loving the prospect and loving the product. That someone will empathize with the prospects' attitudes and feelings and see to it that they are assisted every step of the way to the point of sale.

This strategy also affects the planning of your up-front awareness advertising. Those who respond to your up-front advertising are your best prospects and should receive additional advertising of equal quality and greater quantity. Once you accept that, then you may want to consider whether your awareness advertising should be designed to increase or maximize the public's responses to it.

The best awareness advertising today does not simply hammer away at prospects and nonprospects alike. Rather it is the first step in a continuum of communication which turns interested prospects into one-time tryers and then into longtime customers.

10

Maximized Sales from Share of Mind and Customer Database

The Big Picture

All marketing is, or should be, a continuous process. With rare exceptions, it is hoped that making a sale is not the end of a relationship with a customer but rather the beginning or the continuation. (The rare exceptions are purchases usually made once in a lifetime, such as a swimming pool or an encyclopedia. However, these exceptions are becoming increasingly hard to find, as marketers find that even sales like these can and should be followed by sales of related merchandise and services.)

Yet the thinking of too many marketing strategists until recent years tended to halt with the completion of a sale. Little or no time or money was allocated for creating a special relationship with the company's best customers. Most companies—whether selling goods or services—failed to calculate and record the lifetime value (LTV) of a customer.

At the same time, there has always been a roughly measurable long-term benefit of repeatedly making a sale through repeated advertising. That benefit has been viewed as share of market or share of mind, a quantifiable company asset.

Now a new kind of corporate asset is emerging—the customer database, a computerized compilation of data about each buyer which can be readily accessed to increase revenues and profits. This new asset certainly does not replace share of market nor minimize its importance. Rather, the customer database is beginning to take its place alongside market share as a full-fledged partner in the maximization of corporate sales.

To companies engaged in direct marketing and personal selling, the emergence of the customer database has been evolution rather than revolution. In their good old days, it was known simply as the customer list. And even today, a plain old customer list which happens to be filed in a computer instead of on the Addressograph plates of yesterday can be a company asset worth millions of dollars.

But what turned the customer list into a database was the computer's unique ability to remember—or to find out—other bits of information about customers beyond their names and addresses. With the introduction of super computers, making that information accessible becomes easier and easier at less and less cost.

Thus marketing has come full circle: From the person-to-person selling of the village baker and tailor and shoemaker of centuries ago, to the impersonal purveying of mass merchandise by the giant supermarket and department store, and now back, once again, to highly personalized customer accommodation and cultivation, although on a vast scale.

The computer allows selections from the total customer list based on two, three, four, five, six, or more bits of information known about each customer. It made it possible to select certain customers for a certain product—and to create a product for certain customers.

In the late 1960s, this database technology rushed like a tidal wave onto the large mail-order firms, such as the book and record clubs and the catalog companies, and swept them to higher ground. Since the 1870s they had benefited from a crude manually compiled database—namely, their mailing list of customers. But now, for the first time, they could keep track of and appeal to the individual tastes, financial means, and buying enthusiasms of their members

*or customers, and of the lifetime value (LTV) of each customer
derived from each exposure in each advertising medium.*

*Next it was the turn of service companies such as financial
institutions, airlines, car rentals, telephone services, and hotels (see
Figure 10). Now they too started addressing and satisfying each
customer separately. And because the LTV of a customer—the
aggregated dollar value of total repeat purchases over the years—
was so much greater than in package-goods selling, they were able
and eager to pour millions of dollars into developing sophisticated
systems of individualized customer cultivation. Now the 20 percent
of their customers who were the "heavy users" and provided 80
percent of the revenue could be identified and given the special
attention they warranted.*

*Meanwhile, manufacturers of package goods, soft goods, and
hard goods were receiving each year millions of customer names
and addresses—on sweepstakes entries, rebate applications, service
contracts, warranty cards, information requests—and* throwing
them away! *Marketing seemed to be the last division of a manufacturer's organization to feel the effect of the computer revolution and
be changed by it.*

*Suddenly, this too began to change. Manufacturers began to
realize that this vast reservoir of customer names constantly spilling
over the dam and running out to sea was a source of great power.*

	1870s +	1970s+	1980s +	1990s + ?
Appeal to Prospects	Tangible Product	Intangible Service	Value-Added Benefits	Periodically Replenished Staples
Example	Catalogs and Merchandise Flyers	Money Market Funds	Frequent Flyer Programs	Home Delivery of Dog Food
Use of Customer Database	Repeat Mailings— Additional Offers	Monthly Statement— Cross-Sell of Other Funds	Record of Activity— Customized Plans and Fares	Monthly Statement— Cross-Sell of Other Home-Delivery Offers

FIGURE 10.   The Evolution of Database Marketing.

Today any company that markets goods or services and wants to survive must face the same realization. The computer's radically increased cost-effectiveness in storing, accessing, and manipulating customer files has changed the rules of the marketing game. Regardless of the size or kind of business you are in, now your company too can and should build a customer database—the most potent new marketing force, some say, since the emergence of television.

Your customer database will be your own private marketplace where you can promote additional sales, cross-promote, explore new channels of distribution, test new products, add new revenue streams, start new ventures, and build lifetime customer loyalty— and your competitors can never tell exactly what you are doing until after the fact.

This chapter examines how share of market and customer database can work together to achieve far more for your company than either could separately. By capturing not only the loyalty but also the names and addresses of your end-users, you gain a priceless opportunity to maximize the development of each sale you make by turning it into a continuing profitable relationship.

Are you familiar with the *Law of the Situation?* It is a term coined in 1904 by Mary Parker Follett, the first management consultant in the United States.

Her client was a company that thought it was in the window shade business. But she persuaded them that they were actually in the light-control business. By expanding their concept of what kind of business they were in, she was able to help them expand their business.

"What business are you really in?" is the fundamental question posed by the Law of the Situation. Every company selling to the public can and must broaden its answer to the question even more than Mary Follett did for the window shade company, for even to define their mission as "light control" may have limited their thinking and opportunities. For example, draperies, like window shades, are a form of light control. Matching bedspreads have nothing to do with light control. Yet bedspreads might be a popular and profitable item to promote to the end-users of your draperies.

The New Revised Law of the Situation

Today the real answer to "What business are you really in?" is that you are in the *customer development* business. And the sooner your company comes to that realization—the sooner it casts off the shackles of a narrower definition—the sooner it will be free to expand in surprising new directions.

What is a mint doing selling leather-bound books? What is a giant bank doing selling refrigerators? What is a radio station doing selling tours to listeners? What is a distillery doing selling long underwear?

They are applying the *New Revised Law of the Situation:* namely, that the business you are in is making money any which way you can through developing a continuing, profitable relationship with the buyer of your product or service. And these companies are applying the Law by joining two powerful marketing assets, *share of market* and *customer database*.

How We Define Share of Mind

We want to call it "share of market" rather than "share of mind." What is the difference? In our definition, share of *market* measures the *breadth* of your market penetration, but share of *mind* measures the *depth*.

For instance, you might have a 17 percent share of the facial-tissue market because your product is the cheapest. Your share could start melting away overnight if a competitor seriously undercut your price. But Kleenex tissues has a share of *mind*. It has been an old, familiar, comforting friend through laughter and tears, opening nights and last rites. It has a share of mind that can resist price competition.

When Coca-Cola tried to abandon old Coke soft drink, they found that it too had an impressive share of mind not revealed by market share figures or their costly research studies. In the past, this share of mind might have seemed a vague, unmeasurable asset, but now a price tag can be—and has been—put on it.

When Philip Morris moved to acquire General Foods for $5.8 billion, about $2.8 billion of that represented not physical assets but good will. As one stock analyst pointed out, "If you had to go out and create a brand like Jell-O, it would cost you a lot more than what Philip Morris is paying for it."[1]

The Synergy of Combining Share of Mind and Customer Database

By itself this good will, or favorable predisposition, or share of mind, can accomplish a lot in the marketplace. Not only does it lead to repeat sales, often (although, alas, not always!) the well-established brand name can be successfully extended to other products.

By itself, a customer database can also accomplish a great deal. Thus if you had an in-house list of people who had bought your rowing machine, you could sell many of them additional exercise equipment even of a different brand name and even under a different company name.

But when you join these two forces together, the share of mind and the customer database, it is as if you have ignited a second-stage rocket to boost your company into a higher orbit. Now you can go to customers who are already favorably disposed to your product and company and offer them other products, services, or benefits especially selected to fit their individual requirements and tastes. This deepens the share of mind or customer loyalty. Then their responses feed additional personal information into the customer database. This makes possible more and better benefits and services, which in turn deepens the share of mind— in an endless feedback loop.

Of course, it's not quite that simple. Nothing ever is. But in principle this is the synergistic effect made possible when share of mind and customer database are joined together.

How Jack Daniel Distillery Is Combining Share of Mind with Customer Database

Consider the synergistic interplay between the market share of Jack Daniel's whiskey and the Lynchburg Hardware and General Store operation we told you about in Chapter 8. The list of mail-order catalog customers is not purely a list of Jack Daniel customers, but it seems highly probable that they are heavily represented. And as we pointed out, the brand loyalty (share of mind) strengthens the appeal of the catalog, and as the number of buyers in the catalog database continues to grow, surely catalog sales strengthen the brand's share of mind.

All that quaint old-time merchandise in the catalog—much of it bearing the Jack Daniel logotype—increases the *perceived value* of the bourbon. Furthermore, as the catalog circulation increases among nonusers of Jack Daniel's whiskey, this "free" (self-amortizing) promotion of the brand helps to enlarge the company's share of market and share of mind, which will in due time lead to a larger database of catalog customers, and on and on.

An Easy Way Jack Daniel Could Increase the Synergism

However, we think Jack Daniel is missing a bet. Their charming atmospheric ads about leisurely whiskey making in Lynchburg don't mention the catalog.

In 1984 Brown-Forman spent $3.5 million on Jack Daniel advertising, about 80 percent of it, perhaps $2.8 million, in magazines. Without detracting from the airy, comfortable look of the ads, they found room at the very bottom to add, in 6-point type, "Placed in the National Register of Historic Places by the United States Government."

A nice touch, that! But why not go a step further and add another 6-point line? "If you like old-time memorabilia, write for a free copy of our Lynchburg Hardware and General Store catalog." The line wouldn't affect the look and impact of the ad one whit. The people who responded would probably be mostly Jack Daniel's whiskey drinkers and would be especially good customers for such logotype-imprinted catalog merchandise as the Jack Daniel glassware, the Jack Daniel parlor lamp, and the official Jack Daniel cap.

So the Brown-Forman would score a triple play:

1. They would get a "free" advertising for the catalog in $2.8 million of magazine ads for Jack Daniel's whiskey.

2. They would get more "free" advertising, for Jack Daniel's whiskey, in the pages of the catalogs sent to readers who requested a catalog. (There is no advertising for Jack Daniel's whiskey *per se* in the catalog, although we think there should be. But there is a great deal of indirect sell.)

3. They would get still more "free" advertising for Jack Daniel's whiskey when many of these people order from the catalog and start wearing clothes and serving with glassware and furnishing their homes with lamps and signs and wall thermometers bearing the Jack Daniel logotype—all of which provide constant reminder advertising.

But wait, we're not finished. How about putting a little hang tag on the neck of each Jack Daniel's bottle of whiskey? It could offer a modest premium, such as an iron-on decal or a free copy of the catalog. It would give them, we estimate, annual advertising circulation of around 36 million at a cost per thousand of maybe $1 or $2. A media director's dream! And the replies would add dramatically to their customer database.

What Makes Their Catalog Customer List a Database?

Is the Lynchburg General Store customer list really a database? Isn't that a rather fancy and pretentious name for what is simply a mailing list of customers stored in a computer?

If we define a database as a computer file of names which have, and are selectable by, other bits of information attached to them, then such a file cannot avoid being a database. Whether it is *used* for datamarketing is another question. But as soon as you add a street address, city, state, and zip code to a name, you have made it "segmentable" by computer in a way that would be almost impossible with a large old-fashioned mailing list.

For instance, if we were Jack Daniel, we could tell the computer, "Select from our customer and prospect file only those people living in semi-rural affluent zip zones." And then we could observe if those people are more responsive to special offers of expensive Jack Daniel merchandise.

It is also highly unlikely that Jack Daniel would fail to enter with each customer name the dates and amounts of their catalog purchases. This information provides an additional basis for selecting certain names the way catalog merchandisers do: scoring and selecting of customers according to the Recency, Frequency, and Monetary Value of their purchases. (Obviously someone who has sent in big orders recently and frequently is a terrific customer and can be successfully offered more expensive merchandise more frequently.)

How the Jack Daniel Catalog Could Clone the Best Customers

Other data from sophisticated list compilers that could be overlaid on this list might be lists of automobile owners identified by make, year, and price bracket of car; or homeowners identified by size of lot, value of house, presence of fireplace, etc.; or householders identified by age, sex, marital status, and number and age of children; and so on.

These data could be used to "clone" the best customers of the Jack Daniel catalog. That is, by overlaying these data on the best customers as identified by recency, frequency, and monetary value, one might discover that the majority of the best customers are bourbon drinkers who drive a higher-price foreign car fewer than 2 years old; they are married, are between the ages of 40 and 50, have an average of two teenage children, and own a house with at least three bedrooms on a building lot at least 100 x 200 feet.

Then Jack Daniel could go to a list compiler and say, "Out of all of the mailable names and addresses in the United States, extract for me those that have these characteristics. In other words, clone my best customers. Give me as many people exactly like them as you can."

Sophisticated list manipulation methods, which need not be analyzed here, can easily accomplish this task. And the mailing list thus extracted should respond very well when mailed the Jack Daniel catalog.

The Many Uses of Share of Mind Plus Database

By adding the power of a customer database to the power of share of mind or consumer brand franchise, you can maximize development of your company's overall sales and profits these five important ways:

1. Maximized repeat sales
2. Maximized customer loyalty
3. Maximized cross-promotion
4. Maximized line extension
5. Maximized success of new ventures

Let's examine these one at a time and see how various companies are using each of these capabilities today.

1. Maximized Repeat Sales

As we have indicated, share of mind alone obviously leads to repeat sales. If you like your first box of Kellogg's Raisin Bran cereal, you are predisposed to buy another. If you like your first night's stay at a Holiday Inn, you are favorably disposed to staying at one again.

But if Kellogg or Holiday Inn captures your name and address and stores it in a customer database, they are in a position to send you promotion which will stimulate you to choose their product or service over a competitor's more frequently.

We see at least three basic ways to accomplish this (some overlap is possible—a promotion might use two out of the three at the same time): (1) establish an ongoing rewards program, (2) give preferred treatment to your best customers, and (3) custom-tailor special offers or benefits for special segments.

Establish an Ongoing Rewards Program.   "The more often you buy from us, the more rewards you get" is the basic principle involved here. The Raleigh and Belair cigarette coupons catalog and the Betty Crocker catalog of Oneida stainless and other tableware redeemable in part by proofs of purchase are two previously cited examples. Both promotions illustrate the kind of continuity program that can be established with the aid of a customer database.

But there are inherent limitations to this approach in the package-goods field. If a household buys a 79-cent tube of toothpaste twice a month, the manufacturer cannot afford to provide handsome rewards for repeat purchases. If the reward tied to each purchase is minimal, customers could take 20 years to accumulate enough points to earn a toaster.

One way to overcome this limitation is with an umbrella promotion covering many products, such as the Betty Crocker promotion accepting proofs of purchase from over 200 General Mills products. It also helps to accept a high proportion of cash along with the proofs of purchase for redemption, as we saw in the case of the cigarette promotion.

Still another solution is to offer impressive rewards that don't cost anything to provide. Thus you might be able to negotiate a deal with a motel chain which would permit you to offer a free 1-night stay in a room which would otherwise have stood empty. You gain at no cost a valuable premium, and the motel operator gains at little cost a chance that the customer may stay and pay for a second night.

But it is in the service field, such as air travel, that we have seen the most dramatic development of ongoing rewards programs. There the potential annual expenditure per customer is much higher. The dollars available for promotion and profit are thus much greater. And often a fixed overhead and unfilled capacity make it both possible and profitable to use lavish promotion to sell off empty seats or rooms or berths.

However, when service companies stimulate repeat sales, the sales usually involve not only an ongoing rewards program but also the next principle . . . preferential treatment for good customers.

Give the Best Treatment to Your Best Customers.   There are two magic numbers in customer-database marketing. One of them is 80, and the other one is 20. These are the traditional numbers quoted in the time-honored business truism that you get 80 percent of your business from 20 percent of your customers.

These customers are the ones known in package-goods marketing as the heavy users. If you can steal—or keep from losing—more of this kind of customer, then you should come out ahead of the game. If that is the case, the theory goes, why not concentrate the most care and marketing expenditure on this most productive portion of your market—and make it even more productive?

There is even a fancy buzzword phrase for pursuing the heavy user: *selective database marketing*. Let's look at how selective database marketing is being used by three service industries: airlines, hotels, and cruise ships. Keep in mind that how well your company retains and attracts heavy users can be the cornerstone of its future. Somewhere in these case histories could be the spark of an idea to ignite a new sales concept for one of your operations.

The Frequent Flyer Programs.   Selective database marketing has transformed the airline companies. They were hard hit in the late 1970s by skyrocketing fuel costs and by government deregulation, which removed what was in essence a system of official price-fixing and guaranteed profits. They began to look for new ways to squeeze out a profit.

They discovered—or discovered a new meaning in—the 80-20 principle. They found that 80 percent of their sales volume was coming from 20 percent of their passengers—the "frequent flyer," usually a business traveller.

Furthermore, their day-to-day operation automatically produced a customer database, which was simply lying there waiting to be used. Since business fares are always charged, somewhere in the computer files there was already complete information on how many times Mr. Jones flew Eastern Airlines per year, how far he travelled, how much he spent on air fares, and what his destinations were.

So the airlines developed the programs that every business traveller knows so well by now, the frequent flyer programs that woo and reward the heavy users with free mileage or discounts per thousand miles traveled with one airline.

American Airlines was first with its AAdvantage program in 1981. Soon the other major carriers jumped in, and by 1984 the airlines industry had spent over $75 million on their frequent flyer programs. The Pan Am WorldPass program alone, according to an executive of its advertising agency, accounted for some $300 million in incremental revenue for the airline in 1983. His description of how the program is operated shows how much loving customer care was necessary to achieve that result:

The WorldPass database contains thousands of names, most of them passengers who fly many thousands of miles each year. Each individual's flying record must be monitored and maintained, and appropriate awards determined. This record includes mileage awarded for car rentals and hotel reservations with Hertz, Sheraton, and Inter-Continental Hotels, who have a cooperative arrangement with Pan Am.

An on-line service center takes customer service 800-number inquiries concerning awards due, credits, etc. On-line terminals allow the operators to access a WorldPass inquiree's record in less than one second, to make any necessary changes or to answer a question from a flyer who wants to know how many miles he or she has flown, or how many are needed to reach the next award level.

For the cost of the program and giving away seats, Pan Am gains invaluable information. For example, by following a Mr. Smith's flying history and by referring to his survey responses, Pan Am determined that he flies to London six times a year and that he loves to ski. In his WorldPass communications, Mr. Smith now receives information on ski packages to Chile, Austria and other resort areas.

Pan Am also knows that of those six flights to London, four were on other airlines. Mr. Smith now receives information on special Pan Am flights to London, and on the savings he can achieve by taking these flights.[2]

As you can see, Pan Am's program includes segmentation within segmentation. Each participant in the program receives customized customer care. And this customer service pays for itself and more by providing the information needed for profitable customization of offers.

Marriott's Honored Guest Awards. The Marriott Corporation began its selective database marketing program in 1981 with the introduction of its Club Marquis promotion, designed for its best customers. Membership was open to guests who stayed at a Marriott hotel six times within a specified period. Members received such special services as express check-in and check-out, $200 check cashing, and $200-a-night reimbursement plus complimentary stays at any Marriott hotel in the future if Marriott ever failed to honor a reservation.

Then in January 1984, Marriott launched their Honored Guest Awards program, which obviously seeks to *increase the lifetime value (LTV) of their business travellers*. The program adopted a points system similar to those of the airlines. Members receive points for staying at Marriott Hotels, for flying with any of three participating airlines, for using Hertz Rent-a-Car: 100 points are awarded for each night's stay, *plus 10 extra points for every additional dollar spent on hotel services such as the restaurants and bars.*

Do you see what Marriott has done? They have tempted you mightily not to rush off to a restaurant somewhere else in town for your lunch or dinner engagement, but rather to stay in the hotel and invite your guests over to join you in the hotel bar or dining room. And if you run up a tab of $150, then you will be awarded *1500 points* compared to the measly 100 points you earned by your night's stay.

When you have chalked up 17,500 points—no problem for a frequent business traveler on a generous entertainment account—you are entitled to a weekend anywhere in the world at a Marriott facility. At 150,000 points, you'd get 12 days and 11 nights at any Marriott hotel in the world, two round-trip tickets to any destination serviced by the three participating airlines, and a full-size Hertz car for a week.

The program was launched via precisely targeted no-waste direct mail. Several million mailings went out over a 6-month period to frequent Marriott guests and frequent traveler lists of the participating airlines and Hertz.

Marriott was able to single out its own best customers because it maintains them in a database called MARSHA (Marriott Automated Reservation Systems for Hotel Accommodations). This system enables a hotel manager to write a guest who has stayed at that hotel for more than five times in a year: "I know you've been here many times. You're one of my best customers. Next time you stay here, stop in and say hello. If you ever need anything, let me know." The *very* best customers get a letter from Bill Marriott himself.[3]

That's customer care. It's an outstanding example of giving the most attention to the best source of additional sales, your present good customers.

Marriott is so convinced of the value of this program that they spent an estimated $16 million on it in 1985. Because of this high cost, their competitors were skeptical. Said the executive vice president of Hyatt, "One of us is making a terrible mistake."

We'd bet our money on Marriott.

The P & O Cruises Posh Club.   Graeme McCorkell, president of MSW Rapp & Collins in London, has told us of an impressive demonstration of the power of selective database marketing in the United Kingdom.

In January of 1981, P & O Cruises came to the agency with an interesting problem that their business shares with the hotel trade: a large fixed overhead. It costs much the same in operating terms whether the vessel sails full or half empty.

Thus P & O and other cruise lines are prepared to offer big discounts to fill their ships. But at best a sharply discounted promotion can merely turn a potential loss into a break-even situation. If it fails, it can actually add to the loss. The ideal solution is to find a way to increase the percentage of passengers paying full fare. So P & O asked the agency to fill those empty staterooms with passengers willing to pay the regular fare and to keep the promotional cost minimal.

The agency found that P & O possessed a large list of customers who had sailed with them in the last 4 years. These people were already receiving each new season's cruise program. It would be too expensive to remail this entire list regularly. How could a mailing program be directed to just the likeliest prospects?

If P & O were like a mail-order catalog operation, then the obvious way of sifting out the valuable customers would be to take a look at the Recency, Frequency, and Monetary Value of past customer purchases. However, the cruise business is different. Few people take a cruise annually. Someone who last took a cruise 4 years ago might be just as likely to book this year as someone who sailed only 1 year ago. In other words, there was no large frequent passenger market to tap.

The answer was to let the mailing list select itself. To achieve this, the agency proposed offering the entire list free membership in a club that would give them exclusive privileges and benefits related to cruise travel. It seemed certain that those who responded would be more receptive to subsequent mailings. The agency then developed the POSH Club.

As you may know, the word *posh* was originally an abbreviation for "Port Out Starboard Home." Many years ago, rich passengers on liners travelling east would demand staterooms on the left (or port) side of the ship, away from the sun. Travelling back west, they kept cool in the shade of the right (starboard) side. The origin, connotation, and spelling of this word all made it fit ideally as the name for an exclusive club for P & O customers.

The test and rollout converted 15 percent of the customer list into a hotline of POSH Club members. After that mailing, no more membership solicitations were necessary—ever! Since then, recruitment has been successfully conducted during a cruise: A captive audience is influenced by a relaxed atmosphere, friendly contact with passengers and staff, and a charming POSH Club representative.

The special privileges of POSH Club membership cost P & O very little. They include a bottle of champagne with the captain's compliments to welcome you when you arrive at your cabin, an invitation to a "members only" cocktail party, vouchers toward the cost of shore excursions, opportunities to buy club regalia such as ties and silk scarves, a special award to the most travelled passenger on each cruise, and a quarterly newsletter (which generously reveals details of upcoming cruises).

The most important benefit is the opportunity to travel on specially nominated POSH Club cruises. These are attractive cruises that may otherwise be difficult to sell. (Nobody deliberately plans a cruise that will be difficult to sell, but for operational reasons some itineraries have to include long stretches of ocean between ports.)

For operational reasons, the two *least* successful cruises of 1980 (from the point of view of sales) had to be repeated in 1981. Both were nominated as POSH Club cruises for that year. This did not mean that the cruises were exclusive to POSH Club members, only that POSH Club privileges were limited to the nominated cruises.

Believe it or not, these two cruises—the two *least* successful cruises in 1980—were P & O's two *most* successful bookings in 1981. All from mailing to just 15 percent of the total customer file.

After the rollout mailing, P & O wrote to just 3000 of the newly recruited club members in the London area inviting them to attend a preview of the next cruise program—drinks, snacks, film, and a talk. They got 800 acceptances—a 27 percent response!

Since then, they have held 16 of these "shore parties" a year—and they're still overbooked. And in just a few years the number of special POSH Club cruises had gone up from two to six to cope with the demand.

Where Do You Come In?   Don't make the mistake of concluding from these examples that selective database marketing doesn't fit your company—that it is applicable only to companies like airlines and hotels and cruise lines that have the problem of unsold excess capacity. The basic principle of preferred treatment for preferred customers can be profitably applied to almost any kind of business that maintains a customer database.

Nieman-Marcus, the famous Dallas department store, has started a frequent customer program, the InCircle. Annual purchases of $3000 or more earn members periodic delivery of chocolates. If you spend $12,000 or more, you get caviar.

"We've seen already that the attrition rate for InCircle customers is lower," reported a store executive after the first 10 months.[4]

If you think it's not feasible to start your own selective database marketing program, you may still be able to hook in with that of some other company.

Newmark & Lewis, a New York discount chain, started a frequent buyer program which awards customers who purchase appliances at their stores with mileage points in the Eastern Airlines frequent flyer program. Both Eastern and Newmark & Lewis win new customers.

Publishers Central Bureau, the leader in mail-order sales of remaindered books, has at least several selective database marketing programs. For instance, good customers receive an invitation to enroll in the Member of Preferred Choice Bookplan. It operates just like any no-minimum-purchase book club. Members receive a monthly bulletin announcing the main selection and a wide variety of alternates, all newly published, at discounts up to 30 percent.

We haven't monitored this program, but we would guess that readers of certain kinds of books are offered certain main selections for automatic shipment—that is, people who have bought many art books in the past would be offered an art book, and so on. If so, this would also illustrate our next point.

Custom-Tailor Special Offers, Appeals, or Benefits for Special Segments. Just as there are many solar systems in our Milky Way, there are many different kinds of customer within a customer database. This is an area of development that companies have barely begun to explore. For example, if you are selling breakfast cereal, why not offer one kind of premium to new mothers in your customer database and another kind to retirees? Today's list-segmentation techniques are making this quite practical.

The AT&T Opportunity Calling catalog of discounts and rebates is an ongoing rewards program for long-distance phone service customers. In 1985 the company began moving toward segmentation of its customer database to provide targeted catalogs.

"We are in the process of making a major move toward segmentation," said a company spokesperson. "We are looking at multiple catalogs. Already our research had told us, for example, that people want a back-to-school catalog."[5] Of course when he says "people," what he really means is "some people" out of the total database—those with school children in the home.

2. Maximized Customer Loyalty

There is an old Latin saying, *Qui non proficit, deficit.* In marketing, the opposite is also sometimes true: If you're not losing the customers you already have—if you can maintain and deepen their loyalty—that can be a victory.

The AT&T Opportunity Calling catalog should really be classified as a customer loyalty program rather than a sales stimulation program. Its purpose is to keep you from switching to another long-distance phone service, not to stimulate you to make more long-distance calls.

When the government deregulated phone service, it mandated free and equal competition among companies offering long-distance service. But canny old Ma Bell got the jump on her young whipper-snapper competitors by launching this massive rewards program.

In a stroke of genius, AT&T decided to offer handsome rewards which wouldn't cost them anything and wouldn't require any warehouses and shipping facilities for handling merchandise. They found the answer in negotiating rebates and discounts they could offer on brand-name products and services widely available at retail. And apparently it was easy to find plenty of product and service companies eager to participate—it gave the latter a chance to make powerful sales promotion offers to 22 million residential phone customers at no advertising cost.

Within 2 years after the program was launched, the response rate per catalog had edged up to 5 percent. AT&T had built a mighty defense, backed by a $100 million promotion budget, against attempts by Sprint, MCI, and the other long-distance companies to steal their customers in the government-mandated free-for-all competition. AT&T had issued 3 million certificates and checks with a face value of $50 million. Some 50 percent of the eligible customers in their database said they had used the program or intended to.

What descriptive name should be given to this new kind of marketing? Is it sales promotion? Is it direct marketing? It is neither and both. We prefer to call it MaxiMarketing.

Another way you can sustain customer loyalty through your customer database is to set up a program which will frequently repromote your company's image and positioning—and, ideally, to get your customers or other advertisers to pay for it.

Olin Corporation, whose products include pool-care chemicals, publishes an annual magazine called *Poolife* and mails it to 1.2 million swimming pool owners. An important source of names is letters or calls to Olin for information on product rebates or services.

The magazine contains articles on water care and pool maintenance as well as features on swimwear, computer programs for pool care, food and entertainment ideas. In addition to promoting Olin products, the magazine carries paid advertising by other companies wishing to reach pool owners.

We don't know whether the paid advertising is enough to cover the entire annual expense of $300,000 or so, but, according to a spokesperson, "Advertiser response has been terrific." So any way you figure it, Olin comes out pretty well.

Your customer loyalty promotion to your database can also be financed and justified by its encouragement of future purchases of the same or a better product.

Prince Manufacturing Company, makers of Prince tennis equipment, publishes a quarterly magazine called *Prince* and mails it free to 150,000 requesters. They launched it by sending a test issue to 60,000 in-house names, who were asked to return a postcard if they wished to receive further copies. Some 54 percent returned the cards. Since then additional names have come in from purchasers of Prince racquets who send in the hang tag placed on each racquet.

Each issue includes an interview with a top tennis pro and a guest column of tips from a noted tennis coach. But it also keeps the subscriber aware of the Prince brand name and product line, including new and higher-priced rackets, so that Prince will be favorably positioned in the subscriber's mind when the customer's old racket wears out.

Dierberg Food Stores of St. Louis has provided a striking example of how retailers can promote through a customer database and get others to pay most of the cost. This nine-store chain maintains a database of 150,000 customers. Four times a year it sends them a beautiful 12-page magazine of recipes, the *Customer Club News.* Bound into the center is an envelope of money-saving coupons, some of them cents-off coupons redeemable at Dierberg stores, others coupons by other local merchants and restaurants who pay for the privilege of being included. This outside advertising plus co-op ad money from food manufacturers pays most of the cost of printing and mailing the magazine.

3. Maximized Cross-Promotion

Any company that has a number of different products, services, or divisions under its roof can use its combined customer database to introduce customers who bought one type of purchase or account to its other opportunities.

Of course a "combined customer database" is not necessarily as simple as it sounds. We know of a large bank that is attempting to combine all its accounts into one accessible cross-promotable master list, and it estimates it will take several years to achieve. But once it is achieved, of course, it becomes a priceless asset.

Sears, Roebuck & Company apparently had an awesome vision of the potential of combined databases some years ago and developed a master plan to turn the vision into reality.

The combination of their retail stores and mail-order catalogs with Allstate Insurance, Dean Witter, Greenwood Trust Company, Coldwell Banker Real Estate, the Sears Savings Bank, and now their new Discover card—each with its own database—enables them to cross-promote on a grand scale.

Already someone purchasing a home through Coldwell Banker qualifies for discounts of up to 25 percent on appliances, paint, burglar alarms, and other household items purchased from Sears. And Discover card holders receive a free Sears auto-care booklet of coupons worth up to $99 toward Sears auto products and services. It may take years for Sears to develop all the other possibilities of cross-promotion, such as offering mortgage loans to their real estate clients or automobile insurance to their money-market-fund accounts. But who knows? Some day you may be able to buy a home through Coldwell Banker and charge it on your Gold Discover card!

But you don't have to be a giant like Sears to employ the basic principles of cross-promotion. As long as you have several products or services and the names and addresses of customers, you can contact a customer who has bought one item in your line and promote the others. (This may sound obvious, but if it is obvious, why is it so often neglected and overlooked?)

Black & Decker has a much more extensive line of power tools and shop aids than most customers realize—and more than many stores are able or willing to find shelf space for. We think it would be good Maxi-Marketing strategy for them to build up their customer database and promote their various products directly to selected segments of it.

They could even go a step further and distribute to this database a consumer catalog of their full line of products—taking as much space as they wished to extoll the virtues of each item. Even if the catalog did not encourage ordering directly from Black & Decker, it would put the heat on their retailers for more shelf space, as customers began asking for catalog items the retailers didn't ordinarily stock.

Of course, we would favor a discreet admission in the catalog that any item not found in local stores could be ordered direct. It is hard to imagine that in this day and age retailers would boycott Black & Decker if they did that, especially if an increasing number of customers are coming in and asking for Black & Decker products. And for Black & Decker it would be like opening up miles of additional shelf space.

ChemLawn Corporation, starting around 1969, built with direct-response advertising and direct mail a customer database of 1.4 million households in 106 markets. Their lawn-care service and others captured 40 percent of the $500 million lawn-care market, robbing companies making lawn-care products of a huge market share.

Now ChemLawn is using its customer database to branch out into other areas of home service such as tree and shrub care, carpet cleaning, and indoor exterminating. According to a story in *Advertising Age,* crosspromotion of the customer database is at the heart of their expansion plans:

> The idea behind the strategy, said Jack van Fossen, the company's chairman, is to give ChemLawn a "cross-fertilization" from one service to another with the same clientele. "If we're best at carpet cleaning," he said, "that'll lead us to more lawn-care customers."
>
> Elliott Schlang, an analyst who tracks ChemLawn . . . sees this as part of an over-all approach to the market. ChemLawn's expansions, he said, are

divided into three distinct phases. It establishes new markets in which to do business, saturates those markets, then cross-sells to its captive audience of existing customers.[6]

4. Maximized Line Extension

As we acknowledged, share of mind alone can lead to diversified growth. One path to diversified growth is line extension. If people like your corn cereal breakfast food, they are favorably inclined to try your new rice cereal.

Possessing a customer database and putting it to good use also can give you a powerful additional boost. If you know who and where many of your best customers are, you can say, "You loved our corn cereal. Now try our rice cereal. Here's a 50-cent coupon to get you started!"

Another interesting application of a customer database to line extension is to put your famous brand name on a new product and get it successfully launched without having to fight for shelf space in your usual retail outlets.

Today, establishing a new package-goods product in the retail market costs up to $50 million. Massive television expenditure often is required to make a dent in public consciousness and to convince retailers that the new product deserves shelf space. But if you can go directly to consumers who already know and trust you, you may be able to extend your line with new products without having to travel this horrendously expensive and often unsuccessful route.

And if your new product is not sold in stores at all in the beginning, then your retailers can't complain that by selling direct to the public you are competing with them. This is the strategy obviously pursued by Avon in the introduction of their new Deneuve fragrance. Just as Borland International did with its Sidekick software, Avon started building retail demand with $2 to $5 million in massive mail-order advertising that undoubtedly repaid its cost and more.

Hanes has shown how combining brand image with a customer database can lead to line extension of products sold directly to the public. In the 1970s, they started a mail-order catalog, *L'eggs Showcase of Savings*, to sell slightly imperfect L'eggs pantyhose (seconds) directly to the public. They had no fear of retailer resentment, because factory outlet sale of seconds is such a common practice. The popularity of L'eggs hose helped make the catalog a big success. (Split-run tests showed that the famous name made a decisive difference in results.)

As the business progressed, they noticed they were getting a great many orders for large and extra-large sizes not readily available at retail. So they launched another successful catalog that marketed True Delight pantyhose for larger women (14 percent of the market). This paved the way for the introduction by Hanes of a similar line at retail.

Today, Hanes's direct-marketing division has an annual volume reportedly approaching $150 million, a hefty part of their billion-dollar business overall. And the icing on the cake is that the direct-marketing operation also provides sales promotion support for their retail distribution at extremely low cost. Bound into some of their mail-order catalogs are cents-off coupons good for 50 cents on any L'eggs product purchased at retail, providing coupon distribution in the millions for just the cost of printing the coupons.

La Costa Products, about which you'll hear more in a moment, started with massage oil and shampoo. Within a few years they were able to expand their line to include La Costa Spa wraps and robes, suntan lotions and moisturizers, visors, soaps, cosmetics, mousse, purses and cosmetic cases, men's cologne and shave cream, vitamins and minerals, T-shirts, etc. It would be a monumental marketing project to force such a broad line into the retail pipeline and then to force it out again through national advertising and promotion. But because La Costa Products had access to a database of 250,000 former guests of The La Costa Hotel & Spa, they were able to establish substantial instant distribution of the entire line via mail-order catalog. (And once this base is established, it becomes quite feasible to start adding retail distribution—as indeed may happen in this case.)

5. Maximized Success of New Ventures

One of the most important uses of the customer database is as a launching pad for new profit centers. If it is a huge database, it may provide all the prospects you need. If it is smaller, it can still help launch a new venture by providing a hard core of especially profitable customers immediately while the slow process of building business from outside sources gets under way.

When companies built on selling their products to the public through wholesalers and retailers become interested in direct marketing, a familiar stumbling block is their fear of alienating their retailers by appearing to be going into competition with them. However, with each passing year, as corporate ownership, distribution channels, and retailing chains become more complexly structured, this fear becomes increasingly less realistic.

One solution to the problem when concern is legitimate is to develop an entirely different product line for direct marketing. Then the distributors no longer have any grounds to complain that the manufacturer who supplies them is also competing with them. And the customer database can provide the foundation for building such new enterprises.

Avon has provided an instructive example. In 1972 they saw direct marketing as a possible area of major expansion. They didn't have to worry about retailers, but they did have to be concerned about the reaction of their several hundred thousand "Avon calling" part-time sales agents. This concern seemed to rule out selling cosmetics, fragrances, and skin-care products directly to the public via mail-order advertising. So Avon decided instead to sell women's apparel by mail. This new line would benefit from the good will around the Avon name but would not give their agents any reason to object.

Avon did not have a customer database at the time—but they did have some 2.5 million customers known by name and address. These names were the jealously guarded property of the agents themselves.

So Avon established a system of agent rewards in exchange for customer names, explaining that the names were needed for a new enterprise which would not conflict in any way with the agent's sales. From this they were able to construct a database which became the foundation of today's $150 million Avon Fashions division.

Remington Products has shown how a product manufacturer can use a customer database of warranty-card names to start a new direct-marketing profit center without alienating its retailers. The catalog includes Remington shaving products not sold in stores plus other merchandise, some of it thematically related.

In 1983, after a series of direct-mail tests, Remington mailed its first catalog to 544,000 warranty-card names and drew a 4 percent response. Since then the operation has continued to grow. In due time it could, like the Hanes direct-marketing division, begin to contribute a significant percentage of the company's total annual sales volume.

The *La Costa Spa* has dramatically demonstrated how much can be accomplished in a service business possessing an outstanding share of mind and customer database. This $100 million facility was started in 1966 to pamper the well-to-do. Two weeks at the Spa for two, everything included, can run over $7000.

That La Costa Look, the La Costa mail-order catalog, was the brainchild of William B. Randall. He built the Sea and Ski suntan lotion company, then sold out and "retired" to the fairway at La Costa. Soon he was making massage oil and shampoo under the La Costa label. When former guests started calling and writing for more, he decided to launch a catalog featuring his own extensive line of La Costa products and other famous brands. Within a few years he was mailing a glossy catalog twice a year to 250,000 former guests and 100,000 outside names and getting back an average order of $108, unusually high in the catalog field.

The inside back page of the catalog carries a full-page ad for the Hotel & Spa. Thus the catalog and the hotel support each other. The catalog helps bring guests to the hotel. The hotel guest list provides a rich customer database for the catalog.

Cuisinarts is the leader in a mature product category, food processors. It has fierce competitors, some offering cheap imitations. The original flurry of consumer excitement over food processors has subsided, so you might think that there is little Cuisinarts could do to improve its market position.

But Cuisinarts obviously applied the Law of the Situation and realized that it is not just in the business of selling food processors at retail. Rather, Cuisinarts is in the much broader business of developing sales of any kind for any superior product, by any means, to customers who do home cooking.

So its advertising, product literature, and warranty cards now solicit the names of customers and prospects, to whom Cuisinarts directly sells $18 cooking club memberships, $187.50 stainless steel cookware sets and other kitchen ware, Cuisinarts cookbooks, and $15 subscriptions to their beautiful Cuisinart magazine.

The additional revenue from these incremental sales will help support and justify expanded Cuisinarts advertising in magazines (and now on television). The net result is that Cuisinarts can continue to race ahead in sales, leaving its less enterprising competitors in the dust.

The Bottom Line

If your business facilities burned down to the ground tomorrow and all your physical equipment, fixtures, and inventory were destroyed, but you possessed a product or company name the public trusted, you would still own a substantial business asset.

And if you had also stored in a fireproof vault a computerized list of the names and addresses of a great many of your good customers, you would be the owner of another substantial asset, perhaps equally valuable—a customer database.

The fusion of your brand or company image with a customer database unleashes a new source of corporate power and energy. It permits you to take better care of your present customers, and that helps you win more new customers, in an endless feedback loop.

Building and maintaining a customer database will help you sell most to those who buy most—the heavy users. A customer database will help you retain the loyalty of your present customers despite the best efforts of your competitors to steal them away. It will permit you to sell one of your products to known users of another. It will help you start new lines and entirely new ventures.

As we have seen, it doesn't matter whether you are a manufacturer, a retailer, a personal selling company, or a direct marketer, you can tap into this new source of marketing energy.

One trick of making a customer database program affordable is to get your advertisers or customers to pay for it—or, as AT&T did, to offer something which seems extremely valuable but hardly costs your company anything.

And it doesn't matter how small your business is—you can substitute inventiveness for size and wealth. In this marvelous age of the personal computer, a few thousand dollars invested in computer hardware and software can start you on the road to keeping track of and satisfying the individual tastes and requirements of each of your customers. And you can mail them superb computer-personalized communications with customized offers or reminders.

With today's word-processing, file management, and addressing software, it is feasible with a few keystrokes to send a beautifully typed letter to as few as a dozen customers in your database, saying, "Mrs. Johnson, your size (or favorite color, or the latest book by your favorite author) just came in."

But no matter how small or how large your business is, a key to making it work is never to forget what business you and your company are really in: the business of "customer development," not the business of making and selling widgets.

For this reason, corporate commitment to database marketing must come from the top to reap its full rewards. If, however, you are a product or department or division manager, you can become a hero by demonstrating what database marketing can mean to your company's growth. It is the new frontier in marketing, and you can be one of the conquerors.

11

Maximized Distribution Through Multiple Channels

The Big Picture

You don't have to cross the ocean to find a whole new market. It may be right here under your nose. But to find it, you've got to cast off any preconceptions you may have about single-channel distribution.

As manufacturers seeking to introduce new products bump against the limits of retail shelf space, as stores reaching outward for more business collide with competitors invading their territory and mail-order catalogs competing for the same customers, as mail-order firms find themselves threatened with a dread malady known as "catalog glut," and as companies built on personal selling by or to homemakers find their audience shrinking, every company must review and reconsider its traditional way of doing business.

The race is to the swift. And the swift are those companies who today are rapidly exploring new forms of distribution and discovering the synergistic power of multichannel distribution.

Building a customer database or using an existing customer database in new ways is not always an essential ingredient. But customer databases will become increasingly essential as companies find that they often form a bridge between one form of distribution and another.

By the year 2000 or sooner it may be common to see phone-in drive-in supermarkets . . . movies and computer programs ordered and delivered by telephone . . . fast-food mobile vans that bring hot "meals on wheels" not just to the infirm elderly but to all kinds of households where the adults have paid jobs and are too busy to cook and too tired to go out . . . a new kind of retail outlet that brilliant catalog leader Harold Schwartz has dubbed "star stores"—small shops with little merchandise on hand but with shoppers' video terminals connected to warehouses vaster than Macy's.

But Chapter 11 focuses on possibilities and developments that are right here and now—companies expanding into new forms of distribution that your own company should perhaps be considering.

In the 1950s a curious, little-remembered marketing episode occurred that had profound implications for distribution today. Gathering dust in bookstores across the country was a ponderous one-volume tome, *The Columbia Encyclopedia.* Its retail price was $60, which would be more like $180 in today's dollars, a formidable obstacle to mass sales.

Then the Book-of-the-Month Club obtained rights to print their own edition and to offer it as a premium: "This $60 volume yours for only $6 if you join the Club now and agree to buy . . . ." (That $6 was probably about what it cost the club to print the book and pay the publisher a lease fee.)

It was an extremely successful offer, and for several years the club advertised it widely, spending perhaps a total of $3 to $4 million in publication advertising and direct mail—the equivalent of $9 to $12 million in today's dollars.

You would think that this promotion would surely have killed off any slim chance that retail booksellers still had of selling the volume in quantity. After all, who in the world would pay $60 for a book they could obtain for $6 just for agreeing to buy some other books they would like to own anyway?

But exactly the opposite happened. Once the campaign got well under way, the book suddenly became a brisk seller in the stores! Why? Because people are different.

Some people are responders and joiners, and some are not. Some people need to "kick tires" before they buy, and some do not. And for every one or two people out of a thousand who saw the offer in a magazine or newspaper ad and responded to it, many others were influenced by it but did not respond by joining the club.

Some of these nonresponders obviously became interested in the encyclopedia through the advertising, examined it in a bookstore, and decided to buy it.

The Book-of-the-Month Club did not own the retail rights as well as the mail-order rights to the book. But just think if they had. Then they would have profited doubly, *and their advertising would have been doubly efficient.*

The natural law this episode illustrates, from a direct-marketing point of view, is that for every direct sale generated by direct-response advertising, an equivalent demand is generated at retail. Today, when you combine this natural law with the power of the customer database, you get a new kind of distribution force which cannot be classified either as direct or indirect, because it is both, working together.

The discussion which follows is divided roughly into two areas. We started to label them databased distribution by manufacturers and by retailers, but in today's marketplace, those terms are woefully inadequate.

A service company such as an insurance company or a financial broker is not a "manufacturer"—even though it originates what it sells. And you don't think of a mail-order firm as a "retailer," although most of them are. (That is, they buy merchandise wholesale and act as an intermediary to sell it to the end-user, just as a retail store does.)

So instead we're going to label any company which originates a product or service an "originator" and any company which sells it for them to the end-user an "intermediary." (We would have called the latter a "distributor" except that in the business world that often means something else, an entity which stands between the manufacturer and the retailer.)

You may think that one of the two parts of this chapter which follow doesn't apply to you and your company. If your company is an "originator," what do you care about how to become a better "intermediary"? And vice-versa?

The answer is that the distinctions are blurring and the walls are tumbling down. Aquascutum is an "originator," but now it has its own retail store on Fifth Avenue. The Lands' End catalog is an "intermediary," but much of its merchandise is its own exclusive manufacture and label. Johnston & Murphy, which "originates" quality shoes and sells them through "intermediaries," is now also acting as its own "intermediary" with its own retail shops and mail-order catalog.

So if you're going to review your company's options, you've got to look at the whole picture.

We're going to start by exploring with you the new fusion energy being generated by intermediaries who are employing multichannel distribution.

I. The Power of Combining In-Store and Nonstore Marketing

As we pointed out in the *Columbia Encyclopedia* discussion, if you can capture sales from both the armchair shoppers who are invited to order by mail or phone and the tire-kicker retail shoppers who read and are influenced by your advertising, you can double its efficiency and profitability.

A new breed of entrepreneurial intermediaries have discovered this secret and are using it to unlock the riches of the marketplace. We are talking about companies like Brookstone, The Banana Republic, Williams-Sonoma, Laura Ashley, Royal Silk, Talbot's, Yield House, Eddie Bauer, Jos. A. Bank, and The Sharper Image.

What are they? Are they mail-order firms who are opening retail outlets across the country? Or are they retailers who got their start in the mail-order catalog business?

We think they are MaxiMarketers.

While hidebound traditional retailers watch with fascination, these new intermediary firms get "free" advertising for their retail stores in the millions of catalogs they mail out. And they get "free" mailing lists and "free" delivery for their catalogs when shoppers throng into their retail stores, leave their names and addresses each time they make a purchase, and take home a catalog.

Some traditional stores are waking up to what's going on and are beginning to build their own customer databases and to start or expand their own catalog merchandising.

A. When Nonstore Merchants Open Stores

Williams-Sonoma, a housewares and cookware intermediary, is a particularly fascinating case. It was a retail store, which spawned a major mail-order catalog operation, which in turn spawned a chain of retail stores.

The company was started around 1955 by Chuck Williams, who bought an old hardware store in Sonoma, California, and turned it into a gourmet cookware and housewares shop. Later he moved it to San Francisco, where he called it Williams-Sonoma so his old customers would know his new store was run by that same Williams fellow from Sonoma.

After a couple of decades, he found he had accumulated a customer database of about 10,000 people who had bought from his store but who lived outside the San Francisco area. So he created his first mail-order catalog. Soon, of course, he began mailing the catalog to outside lists as well.

This created a nationwide demand for his unique merchandise which not only boosted his store sales in San Francisco but made it possible to open other stores. By 1983 he had 11 retail outlets. By 1985 the number had risen to 19. And the sales volume rose accordingly, from about $4 million in 1979 to about $40 million in 1983!

What makes the Williams-Sonoma story especially significant is that it is one of the few cases we could find where an effort has been made to measure the effect of catalog circulation on store sales. Here is the report of Pat Connolly, vice president for mail-order sales, in a panel discussion in 1982:

> The mail-order business comprises more than half of our business right now, but each of the stores has registered impressive growth gains because of the catalog, a growth rate about 30 per cent per store. In one of our stores, we increased the sale 300 per cent in four years. This was a store that was in existence for six years before we started to promote it. Then in our San Francisco store we more than doubled the sales in three years, and that store had been there for 22 years.
>
> We've always tried to measure the excess store sales that result from catalog mailings. If you have a store and you're mailing catalogs, it is very difficult to really know how much benefit you're getting in the store from the catalog. You know that sales go up, but you're really not exactly sure to what extent the catalog is responsible.
>
> This summer we did an extensive study looking at results that we've had for the past three years. We found that in our business we can get about a 30 per cent lift if we mail our catalog in a store area. That's 30 per cent additional incremental sales in the store.[1]

Another important discovery the company made was that the completion curve of the resulting store sales was the same as that of the catalog sales.* That's important news to retailers who may not realize that one of their catalogs or flyers can still be generating retail sales in their stores a month or two later.

Williams-Sonoma carries about ten times as many items in the stores as they do in their catalog—but every item that is in the catalog is also in the stores. To reap the full retail rewards of a catalog-store mailing, make sure that your stores are well-stocked with all the catalog merchandise. Otherwise a customer who visits a store seeking to buy a particular catalog item may simply turn away in disappointment and leave if the store is out of stock. And Connolly points out, "In mail order you can back order, although it's very painful. In retail when the customer leaves, you've just lost the sale."

One final important point: The names collected from people who visit the store prove to be an extremely productive catalog mailing list, better than most outside rented lists. Points out Connolly: "They've had a pleasant experience with the store; they're familiar with the quality of the merchandise, and this experience breaks down the resistance to mail order that they may have had."[2]

For some reason, the Williams-Sonoma catalogs we have received list only the cities in which they have retail shops, not the street addresses as well.

The Sharper Image is sharper in this respect. One of their recent catalogs devoted three-fourths of the entire back page to a prominent listing of their stores, including their addresses, and a strong pitch for the retail trade:

Stores To Satisfy Your Curiosity

As soon as you step inside the door of a Sharper Image Store—you know you've entered a magical place.

Because in our store all the ingenious products The Sharper Image is known for are out in the open—waiting for your touch. Test out and try anything that attracts your curiosity—in a relaxed, unhurried atmosphere.

One cannot help wondering if this stronger pitch for a store visit does not result in incremental store sales even greater than Williams-Sonoma's 30 percent—without subtracting anything from the catalog sales.

Laura Ashley, Inc. is a spectacular example of the potential of database-powered multidistribution by a combination originator and intermediary company. This British-based manufacturer-retailer of home furnishings and women's apparel, with around 200 stores internationally, grew an average of 46 percent annually between 1975 and 1985,

---

* The completion curve simply means that when you mail out a catalog or an offer and plot the daily response on a graph, half of your results will be concentrated in a tall hill within a few weeks after the first response arrives. The remainder of the replies will be spread out in a long declining slope spread out over a period of months.

when it achieved a worldwide sales volume of $150 million. About half of this volume was accounted for by its U.S. operations.

The company was started around 1955 by Laura and Bernard Ashley. She began designing prints for tea towels, and he built a very simple screen-printing device on their kitchen table. Gradually they developed a wholesale business selling their own scarves, towels, and home furnishing and accessory items to U.K. department stores.

Next they opened their own store to showcase their collection and found they liked the retail business better than wholesale. So by 1963 they had abandoned the wholesale business and were concentrating on opening up retail shops in the United Kingdom.

One thing that made their operation unusual from the beginning was their decision to retail only products of their own design and manufacture. Even today this is true of 90 percent of their product line.

Laura Ashley entered the U.S. market in 1974 and within 10 years had established 63 stores and built an annual sales volume of $70 million.

A key ingredient in this meteoric success was their building of a catalog customer database and the constant interplay between catalogs and stores. When they decided to open a store in Denver, for instance, they were astonished to find that they already had 9000 customers concentrated in a small area of the city. It didn't take much additional promotion to make the store they opened in that area an instant success. And they are able to use their catalog customer database in this way to identify promising locations for the 15 new stores a year they plan to add.

Their central database at their U.S. headquarters in Carlstadt, New Jersey, captures and retains three kinds of records: people who have ordered a catalog from a direct-response magazine advertisement, people who have ordered from a catalog by mail or phone, and people who have purchased in a store. Presumably this makes it possible to track the efficiency of a magazine advertisement even in terms of resulting store sales as well as mail and phone catalog sales.

Although new fashion catalogs are automatically mailed free to the entire database (and the more expensive home-furnishings catalog is given to their best customers), they are also able to *sell* a great many copies. The stunning beauty and quality of the catalogs make people willing to pay for them, and the fact that they have paid means that expensive catalogs are not wasted on uninterested prospects.

They sell the home-furnishings catalog for $4 in their shops and also sell some 100,000 copies in bookstores around the country. They also successfully tested selling their fashion catalog in bookstores for $2.

Their direct-response ads in magazines offer a catalog "subscription" (actually eight catalogs within 2 years) for $5. They expected to sell 85,000 to 90,000 catalogs this way in 1985.

They laughed at the line in the *Newsweek* story about them which said that their remarkable growth has been achieved "with little or no advertising."[3] That mistaken observation bespoke a common misunderstanding of the value of a store catalog as store advertising.

Their customer database was around 500,000 at the beginning of 1985 and was growing at the rate of 50,000 names a month.

Remember Chapter 10's discussion of how to clone your best customers? Apparently Laura Ashley is seeking to do just that. In an interview in the beginning of 1985, their vice president for U.S. marketing, Jim Frain, said:

> We're looking at the customer base that we have been developing, and fine-tuning the demographic profile in very local neighborhoods all around the country. So what we're working on very painstakingly right now is precisely identifying those neighborhoods within a ZIP code and whether they're subscribers to certain magazines and customers of certain stores.[4]

Translation: We're identifying neighborhoods with the highest concentration of grade-A Laura Ashley customer clones, so that we can distribute catalogs and open stores in those neighborhoods. This is the synergistic promotion and distribution of the future.

Royal Silk is another success story of an entrepreneurial young company which found, like Laura Ashley, that some people are armchair shoppers and some need to touch the merchandise before buying. Pak Melwani founded the company in 1978 to sell exclusive, affordable, imported silk garments for women by catalog. Within 7 years he was mailing 20 million catalogs a year and had achieved an annual sales volume of $30 million.

Melwani had previously invested unsuccessfully in a retail gift shop that had left him with little taste for retailing. But after he began mass mailings of his Royal Silk catalogs, people started coming into his corporate offices in Clifton, New Jersey, asking if they could buy catalog items on the spot.

This led to the opening, in 1982, of the first Royal Silk store, in Clifton. In a couple of years it was doing an annual volume of $1 million and encouraged the company to start opening additional stores, including their flagship store on lower Fifth Avenue in Manhattan.

You will recall our advocacy of double-duty advertising. Royal Silk does *triple*-duty advertising in selected magazines. The ads (1) offer an item for purchase by mail or phone, (2) offer a free catalog, and (3) promote store traffic by listing the store addresses.

According to Gerald Pike, the company's vice president, "We include our stores' addresses in the print ads, and they support the entire operation. We can add the address at no additional cost."

Another advantage of the catalog and store combination that Royal Silk has found is that their respective seasonal peaks and valleys tend to balance out. In December, the strongest retail month of the year, the catalog business is very slow. But in January it's just the opposite.

Brookstone is famous for its catalogs of "hard-to-find tools and other fine things." They also deserve to be famous for their remarkable stores. It's not easy to invent an entirely new kind of store, but Brookstone has done it. Each store is a kind of walk-in catalog. Or it could be described as a kind of museum of contemporary gadgetry in which everything on display is for sale.

As you enter, instead of picking up a shopping basket, you pick up one of the clipboards, each with its own pen and order form. Displayed on counters or in showcases throughout the store are the items in stock— just one of each—*with the catalog description alongside*. Thus the store combines the informational advantage of a catalog with the look-touch advantage of a store.

You write the name and order number of the items you want on your order form, exactly as if you were ordering from the catalog, and hand it to the clerk behind the sales counter. A trolley delivers your order form to invisible elves in the back room or basement who pick your items off the shelves and send them back to the sales desk via the trolley. Thus valuable street-floor or up-front space is not crowded and cluttered with stacks of cartons of identical items, nor is it necessary to flag a busy clerk and ask him or her to get you what you want.

It is true that aspects of the system are uniquely suited to Brookstone and similar operations. But there are also clues here to the future of many different kinds of retailing which deserve to be carefully observed and pondered.

B. When Stores Add Catalogs

Al Schmidt, a noted catalog management executive, tells of reading about a family store in Fayetteville, Arkansas, that was going through hard times. The family instituted a rigorous program of cost reduction. They changed four-bulb fixtures to two-bulb fixtures. They changed 150-watt bulbs to 75-watt bulbs. And they gave up putting out a Christmas catalog for the first time in 25 years!

This story illustrates a common retailer mentality about store catalogs—namely, that they are an expense item, to be expanded when sales are good and cut back when sales are poor.

Such an attitude makes it difficult for most retailers to see the possibility of a store catalog as a separate self-sustaining profit center which can also generate store traffic at no additional cost.

There is also a third possibility, largely unexplored. And that is to construct a customer database which will accurately record and total both the mail and phone sales and the in-store sales resulting from featuring an item in a catalog. Then, even if the mail or phone results alone are not enough to make the catalog profitable, it may be possible to determine that the combined sales results are directly profitable—quite apart from the serendipity of store traffic generated.

We believe database marketing is and will be the secret weapon of the most successful retailers of tomorrow. But merely designing and implementing your customer database correctly is not enough.

To force (or to permit) a store catalog to stand on its own two feet requires a drastic change in thinking, management structure, and operating procedures that many stores are still not able to accomplish.

This is not surprising. Retailing has been evolving for over 100 years. It has developed its own customs, lore, habits, language, sales techniques, and accounting procedures, by this time all highly developed and deeply ingrained.

Mail-order catalog marketing is about as old and has also developed its own customs, lore, habits, language, sales techniques, and accounting procedures. And they are so different from the store retailer's that it is hard for retail management to make the proper mental adjustment when they attempt catalog marketing.

To take just one example of the difference in the way of thinking: Let's say that in February a mail-order catalog manager runs a small ad in *Better Homes & Gardens* for $6000 to offer a free copy of a catalog and receives 6000 replies. Then the manager has the expense of, let's say, $1500 for printing and mailing a catalog to each of these prospects. The total investment is now $7500 or $1.25 per prospect.

From a store retailer's point of view, the advertiser has spent $7500 that month *and has no sales to show for it.* A disaster!

But let's say the catalog manager knows from past experience with ads in *Better Homes & Gardens* that 10 percent of these prospects will make one or more purchases. That makes the advertising cost of acquiring a customer $1.25 multiplied by 10, or $12.50. The manager also knows from analysis of the customer database that the lifetime value (LTV) of each of these customers is an estimated $131.17. That is, based on past experience each of these customers should spend an average of $131.17 over the next 3 years. And the gross produced for advertising and profit, after the cost of merchandise, overhead, and repromotion has been deducted, should be $18.50. So the company has provided for a future gross profit of $6 ($18.50 minus $12.50) per customer times 6000 customers, or $36,000.

This simplified calculation leaves out the cost of money and other considerations. But it provides a glimpse of the catalog marketer's lifetime customer value point of view. It is entirely different from the retailer's daily and monthly sales quota outlook.

A common handicap of store catalogs based on traditional retail psychology is that they are vendor-driven rather than market-driven. Rather than let past public responses dictate the selection of unique merchandise for the catalog, the store will fill the catalog with dozens of similar items that have little mail-order appeal but are subsidized by generous vendor co-op advertising money.

Bloomingdale's by Mail, Ltd., which has scored such a brilliant success as a free-standing profit center under the inspired management of Barry Marchesault, has sought the best of both worlds. Marchesault selects merchandise of highly likely mail-order appeal—but may not observe the limits of strict mail-order requirements in allocating space for vendor-supported items. The result is that he can afford a more handsome and lavish catalog than would be justified by mail-order sales alone. Thus the catalogs reinforce and strengthen the Bloomingdale image with retail shoppers while yielding excellent mail-order profits.

Bloomingdale's by Mail was established in 1978 as a separate profit center, with separate management; within 7 years it had built a database of 800,000 non-charge-account customers. Catalog sales were projected to reach $70 million in 1985 and projected to climb to $200 million in 1990. That would make the operation Bloomie's second largest "store," right behind its flagship store in Manhattan.

If you are in store management, how can your company overcome the limits of retail thinking and successfully establish a self-sustaining catalog operation? The easiest way is to hire a mail-order catalog manager with a proven track record and give him or her *carte blanche*. The only trouble with that—Catch-22—is that the retailing "mind set" up and down the line of store management may make it impossible for such an executive really to achieve *carte blanche*.

If there is one person in the world who understands the truth of this, it's Al Schmidt. He experienced it both ways.

Brooks Brothers was having trouble in 1978 with modernizing their catalog operation and invited Schmidt to join them as vice president for direct marketing. In his first few days, he outlined the changes he felt were necessary to make the operation a success:

- A commitment of money for circulation expansion
- Dedicated stocks, separate inventory for filling orders
- Use of third-party credit cards—Visa, MasterCard, American Express, Diner's Club

- Exchanging and renting of house mailing lists
- The use of a toll-free 800 number for phone orders
- Separate fulfillment facilities for catalog orders
- Different merchandise direction for the catalog, emphasizing unique mail-order items, rather than following the department-by-department approach of the typical retail store
- Use of outside expertise for list maintenance and merge/purge (purging duplicate names from lists used)

According to Schmidt, the chief executive officer was able to recognize the validity of these needs and to see that the means were provided to meet them.

Before Schmidt began, Brooks Brothers had routinely mailed out catalogs three times a year to a list of 300,000 customers who had made at least one purchase sometime within the last 5 years. There was no analysis of results. It was just considered good store promotion.

Within a few years, Schmidt had Brooks Brothers mailing 15+ million catalogs a year and earning an 18 percent pretax profit on sales from them as well as generating substantial store traffic in their 36 retail locations.

In 1981, Schmidt launched the Brooksgate catalog for young men with an initial mailing of 500,000. In addition to the mail-order results, *sales in the Brooksgate departments of the Brooks Brothers stores went up 70 percent.*

But later, Schmidt recounts, when he moved on to a similar position at another well-known store, he was not able to achieve a similar success because he could not overcome the retailing "mind set" of the management:

- They wouldn't budget money for circulation expansion.
- After a year, they still wouldn't permit the use of third-party credit cards. (They feared it would hurt use of the store's own card, which is very profitable for a store.)
- They wouldn't let him establish separate stocks for catalog orders. "My staff that was picking mail-order orders was still fighting over the counters with customers for the merchandise to fill orders."[5]

Schmidt's requirement of expanded catalog circulation is worth additional comment. Although your retail customer database is a valuable starting point, your independent mail-order catalog operation will need more prospect names to feed on. This will necessitate the rental of and exchange with outside lists of responsive mail-order buyers. The result will be an expanded catalog customer database which can also be of great benefit to your in-store marketing, especially if you have a number of stores.

If you're a retailer who would like to emulate the success of the Brooks Brothers catalog, you would be well-advised to find a catalog expert like Al Schmidt, retain him or her as a manager or consultant, and provide the unstinting backing and commitment necessary to get the job done.

Because foot-dragging can occur in the ranks of store management personnel who resist change, we also suggest a store policy of educating a few selected middle and junior managers in direct marketing in general and catalog marketing in particular.

Send them to the conventions of the Direct Marketing Association, as some smart retailers already do. Take out a few subscriptions to the leading direct-marketing trade publications—*Direct Marketing, DM News, Catalog Age*. It could be one of your best investments in planning for retailing of the future.

An Opportunity for the Specialty Retailer.   You say you're a very small specialty shop? You say that the $150 million success of Laura Ashley means nothing to your modest operation?

You may be right. But don't decide too quickly. As long-time practitioners of direct-marketing advertising, we would be the first to warn hopeful amateurs of the odds against starting a mail-order catalog operation from scratch and making a fortune. Although it has been done and can be done, all you hear about are the successes.

What you don't hear about is the high mortality rate. For every successful business started by filling orders at the kitchen table or in the garage, there are hundreds of failures.

But if your mail-order venture is based on a successful specialty shop with some claim to uniqueness—and if you start with a core mailing list by assiduously collecting the names and addresses of every single customer in your shop and storing them in your computer, along with information about when, how much, and what they bought—you will have *doubled* or *tripled* your chances for success.

You won't be under pressure to grow too quickly. You can start with a catalog just for your customer list and nurse it along—"get the bugs out" of merchandise selection, inventory control, and fulfillment.

You can add to your catalog circulation at comparatively low cost by handing out copies to store visitors whether they buy or not, saving the cost of postage, list rental, and lettershop services. And with today's incredibly affordable computer hardware and software, you can pioneer in ways to tailor your communications with your customers to their individual tastes and needs.

Here is the story of an unusual small specialty shop that added a catalog and within 5 years was able to multiply its catalog sales volume 200 times.

Good Things Collective was started around 1977 by David Jockasch, who might be described as an alternative lifestyle entrepreneur. He came to the Northhampton-Amherst area of Maine in 1977 and started developing a wholesale-retail business selling homespun unisex clothing. He operated it as a sole proprietorship until 1981, when it was incorporated as a worker-owned business, beginning with six owners.

In 1979 the business moved into a retail store in Northhampton and started a mail-order catalog business in the back of the store. The catalog was considered a sideline, but its business expanded more quickly than the store's did—within 5 years, catalog sales volume rose from $20,000 to $500,000, 70 percent of the company's total sales volume.

By their own account, their database started with "friends, friends of friends, people that were referred to us." Gradually they expanded by advertising in alternative lifestyle magazines like *Mother Earth News* and *New Age,* and they mailed to some outside rental lists.

By 1984 their catalog circulation was 100,000. Many established big-name catalog merchants would consider this a laughably small number for a national catalog. But to us it means that Good Things has built its catalog operation cautiously, sensibly, on solid ground every step of the way. And it is a natural supplement to its retail operation.

At last report, the company had moved to a larger store and had moved its catalog operation out of the back room and into a 5000-square-foot warehouse in Easthampton. They had customers in 50 states and were analyzing their database to see where their mail-order sales were strongest. This enabled them to at least toy with the idea of opening additional stores in places like Boulder and San Diego.

The Good Things story demonstrates that even a small specialty store with something unique to offer can go national with a mail-order catalog and then can use sales from the catalog as clues to good locations for additional stores.

II. The Power of Database Distribution by Originator Companies

Suppose you are an "originator" company rather than an "intermediary" or retailing operation. How can you build a customer database and use it to expand your distribution without alienating retailers or agents and forfeiting your chances for optimum intermediary distribution?

We're going to propose four ways: (A) Round out your line and plug the geographical gaps in your market. (B) Use an intermediary's database. (C) Use the power of either-or selling. (D) Sell direct first and force retail distribution.

As you will see, these approaches may benefit from but are not limited to your own customer database. Although a database made up of present buyers from *the businesses you are now in* is a valuable jumping-off place, this does not mean you should necessarily be limited to this comparatively narrow base. Unless you have a huge customer base, like Sears or Avon or American Express, you may find it not only desirable but necessary to graze on outside databases to feed your own.

A. Round Out Your Line and Plug the Geographical Gaps in Your Distribution

It is a common experience for an originator company to have a broader line than many of its retail outlets are able or willing to carry or to have spotty geographical distribution. Using and/or building a customer database can help you round out your distribution without upsetting your good relations with your intermediaries. And it may lead to valuable diversification.

Pfaltzgraff has always occupied a unique niche in the dinnerware business. It offers a comparatively few number of patterns but as many as 50 to 100 different matching pieces. As a result, many customers become Pfaltzgraff collectors. They start with a set of dinnerware and then keep adding serving accessories and decorative items in the same pattern.

Around 1975, the company considered supplying these collectors by mail. Explains Jerry King, the company's director of direct marketing:

> We found that as small lamps and other items were increasing in price, more and more retailers were reluctant to carry 100 items in a given pattern. We began to get an increasing number of letters and phone calls from consumers throughout the country saying, "I started collecting your Yorktown pattern. I've bought every piece that my local retailer carries. But I know you make a lot more. Can I buy them directly from you or how can I get them? Where's another dealer in my area that I can check?"
>
> From a marketing standpoint, there's nothing worse than having a product that you want to sell and a consumer on the other end who is quite eager to buy, with no way to get it to them. So we began to pursue mail order as a way, not to compete with our retailers that were out there, but as a way to supplement that channel of distribution, as well as to keep people interested in buying Pfaltzgraff products to round out their collection.[6]

It is interesting to observe how the operation evolved: First they sent postcards to their customer file offering their catalog *Country Notebook*. To fill out the catalog, they found and added other handcrafted items. Then a consultant proposed expanding the catalog circulation by testing outside lists. They found they could use outside lists, but since these customers were not Pfaltzgraff collectors, the other handcrafted items in the catalog sold better. So they stepped up their search for unusual handicrafts and increased the number of pages devoted to them.

At last report, to serve their known Pfaltzgraff buyers better, they were returning to their original objective and were putting together a second catalog of strictly Pfaltzgraff products to be mailed to all known Pfaltzgraff customers.

The Pfaltzgraff case is a striking example of how selling to your customer database can lead to other, unexpected profit opportunities while achieving your original objective.

B. Use an Intermediary's Database

Suppose you don't have a database of your best customers and prospects, and your intermediaries do? Or you still have legitimate concerns about using your customer database in a way that might seem to be competing with your own intermediaries?

Well, if you feel you can't or don't want to sell directly by mail to *your* database, you can help your intermediaries sell by mail to *theirs*. It is like opening up a whole new channel of distribution while strengthening your relationships with your intermediaries.

Simon & Schuster blazed a trail with this approach in the early 1940s. Large beautiful books filled with expensive color plates at affordable prices were unheard of at that time. Publishers of such deluxe editions were caught in a vicious circle. They felt they had to charge a high price per copy because they would sell so few copies and they needed to amortize the cost of the plates. But the reason they would sell so few copies was that they charged such a high price per copy.

Richard Simon, an outstanding publishing visionary, was determined to break out of this trap with an impressive volume of color plates called *A Treasury of Art Masterpieces*. If the cost of the color plates could be spread out over a far greater press run, the book could be sold profitably at a reasonable price. And the reasonable price would enable them to sell far more copies than usual.

But how could they be sure? If they guessed wrong and were stuck with thousands of unsold copies, it could be an expensive mistake. Simon and his colleagues decided that the answer lay in getting in a large number of orders before the books were printed.

They prepared a beautiful direct-mail piece with a sample of the color printing and persuaded a few bookstores with mailing lists of charge customers to test it under the bookstore's name, with the orders coming back to the bookstore. A special prepublication price was offered to stimulate orders for a book which did not yet exist.

The tests proved successful, and Simon & Schuster was then able to go to all the bookstores who had mailing lists and say, in effect, "Look, here are the results that Kroch's in Chicago got with this mailing. You can do the same. We'll provide you with as many copies of the mailing as you need, and we'll arrange to have the letterhead and envelopes and reply form imprinted with your name."

The promotion was a huge success, and opened the way to a new era of beautiful "coffee table books" at affordable prices. And the basic principle, of selling through your intermediaries' databases rather than directly to your own is still sound today.

Of course, you needn't limit yourself to your existing network of intermediaries. You can prepare a professional mail-order mailing and promote its use by any company that has a database, whether it has a store or not.

Don't forget that catalog firms and other direct marketers who buy wholesale and sell retail are retailers too, even though they don't have a retail store.

This realization allows you to approach direct-marketing companies with huge mail-order customer databases and offer them not only your product line for mail-order sales but also your pretested mail-order promotion, just as Simon & Schuster did with booksellers. This can open up a whole new market for your company. And none of your existing retailers can object to this mail-order competition because they have a completely fair and equal opportunity to send the same pretested mailing to their own customer database.

Bell & Howell made history in the 1950s by selling huge numbers of home-movie outfits in this way. They had about one-third of the retail market and didn't want to endanger it. But many people who were prospects for a home-movie outfit had never set foot in a camera store and wouldn't know exactly what to ask for if they did. That untapped market seemed a natural for mail-order sales if it could be done without upsetting the retailers.

Maxwell Sroge, promotion manager of Bell & Howell (later to found a prominent advertising agency and publishing firm in the direct-marketing field) approached a pioneer mail-order syndication expert named Al Sloan. The latter's specialty was preparing powerful direct mail with an irresistible offer of a manufacturer's product. Then he would persuade companies with large customer databases, such as the Columbia Record

Club or Encyclopedia Britannica, to mail the offer to their own customers, under their own name.

In this way, such companies were in effect buying wholesale from the manufacturer and selling retail through the direct-mail piece, and the direct mail furnished by Sloan was simply their dealer aid that created the sales. And the manufacturer could not be accused of favoring mail-order companies with a special deal, because any store with a list of charge accounts was free to use the same mailing in the same way.

But because of Bell & Howell's concern about their dealers, they made available to Sloan a good but obsolete camera and a projector with a 2-year-old design which could no longer be sold at retail. And they required that the outfit be offered to the customer at $149.95, full retail price, even though dealers were discounting cameras and projectors heavily.

However, Sloan was still able to make the offer irresistibly tempting to prospects through such motivation devices as free trial, installment payments, and the inclusion of little extras that made it seem like you were getting a whale of a lot for your money. The mailing also offered soothing reassurance about the outfit's completeness and ease of use that the anxious prospect might not have found in a busy store.

The first year, through Al Sloan, Bell & Howell sold 30,000 camera and projector outfits. The second year, they sold 90,000. And sales continued to grow for years thereafter. Some years, according to Sroge, they amounted to 10 to 15 percent of the entire 8-mm, home-movie market.

Times have changed. Oceans of water have passed over the dam. Clearly in today's demassified product-flooded market the Bell & Howell formula would not still work as well. The practice of syndication has changed to largely one of offerings through statement stuffers mailed to databases such as charge-card and oil company accounts or enclosed in shipments of mail-order merchandise.

But the basic principle of syndication is still valid, and new applications of it are undoubtedly waiting to be discovered. For instance, a winery might prepare a syndicated mailing on a wine-of-the-week club and offer to provide it to their retailers at cost, imprinted with the retailer's name throughout.

Third-party promotion is closely akin to syndication and is another way to use someone else's database to sell your product or service. The most common use today is by insurance companies who will underwrite a policy that a club, company, association, financial service, or publication will offer to its customers as a special benefit. One of the more startling examples in recent times was the announcement that *Reader's Digest* was going to sell Metropolitan Life Insurance policies to its subscribers by mail.

C. Use the Power of
Either-Or Selling

You will recall that Chapter 10, in discussing cross-sell to your customer database, mentioned that Black & Decker has a line of power tools and shop aids that is more extensive than many stores are able or willing to carry. We suggested that they could mail a catalog to their warranty-card names with a discreet suggestion that these products could be obtained directly from Black & Decker if they were not available at the nearest retailers.

Keep in mind that this method of offering your products *either* at a local store *or* directly from the manufacturer in direct mail to your customer database is like a hot-cold water faucet. It can be set any way that suits your marketing needs and objectives.

If "hot" represents retail sales and "cold" represents direct sales, you can turn your faucet to mix 90 percent hot and 10 percent cold—or vice versa. Your mix is determined by how much emphasis you place on completing the transaction at a retail location and how much on ordering direct from your company, the originator (see Figure 11).

For instance, if you wanted to build a fire under your dealers with a 90-hot, 10-cold mix, your mailing would include either a list of retailers or a computerized imprinting of the name and address of the nearest dealer. It might also include a discount certificate to be presented to the dealer. And the possibility of ordering direct would merely be included as an afterthought: "If you can't find our product or are unable to visit our retailer, call this number or send your order directly to the following address."

But if you wanted to maximize your direct orders and profits with a 10-90 mix, then you would include an order form and reply envelope in your mailing, and the possibility of purchasing at retail would be included but downplayed. The great advantage in this latter course is that if you have limited resources, it may help you to stretch your budget and generate your own capital. The more direct responses you get, the more profitable your mailing, and the more profitable your mailing, the greater number of outside mailing lists you can profitably use in addition to your own customer database. And the more mailings you send out, the more you will affect retail sales, even if retail availability is downplayed.

So the choice might be between being able to send a 90-10 mailing to only 500,000 customer database names or sending a 10-90 mailing to 5 million customer and outside list names. In the latter case, you might get as many additional retail sales while profiting from a great many more direct sales.

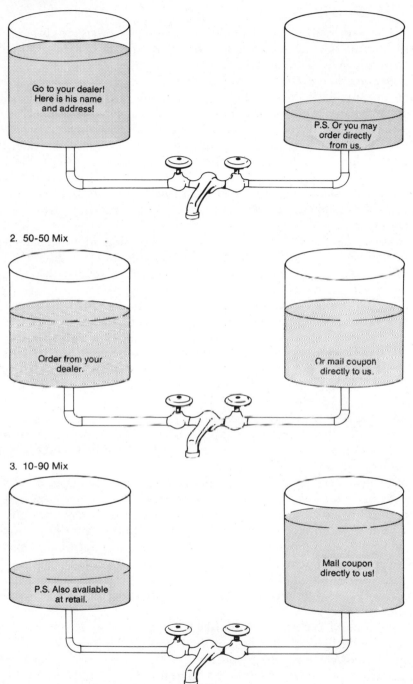

1. 90-10 Mix

Go to your dealer!
Here is his name
and address!

P.S. Or you may
order directly
from us.

2. 50-50 Mix

Order from your
dealer.

Or mail coupon
directly to us.

3. 10-90 Mix

P.S. Also avaliable
at retail.

Mail coupon
directly to us!

FIGURE 11.   Three Ways to Do Either-Or Selling.

If you are really worried about your retailers, there is always the possibility of starting with a 90-10 or 60-40 mix and then gradually changing it to 40-60 or 10-90.

Columbia Record Club was launched with this approach in the mid-1950s. Columbia Records, the parent company, was so concerned with possible resentment by record dealers that all the plans for the club were prepared in total secrecy. When the first club advertisements appeared, they offered the alternatives of taking the reply coupon to a dealer or mailing it directly to the club. On the very same day, every record dealer in the country received by Western Union delivery a complete sales kit which would enable them to enroll and profit from club members. Thus Columbia forestalled a dealer rebellion which they felt might have bankrupted them.

Later, as dealers discovered that club advertising stimulated rather than robbed from retail sales, Columbia was able to gradually turn the faucet toward "cold," until finally all references to retailer availability were elminated. And everyone lived happily ever after.

What if a company like Black & Decker pursued a similar strategy? It might start by mailing its customer database and perhaps selected outside lists its catalog showing its full home-workshop line and enclosing a credit certificate to be presented to the dealer—no mention of ordering direct. Dealers would be delighted by this manufacturer support, and impressed by the number of customers coming in to ask for specific Black & Decker items.

Then the next edition of the catalog might introduce the suggestion of ordering directly but still not provide an order form. And each subsequent edition would turn the faucet a little more in the direction of direct orders, meanwhile increasing the circulation.

If the dealers continued to experience customers coming in to ask for specific Black & Decker catalog items, as all direct-marketing experience indicates that they would, most dealers would not notice or care about the gradual turning of the faucet. (The few dealers who did grumble could surely be accommodated in some way by a management committed to growth and development.) And eventually Black & Decker might end up with a second channel of distribution, direct marketing, which would add a new revenue stream while supporting their first channel, retail distribution.

Keep in mind that we are using Black & Decker only as an example of the kind of business which might profitably adopt this strategy. Is there a principle hidden here which you might be able to apply to your own company's products and method of operation?

D. Sell Direct First and Force Retail Distribution

Reality is more complex than our simplified diagrams suggest. From our discussion so far, and from our diagram of the MaxiMarketing model, you might assume that we are insisting that marketing development should always follow the same unchangeable sequence: manufacturing to awareness advertising to activation to retail sale to customer database to direct marketing.

This is not necessarily the case. Sometimes marketing development happens like this: manufacturing to awareness advertising to activation to direct-marketing purchase to customer database to retail distribution.

In other words, instead of retail sales producing a customer database which in turn results in mail-order sales, the process can happen the other way around.

After World War II, an ex-G.I. named David Margulies was looking for a way to get started in business. While stationed in Italy he had discovered a marvelous little hand garlic press unknown in the United States and decided he could make a lot of money distributing it over here. But when he made the rounds of store buyers, he ran into a stone wall of indifference.

Believe it or not, at that time, there were almost no mail-order specialty catalogs such as those in the big bundle your mail carrier delivers to your home. But magazines like *Better Homes & Gardens* and *House Beautiful* were beginning to run shopping columns of small mail-order ads offering unique, intriguing items.

Margulies decided to advertise his garlic press in this way. His first ads made money, so he ran his little ad again—and again—and again, in more and more magazines.

Then an astonishing thing happened. The same store buyers who had turned a cold shoulder to Margulies now began to call him up, saying in effect, "Send me a gross of those damned garlic presses of yours. My customers are driving me crazy asking for it."

Giorgio is the most startling latter-day example of this pathway to marketing success. In 1963 Fred and Gayle Hayman bought a foundering women's boutique in Beverly Hills and built it into a prestigious landmark establishment.

In 1981 they introduced their own distinctive fragrance, at $150 an ounce. And taking advantage of the new technology of Scentstrips, they did something unheard of for a prestige brand—they started selling by mail, using both direct mail and upscale magazine advertisements with a bound-in Scentstrip and reply card.

In 1982, the first full year of sales, total sales volume for the fragrance was $1.2 million. The next year, the total was $15 million, two-thirds by mail order.

Then, according to Jim Roth, Giorgio Parfum's senior vice president, *"The demand triggered by Giorgio's magazine exposure brought retailers to Giorgio's door in hordes."*[7] (Italics added.)

They began adding retail outlets and introduced men's cologne and other extensions of the line. In 1984 sales for the entire company went up to $60 million. By 1985, Giorgio's products were being sold in 250 retail outlets, and total annual sales for the company were projected at $110 million!

Calvin Klein's Obsession, presumably taking note, opted for a similar strategy when it was introduced. Other magazine advertisements for fragrances with bound-in mail-order reply cards were co-op advertising efforts, with the order coming back to a department store, but the Obsession ads boldly solicited customers' orders to come directly back to the manufacturer.

Did this hurt their retail sales in department stores? On the contrary. At the end of the year, department stores were reporting that Obsession was one of the hottest-selling fragrances of the Christmas season, and it ended up the number-2 fragrance in the United States in its first year. Did any stores decide to boycott Calvin Klein fragrances because of direct competition with their own selling efforts? Of course not. Not while customers are asking for and buying Obsession in record numbers.

The Calvin Klein experience could be a turning point—proof that a respected brand name can do double-duty advertising: reaping direct sales from consumers beyond the reach of department store retailers while stimulating retail sales for those same stores. And by direct sales of additional items in its follow-up literature, Obsession is providing further proof that today retail distribution and mail-order sales of the same merchandise can comfortably coexist.

It will be exciting to see advertisers like Giorgio and Obsession take the next step: multiple-split-run testing of different copy and visual approaches to maximize direct sales and, correspondingly, the retail effect.

The Bottom Line

Names are salespower. Names in the hands of catalog merchants can reveal the best locations in the nation to start retail outlets and can fill them with customers the very first day.

If you're a store merchant, names on retail-customer bills of sale and in customer charge account rolls can provide a springboard for another profit center that requires no high-rent mall location.

If your company originates products or services, the names already inside or added to your customer database can help you broaden your line and widen your geographical distribution. And names in computer files that are not yours—the names belonging to other originators or to your intermediaries—can be a source of marketing power to you as well. They can enhance your present channels of distribution and open up new ones.

So if you want more distribution—new distribution—better distribution—think names. Save names. And use names—pull new customers directly to you and/or to push them, clamoring for what you have to sell, to retail locations or sales agents.

12

What Happens Next?

We have taken you on a long journey, commenting along the way on what we see happening today in advertising, promotion, and distribution. Together we have explored a complex landscape in which the natural law of survival of the fittest is constantly evolving strange and marvelous new forms of functioning.

Now you are "back home" at your desk, wondering exactly what you can do first to make use of what you have observed.

We can't give you a complete answer. The answer in each case depends on who "you" are, what field you are in, and where your company stands. But what we can do is invite you to look back over the ground we have covered and think about the new realities of the marketplace and what they could mean to your company's strategic direction in the future.

Over and over in the offices of business executives, from the product-manager level to the executive vice president for marketing and the chief executive officer, we hear a growing concern about waste and inefficiency in marketing expenditures. There is widespread realization that too much of the $100 billion or so now spent on advertising each year is expended with a shotgun approach that scatters the sales message indiscriminately on prospects and nonprospects alike.

Business leaders at the highest corporate levels are pushing their advertising aides and media specialists to take a closer look at the new alternatives to the clutter in familiar mass advertising.

We predict that in their investigations these specialists will zero in on two considerations that will be given increasing weight in deciding how and where media dollars will be spent. We are talking about two of the themes that run through this book: accountability and addressability.

Accountability

It has become too costly to plan advertising budget allocations on the basis of what *ought* to be generally worthwhile.

Yes, it is true that there probably always will be certain expenditures for good will which are valuable and yet difficult to assess. How, for instance, can Macy's measure the effect on store sales of the annual Macy's Thanksgiving Day parade in New York City?

But most advertisers of products, services, and establishments who devote their advertising to building favorable awareness can, at the very least, incorporate a direct-response element as an index to performance. Inviting a direct response of some sort can measure comparative creative impact, comparative positioning effectiveness, and comparative media performance.

And with today's computer-tracking and electronic-monitoring capabilities, many advertisers can now go a step further. Until now, it has been a common practice to say, in effect, "All this advertising produced all these sales—we think!" But now it is increasingly becoming possible to say, "This *particular* advertising produced exactly this many dollars of sales." And if your company is not able to say this, maybe it's time to set up a study group to explore how it might be *made* possible—whether through direct-response offers that identify prospects and then track sales over months and years of performance, through cash-register scanners in test markets, through better tracking of the leads given to the sales force, or through a combination of activities.

Credibility goes hand in hand with accountability. A great deal of advertising is simply disregarded or disbelieved—because, we have argued, it does not address the whole brain. The responses or sales you track from your advertising will tell you how well it is being received and believed by your target prospects. Measuring the effect of one advertising approach against another in a real-life advertising environment filled with clutter and competitive advertising—and then adopting the approach for which the public has "voted" through its responses or purchases—will enable you to improve your advertising's credibility.

Addressability

We have entered the Age of the Addressable Consumer. For the first time, you can know all your prospects and customers, not as a large faceless mass, but as individuals, by name and address.

Your advertising can call for interested prospects to take two steps forward from the crowd and tell you who they are and where they live. Then, thanks to the computer, you can subdivide these volunteers into groups any way you choose according to their similarities of lifestyle, leisure pursuits, age, income, purchasing patterns, brand preferences, etc.

Next you can privately *address* each member of each of these subgroups as an individual, with a courteous and flattering appreciation of how her or his needs and financial means differ from others'. More than merely addressing such an individual—after all, an "address" is only a one-way communication—you can carry on a mutually rewarding *dialog* by mail and phone.

Finally, this newly affordable addressability enables you to develop an ongoing relationship between your company and an individual customer, and by means of the tools of data processing you can track the relationship's progress and long-term profitability.

With one-on-one computer-assisted marketing, you can recommend to individual customers which of your company's other products or services they might want to try. You can even create new products or services especially for groups of customers with similar characteristics.

The State of the Art—
Or Lack Thereof

Addressable marketing is still in its infancy. Many companies have developed some capability for customized communication and service to special market segments but don't yet know how to make full use of it. For example, Radio Shack has one of the largest retail customer databases in the country, 30 million names and addresses of people who have made a purchase within the last year. And they boast of capturing in their computer files some 24 history segments on each of these customers. Yet after one of us purchased a Radio Shack Model 100 portable computer, a purchase totaling with accessories roughly $1000, we never received a letter from Radio Shack saying: "Good news, Mr. Collins! Now you can add a portable disk drive to your Model 100 system!" Nor any other communication about the Model 100. This typifies sellers who possess valuable information about a customer but fail to make use of it.

One of us also spent hundreds of dollars ordering lawn and garden equipment from the Sears "big book" . . . but never received their specialty catalog of lawn and garden equipment until it was specifically requested.

If you belong to more than one of the airlines' frequent flyer programs, you know that each has its own system for influencing the frequent flyers in its database. Ultimately, the airline that addresses the heavy user in the most helpful way has a better chance of coming out on top in the lucrative business traveler market.

Each of the major airlines now has direct-marketing specialists working with them to enhance the value of their customer database by devising targeted mail and phone programs aimed at each segment of the list. The attention the airlines give to communicating individual sales messages to their best customers will soon be emulated in other industries.

We predict that by 1990 most service companies and many product manufacturers will be spending as much time and money maximizing their relationships with known customers as they now do on their brand-image advertising to the world at large.

Even the smallest shop or service can use this new capability to run rings around their giant competitors, who always run the risk of getting bogged down by bureaucratic slowness in responding to a changing world. Any small business that can afford an advanced desktop computer plus the right printer and readily available software can maintain a customer database and develop a superb minicampaign of customized sales communications for specific segments of a prospect or customer list.

The Story of Joe Girard, MaxiMarketer

Thomas Peters's and Robert Waterman's book *In Search of Excellence* tells of a lone saleman's success in applying much of what we have been talking about.

Joe Girard was the car salesman who sold more new cars and trucks each year, for 11 years running, than any other human being. Joe's success was based on his realization that the sale is only a brief encounter between him and his customer and that without a commitment on his part to establishing an ongoing relationship with the buyer, that encounter can lead nowhere. Read how Joe's commitment to database marketing established a lifetime relationship with the 13,000 names in his file—a relationship that naturally led to second, third, and fourth sales, as well as to prime prospect referrals:

> "There's one thing that I do that a lot of salesmen don't, and that's believe that the sale really begins after the sale—not before. . . . The customer ain't out the door, and my son has made up a thank-you note."
>
> Joe would intercede personally, a year later, with the service manager on behalf of his customer. Meanwhile he would keep the communications flowing.
>
> Joe's customers won't forget him once they buy a car from him; he won't let them! Every month throughout the year they get a letter from him. It arrives in a plain envelope, always a different size or color.[1]

Joe Girard is a MaxiMarketer with a pioneering understanding of the difference between just making a sale and getting a customer for life.

The basic principle he followed in the late seventies is now being pursued in the mid-eighties by the Ford Motor Company. They are experimenting on a vast scale with database marketing in their far-flung operations.

Joe Girard and the Ford Motor Company both know what it can mean to get really close to the customer. And each stands to gain from applying the MaxiMarketing model—whether it's with a customer card file or a mainframe computer.

Closeness to the customer is what MaxiMarketing is about every step of the way, from "making friends" in up-front awareness advertising that generates names of interested prospects—through follow-up communications which build a bridge between the first impression and the sale—to the later interactions that keep you in touch with the customer after the first sale is made.

As Professor Theodore Levitt said in his classic book, *The Marketing Imagination,* "The purpose of business is to get and keep a customer." Or, to use Peter Drucker's more demanding construction, "to *create* and keep a customer."[2]

The same theme was sounded by Peters and Waterman in *In Search of Excellence.* One of their eight attributes of successful companies is "staying close to the customer." Inviting responses to your advertising—and responding to the responses—is the fundamental step in starting a relationship you can extend indefinitely.

Wrapping It Up

All the characteristics of MaxiMarketing can be combined into a comprehensive definition: *MaxiMarketing is the new direction in marketing in which the prospects who are potentially your best customers are identified, located, persuaded, motivated, converted, and cultivated in a way that maximizes sales and profits.*

Or here's an even shorter one: *MaxiMarketing is a continuum which turns likely prospects into long-term customers.*

The Marketing Revolution the Computer Made Possible

The computer's ability to maintain a customer database—whatever the size of your company—is one of the most revolutionary marketing developments in a century. We are in the early decades of that revolution and can barely see the outlines of where it may lead us.

The new MaxiMarketing which this computer capability makes possible shifts the focus from making a sale to concentrating more marketing dollars on having that sale lead to a long-term profitable customer relationship. The computer which was once viewed as an impersonal threat that would regiment society has turned out to be the key to permitting companies to serve their customers far more personally than before.

Each step in the process is logically linked to the next:

- You target prospects who are clones of the best customers in your customer database.

- You find them and communicate with them in the most likely media.

- You appeal to them with whole-brain advertising that invites a response taking them one step closer to the sale.

- You design sales promotion and follow-up advertising which will deepen your relationship with them, not just make a sale.

- You obtain their names and addresses and feed them into your customer database, your company's private advertising medium.

- And through the database you begin to develop additional sales of various kinds, perhaps even different channels of distribution.

This continuum adds up to much more than the sum of its parts, because it makes possible a single unifying marketing strategy. The piecemeal approach to advertising, promotion, public relations, and all aspects of communicating with the consumer is replaced by a wholistic new approach involving *addressability* of the needs and wants of your potential and actual customers and *accountability* of cost-effectiveness every step of the way.

Now what?

How do you begin—in a manner appropriate to your position in your company—to review your company's advertising, promotion, and distribution practices with an eye to the MaxiMarketing model?

Instead of giving you a neat little list of things to do that may not apply to your situation, we have put together a list of questions based on what we have covered in this book. These questions have been designed to spark your ability to generate new ideas. After applying them to your own company's products and practices, you should end up with a scratch pad or notebook filled with things to do and pursue.

If Your Company Is the Originator of a Product or Service . . .

■ How many different types of targeted prospects for your product or service can you identify and describe? What are the most efficient new media to reach and sell them?

■ How much advertising to nonprospects do you estimate is involved in each type of media you use? How might this percentage be reduced?

■ Does your advertising have an appeal or offer which separates the prospects from the nonprospects and the hot prospects from the warm prospects? If not, how could it?

■ Have you graded your media expenditures with a performance index based on direct response?

■ Are you able to compare with any exactitude public reactions to different approaches in your awareness advertising using a real-life media environment?

■ Could you convince the person sitting next to you at a dinner party of the merit or superiority of the product or service your company is advertising? Does your present advertising do as good a job?

■ Does your current advertising ask prospects to do something more specific than predispose the target audience to making a purchase some day? What can you add for activation?

■ Have you tested more than one creative approach to getting the public to respond to your current sales promotion offer?

.■ How do you know that the sales promotion advertising your company is using is the most response-producing and brand-building approach possible?

■ How much of your advertising does double duty? Can you think of ways to make your advertising do more than one job (as suggested in Chapter 8)?

■ What if you could get many pages of advertising in an issue of a magazine without having to pay for more than one of them? Could you or your advertising agency find ways to fill those pages that could increase your sales? What would happen if you prepared those additional pages and mailed them to prime prospects who responded to your single-page ad?

■ If a television station or network offered you time for a 30-minute commercial message for the price of 30 seconds, how would you use it?

■ What if you prepared a 30-minute commercial and tested it on cable or via a videocassette offer? How might you increase distribution of the 30-minute commercial at little or no cost?

■ When people see your commercial message or read your ad, do they know what to do about it? Do they know how to get in touch with you if they have questions or want more information? When they get in touch, do you save the name? If you save the name, how well and how often do you contact the inquirer to build sales and loyalty?

■ Is what your company sells adaptable to third-party or syndicated sales by mail and phone? Is this potential being exploited to build alternative distribution out of sight of your present dealers?

■ How might your company help your retailers make more use of direct mail to promote your product or service than they can manage to do by themselves?

■ Does your company save the names and addresses of all the prospects and customers who communicate with you by mail or phone? If so, are these names entered in a computer databank? If they are being put on computer, are they being correctly formatted for a wide variety of promotional and analytical uses?

■ If you have customer and prospect names and addresses in the computer, how are they currently being used? What possible additional uses can you think of? How could you enrich your knowledge of each of these individuals by overlaying your list with outside list data?

If Your Company Is a Store
or Group of Stores . . .

■ Which of the previous questions apply to you—and what can you do about them?

■ What percentage of your customers do you estimate you have on file? Are they all on computer? Are they—or could they be—selectable by recency, frequency, and total amount of purchases? By any other criteria? By overlaying data from outside lists?

■ Do you mail or distribute advertising to a customer database or prospect list, or merely to the public at large? Can you track the resulting sales?

■ If you mail a catalog or sales flyer that invites purchases by mail or phone, are you also able to track the effect of the mailing on store traffic and in-store sales?

■ Would it be feasible to test a mail-order catalog which would reach beyond your immediate trading area?

■ Do you retain and compile the name and address of each person who buys something in your store? Is there some way you could also capture and enter the names and addresses of people who simply visit but do not buy?

■ If you could know 15 things about each customer in your database, what 15 things would you choose to know? Is your database set up so that you could add the information and have it easily accessible for future use? How could you make profitable use of the information?

■ Do you know who your best customers are by name and address? Do you do anything to make them feel especially appreciated?

■ Do you ever give equal, and simultaneous exposure to two different advertising approaches and see which sells the most? If not, how might you do that?

■ Can you precisely rank each of your advertising media and insertions by performance? Can you think of other media you might be interested in trying? If so, could you measure how they compare in effectiveness with your present media?

■ How might you form a strategic alliance with another advertiser, either local or national, so that each of you profitably promotes the other?

■ How might you frequently repromote to your best customers by mail in a way that would pay for itself or not cost you anything?

- How can you use a national mail-order catalog as a basis for opening up new store locations with virtually assured success?

If Your Company Is a Mail-Order Marketer of Products or Services . . .

- Which of the previous questions apply to you—and what can you do about them?

- Does your direct-response advertising also create a demand at the retail level for what you are selling direct? Are you able to benefit from this demand? If not, is there some way that you could?

- Have you and your associates recently brainstormed ideas for additional products you could sell to your customer database?

- Have you overlooked any promising possibilities for profitable third-party sales of your product or service? See how many you can list.

- Can you define and describe the image you present to the public? Is there any way you could sharpen and improve that image while pursuing your direct-marketing goals?

- Are there new kinds of media you could be testing but have been overlooking? Videocassettes? Card decks? Call-in radio shows? Thirty-minute commercials on cable? Telemarketing?

- How might you customize your product or service to increase its appeal to different groups of prospects and customers? How would you find them and convey this news to them?

- Could you benefit from increased promotion of name-brand merchandise backed by co-op ad money allowances?

- Is your company doing enough of the direct-response testing that historically has given your kind of business a unique advantage over other forms of selling?

- What is keeping you from using the transaction data in your files to identify prime retail locations for your products or services? How might you open up distribution within existing retail channels or on your own?

If You Are Part of a Corporate Conglomerate . . .

As part of a large corporate entity with many products, services, distribution channels, divisions, companies, etc. under one corporate umbrella, all the foregoing questions should be of keen interest to the top management of your parent company. MaxiMarketing presents significant opportunities for the kind of synergy that mergers and amalgamation promise more often than they deliver.

Depending on your own position in the corporate structure, you may not have the power to use MaxiMarketing principles in making all the many pieces of your parent company work together better. But you might be able to recommend a corporationwide inventory of the customer names being accumulated and the cross-promotion opportunities which are currently being neglected.

By the mid-eighties, many of the packaged-goods giants, including General Foods, RJ Reynolds, Colgate-Palmolive, and Bristol-Myers, were addressing their direct database marketing needs at the corporate level. Colgate-Palmolive had put in place an educational program aimed at the general managers of more than 80 companies in their far flung worldwide operations. Each month, the top person in the operation received an informative "lesson" from headquarters in New York explaining some aspect of the new one-to-one database marketing discipline.

Seven Models to Consider

There is another way to get your company started. Some of our clients have found the following approach helpful in "getting a handle" on the MaxiMarketing continuum when we discuss the subject.

We have identified seven models for using a customer database to maximize sales and profits. These seven models represent a checklist of development possibilities. See what each of them suggests to you as a way to turn likely prospects into tryers and tryers into loyal customers.

1. The Educational Model. You develop continuing interaction with your customer database through useful information provided periodically. The information may itself be a profitable product, as in the case of *The Pleasures of Cooking* magazine sold to Cuisinart customers for $18 a year. Or the information may be a free publication that sells or promotes additional products, such as the publications sent free periodically to buyers of Shopsmith power tools, Garden Way rototillers, or Prince tennis rackets. Best of all, perhaps, is information which (*a*) is itself sold and (*b*) is the vehicle for selling additional products, such as the Cuisinart Cooking Club newsletter or Harrod's magazine (a dazzling catalog which sells for $5.95 a copy!).

2. The Complementary Model. You develop an entirely new business offering products or services which complement your customers' and prospects' known lifestyles, tastes, and interests. Thus the Kohler mail-order catalog of tasteful bathroom accessories appeals to the upscale Kohler customer or prospective buyer of Kohler plumbing fixtures without competing with Kohler dealers. Kohler keeps its name in front of likely prospects who may at some time be in the market for a whole new (Kohler) bathroom and produces a positive supplementary revenue stream while doing so.

3. The Contractual Model. You use your corporate good name (and perhaps your customer database) to contract for periodic delivery of an appropriate product or service to your market. Thus Johnson & Johnson, a trusted name in baby powder, was able to build a substantial business based on monthly shipment of educational infant toys to new parents. General Foods proved that coffee, always considered only a supermarket staple, could be sold directly to consumers with a contractual bimonthly home-delivery program for its Gevalia coffee. A significant consideration in the contractual model is that the total sale to one customer is much larger than when selling a single item, and therefore the allowable advertising cost for signing up a new customer can be much larger.

4. The Rewards Model. The frequent flyer programs, the Raleigh and Belair cigarette coupons, the Betty Crocker premium catalogs, and the AT&T Opportunity Calling catalog are just a few examples of encouraging a continuing relationship by providing continuing rewards for purchase of the basic product or service. Such a program permits you to renew your acquaintance with the customer frequently in a highly favorable atmosphere. Countless variations can be used to build a long-term profitable relationship with your best customers.

5. The Value-Added Service Model. If you sell a commodity product, you can add a differentiating service to it. Clairol, by including in its advertising a toll-free number people could call with their questions about hair coloring, wrapped a service around the product and made the product more valuable. Sylvania Lighting is now wrapping a service around its diverse lighting products by installing a consumer hot line in its retail outlets that allows direct inquiries and ordering at the point of sale. The Nikon instruction videocassette included with the purchase of one of their new cameras wrapped a service around the product and made it more desirable.

Does your company have a mature product with a flattening sales curve? Wrapping a service around it might give it a whole new lease on life.

6. The Affinity Group. Customers who purchase your product or service share a special interest that draws them to what you offer. You can make this interest the focus of creating an affinity group with whom you can communicate on a regular basis—and have the consumer pay for it. The Barbie Doll Club in France with over 350,000 paying members is a private database that enables Mattel to keep youngsters advised of the latest Barbie Doll fashions and what's happening in the imaginary world of Barbie and her friends. The International Airline Passenger Association is an affinity group of air travelers who are offered insurance and other services at attractive rates. The Neiman-Marcus InCircle is an affinity group of affluent shoppers who are interested in the best of the best and are willing to pay for it.

7. The Third-Party Model. Use other companies as surrogate direct marketers of your products by using their database. Think of Bell & Howell selling hundreds of thousands of home-movie outfits this way, and Metropolitan selling life insurance policies through partnership with *Reader's Digest.* Your company can prepare the promotional material and make it available to mail-order merchants, as Bell & Howell did. Or you can simply encourage mail-order merchants to promote your product and provide as generous a co-op ad money allowance as is consistent with your standard dealer program.

These seven models do not encompass everything you might do to turn prospects into long-term customers. But you may find them useful as a way to start thinking about what you and your company might do.

We will conclude by repeating the quotation from Bill Bernbach which we chose for the epigraph of this book: "Those who are going to be in business tomorrow are those who understand that the future, as always, belongs to the brave."

It also belongs to the quick.

Again and again—couponing is just one example—we have seen that when everybody jumps into a good thing, a law of diminishing returns gradually sets in. But you have also seen, with advertisers as diverse as IBM and the Columbia Record Club, that when a company establishes a strong early lead with a new concept and works at maintaining it, it is very hard to catch up with them and overtake them.

So if your company is brave and quick, you can enter the 1990s as a leader in MaxiMarketing and use this new way of thinking about advertising, promotion, and one-to-one marketing to gain an edge in the battle for market share.

And if you personally are instrumental in making this happen, you will experience the excitement of being on the cutting edge of change. And you might end up with a few more stars in your career crown.

Notes

Preface

1. Jeffrey Hallett, "Getting Ready for the New Economy," *Advertising Age,* June 21, 1984, p. 12.

Chapter 1

1. "Marketing: The New Priority," *Business Week,* November 21, 1983, p. 96. Reprinted with permission.
2. Alvin Toffler, *The Third Wave,* William Morrow and Company, New York, 1980, p. 248.
3. John Naisbitt, *Megatrends,* Warner Books Inc., New York, 1982, pp. 231–232. Copyright © 1982 by John Naisbitt. Reprinted with permission.
4. "'Old' Coke Coming Back after Outcry by Faithful," *The New York Times,* July 11, 1985, p. D4.
5. Lisa Belkin, "Shopping Is Getting a Lot More Complicated," *The New York Times,* August 8, 1985, pp. A1 and C12.
6. Michael Schrage, "The Message Is the Message," *Adweek,* April, 1985, p. 2. Reprinted with permission of *Adweek.*
7. James Cook, "You Mean We've Been Speaking Prose All These Years?," *Forbes Magazine,* April 11, 1983, pp. 142–149. Reprinted by permission of *Forbes Magazine.* Copyright © Forbes Inc., 1983.
8. Naisbitt, op. cit., p. 14. Copyright © 1982 by John Naisbitt. Reprinted with permission.
9. "Marketing: The New Priority," *Business Week,* November 21, 1983, p. 99. Reprinted with permission.
10. Ibid.
11. Diane Mermigas, "Executives Discuss Ways to Snap Zapping Trend," *Electronic Media,* July 26, 1984, p. 10. Copyright © 1984 by Crain Communications, Inc. Reprinted with permission.
12. Mike Drexler, "DDB Says Split 30s Are Here to Stay," *Adweek,* January 28, 1985, p. 28.
13. Tom Delaney, "Polaroid Pans to New Products in Refocus of Media Spending," *Adweek,* January 7, 1985, p. 4.
14. Tom Delaney, "Campbell Plans 'Less But Better' for Products, Ad Budget," *Adweek,* March 18, 1985, p. 4.
15. Tom Delaney, "GF Expects to Stir Up Media Strategies," *Adweek,* April 8, 1985, p. 28.

Chapter 2

1. Theodore Levitt, *The Marketing Imagination,* The Free Press, New York, 1983, p. 115.

Chapter 4

1. Brian Lowry, "Julia Child Serves Advice," *Advertising Age,* July 8, 1985, p. 53.
2. Ralph Gray and Dottie Enrico, "Edsel Ford Questions Women's Books," *Adweek,* August 12, 1985, p. 54B.
3. Leonore Skenazy, "Ads against Wall in Video Background," *Advertising Age,* February 28, 1985, p. 6.
4. Maureen McFadden, "Campbell Testing Offbeat Recipes," *Adweek,* September 30, 1985, p. 46.
5. Ronald Alsop, "Advertisers Bristle as Charges Balloon for Splashy TV Spots," *The Wall Street Journal,* June 20, 1985, p. 27.
6. Ibid.
7. Joe Mandese, "Reinhard to Cable: Focus on Quality," *Adweek,* April 1, 1985, p. 62.
8. Henry A. Johnson, "Computer Technology Is Key to Segmentation and Service," *Direct Marketing,* June, 1985, p. 66.
9. Christine Dugas, " 'Ad Space' Now Has a Whole New Meaning," *Business Week,* July 29, 1985, p. 52. Reprinted with permission.
10. Ibid.
11. Dan Abramson, "Hasbro Pulls 300,000 Orders with Inserts in Christmas Toy Packages Related to Retail," *DM News,* April 15, 1985, p. 7.

Chapter 5

1. Stephen Fajen, "All in a Day's Work," *Advertising Age,* April 22, 1985, p. 20. Reprinted with permission of *Advertising Age.* Copyright © 1985 by Crain Communications, Inc.
2. Stanley E. Moldovan, "Copy Factors Related to Persuasion Scores," *Journal of Advertising Research,* December, 1984/January, 1985, pp. 16–22. Reprinted with permission of *Journal of Advertising Research.* Copyright © 1984 by the Advertising Research Foundation.
3. Edward M. Tauber, "Editorial: The Never-Ending Question," *Journal of Advertising Research,* December, 1984/January, 1985, p. 9.
4. Stephen Fox, *The Mirror Makers,* William Morrow and Company, New York, 1984, p. 113.
5. Ibid., p. 188.
6. Ibid.
7. David W. Stewart and David H. Furse, "Analysis of the Impact of Executional Factors on Advertising Performance," *Journal of Advertising Research,* December, 1984/January, 1985, pp. 23–26.

8. Benjamin Lipstein, "An Historical Perspective of Copy Research," *Journal of Advertising Research,* Vol. 24, No. 6, pp. 11–14. Reprinted with permission of *Journal of Advertising Research.* Copyright © 1984 by the Advertising Research Foundation.
9. "Copy Testing Is Still a Nebulous Area," *Advertising Age,* December 1, 1975, p. 54.
10. Ibid.
11. Ibid.
12. "Impediments to Marketing Productivity," talk by Alvin Achenbaum before New York chapter of the American Marketing Association, February 7, 1985.
13. Ed Fitch, "Insurer Finds Laughter Is Best Medicine," *Advertising Age,* January 11, 1985, p. 36.
14. Ibid.
15. Anthony I. Morgan, "Point of View: Who's Killing the Great Advertising Campaigns of America?" *Journal of Advertising Research,* December, 1984/January, 1985, pp. 33–35. Reprinted with permission of *Journal of Advertising Research.* Copyright © 1984 by the Advertising Research Fund.
16. Brian Moran, "Ashton-Tate Pulls Plug on TV Campaign," *Advertising Age,* September 17, 1984, p. 88. Reprinted with permission from *Advertising Age.* Copyright © 1985 by Crain Communications, Inc.
17. Ronald Alsop, "Liquor Ads Look Less Macho as Female Drinking Increases," *The Wall Street Journal,* June 6, 1985, p. 31.
18. Victor O. Schwab, *How to Write a Good Advertisement,* Wilshire Book Company, Hollywood, California, 1962, p. 186.
19. John Caples, *Tested Advertising Methods,* Fourth Edition, Prentice-Hall Inc., Englewood Cliffs, New Jersey, 1974, p. 3. Reprinted with permission of the publisher. Copyright © 1974 by John Caples.
20. Ibid, p. 10.
21. David Ogilvy, *Confessions of an Advertising Man,* Athenium, New York, 1963, pp. 94–95.
22. Harold J. Rudolph, *Four Million Inquiries from Magazine Advertising,* Columbia University Press, New York, 1936.
23. Thomas Whiteside, "Cable," *The New Yorker,* June 3, 1985, pp. 82–103. Reprinted by permission; © 1985 by Thomas Whiteside.
24. Achenbaum, op. cit.

Chapter 6

1. Stephen Fox, *The Mirror Makers,* William Morrow and Company, New York, 1984, p. 26.
2. Ibid., p. 50.
3. Quoted in Fox, op. cit., p. 50.
4. Claude Hopkins, *My Life in Advertising/Scientific Advertising,* Crain Books, Chicago, 1966, p. 124.

5. Fox, op. cit., p. 185.
6. Martin Mayer, *Madison Avenue, U.S.A.*, Harper & Brothers, New York, 1958, p. 47.
7. Rosser Reeves, *Reality in Advertising*, Alfred A. Knopf, New York, 1961, p. 153.
8. David Ogilvy, *Confessions of an Advertising Man*, Athenium, New York, 1963, pp. 111–112.
9. Advertisement by *The Wall Street Journal* in *Advertising Age*, May 14, 1984, pp. 18–19.
10. Fox, op. cit., p. 43.
11. Ibid., p. 70.
12. Quoted in Fox, op. cit., p. 70.
13. Fox, op. cit., p. 71.
14. Ibid., p. 73.
15. Ibid., p. 183, and Pierre Martineau, *Motivation in Advertising*, McGraw-Hill Book Company, New York, 1957.
16. Fox, op. cit., p. 179.
17. Laurie Freeman, "Lou Centlivre Has One Thing in Mind: F-U-N," *Advertising Age*, July 25, 1985, p. 3. Reprinted with permission of *Advertising Age*. Copyright © 1985 by Crain Communications, Inc.
18. *Credits*, Vol. 3, No. 3, p. 18.
19. Reeves, op. cit., p. 81.
20. Fox, op. cit., p. 253.
21. Ibid., p. 48.
22. "Impediments to Marketing Productivity," talk by Alvin Achenbaum before New York chapter of the American Marketing Association, February 7, 1985.
23. *Art Direction/The Magazine of Visual Communication*, May, 1983, p. 45. Reprinted with permission of Art Direction Book Company, 10 E. 39th St., New York, N.Y.
24. Martineau, op. cit., quoted in Reeves, op. cit., p. 78.
25. John Marcom Jr., "Computer Firms Confused on How to Advertise to Changing Market," *The Wall Street Journal*, September 19, 1985, p. 35. Reprinted by permission of *The Wall Street Journal*, © Dow Jones & Company, Inc., 1985. All Rights Reserved.
26. Jeffrey Lener, "Why Is Software So Hard to Sell?" *Adweek*, April, 1985, p. 18.
27. Herbert D. Maneloveg, "Public Wants More Product Info," *Adweek*, October 7, 1985, p. 40. Reprinted with permission of *Adweek*.
28. David Ogilvy, *Ogilvy on Advertising*, Crown Publishers, New York, 1983, p. 205. Text copyright © 1983 by David Ogilvy. Compilation copyright © 1983 by Multimedia Publications, Ltd. Used by permission of Crown Publishers, Inc.

Chapter 7

1. Don E. Schultz and William A. Robinson, *Sales Promotion Management*, Crain Books, Chicago, 1982, pp. 71, 125.

2. Ibid.
3. William Meyers, "Trying to Get Out of the Discounting Box," *Adweek,* November 11, 1985, pp. 2–4.
4. Achenbaum, op. cit.
5. Schultz and Robinson, op. cit., p. 415.
6. Louis J. Haugh, "Questioning the Spread of Coupons," *Advertising Age,* August 22, 1983, p. M-31. Reprinted with permission of *Advertising Age.* Copyright © 1983 by Crain Communications, Inc.
7. Ibid.
8. Mary McCabe English, "Like It or Not, Coupons Are Here to Stay," *Advertising Age,* 1983, August 22, 1983, pp. M26–28. Reprinted with permission of *Advertising Age.* Copyright © 1983 by Crain Communications, Inc.
9. Achenbaum, op. cit.
10. Haugh, op. cit., p. M-32. Reprinted with permission of *Advertising Age.* Copyright © 1983 by Crain Communications, Inc.
11. Nancy Giges, "Coupon Loss Put at $500 Million," *Advertising Age,* March 4, 1985, p. 75.
12. Irene Park, "The Min/max Approach to Couponing," *Marketing Communications,* March, 1985, p. 32.
13. Haugh, op. cit., p. M-29. Reprinted with permission of *Advertising Age.* Copyright © 1983 by Crain Communications, Inc.
14. Robert Prentice, *Advertising Age,* May 8, 1985, p. 24.
15. Ibid.
16. Park, op. cit., p. 33.
17. Haugh, op. cit., p. M-32. Reprinted with permission of *Advertising Age.* Copyright © 1983 by Crain Communications, Inc.
18. Pamela G. Hollie, "A Fragrance Explosion." *The New York Times,* October 21, 1984.
19. Copyright United Feature Syndicate. Reprinted in *Advertising Age,* August 22, 1983, p. M-26.
20. Achenbaum, op. cit.
21. William A. Robinson, "Virginia Slims Come a Long Way in 17 Years," *Advertising Age,* May 30, 1985, p. 30.
22. Wendy Kimbrell, "Football Promotion Scores for Wendy's," *Advertising Age,* May 2, 1985, p. 28.

Chapter 8

1. Jerrold Ballinger, "Developer of Co-Op Ad Plans Says Only Half of $15 Billion in Available Funding Is Used," *DM News,* May 1, 1985, p. 11.

Chapter 9

1. Charlene Watler, "Like the Dress Pictured in This Ad? That's Too Bad, You Can't Have It," *The Wall Street Journal,* May 10, 1985, p. 37. Reprinted by permission of *The Wall Street Journal,* © Down Jones & Company, Inc., 1985. All Rights Reserved.

2. Jack Maxon, Letter to the Editor, *Advertising Age,* January 14, 1985. Reprinted with permission of *Advertising Age.* Copyright © 1985 by Crain Communications, Inc.
3. *Boardroom Reports,* September 15, 1985, p. 15. Reprinted with permission.
4. Arch G. Woodside and William H. Motes, "Image versus Direct-Response Advertising," *Journal of Advertising Research,* August, 1980, pp. 31–37.

Chapter 10

1. Stuart Weiss, "What's Invisible and Worth $55 Billion?" *Business Week,* October 14, 1985, p. 132.
2. Robert Drummond, "Flying High," *Marketing Communications Magazine,* October, 1984, p. 49. Reprinted with permission, *Marketing Communications Magazine,* Media Horizons, New York, N.Y.
3. "Marriott Tests Direct Response Waters for Honored Guest Awards Program," *ZIP Target Marketing,* March, 1985, p. 13.
4. John Paul Newport Jr., "Frequent Flier Clones," *Fortune,* April 29, 1985, p. 201.
5. "AT&T Enters the Specialized Catalog Field, Plans Segmented Opportunity Call Editions," *DM News,* October 15, 1985, p. 6.
6. Gary Levin, "ChemLawn Branches Out So Profits Grow," *Advertising Age,* June, 4, 1984, p. 4. Reprinted with permission of *Advertising Age.* Copyright © 1984 by Crain Communications, Inc.

Chapter 11

1. "Retail Store, Mail Order Catalog: Synergistic Growth," *Direct Marketing,* April, 1983, pp. 44–60.
2. Ibid.
3. "Laura Ashley Breaks New Ground in Building Retail Customer Base," *Direct Marketing,* February, 1985, pp. 72–81.
4. Ibid.
5. Al Schmidt, Jr., "How Retailers Can Profit from Mail-Order Catalogs," *Direct Marketing,* October, 1984, pp. 112–124.
6. "Manufacturer Complements Retail with Mail Order Catalog," *Direct Marketing,* September, 1983, pp. 72–77.
7. "Giorgio's Star Rises Beyond Beverly Hills," *Advertising Age,* February 27, 1984, p. M-29.

Chapter 12

1. Thomas J. Peters and Robert H. Waterman Jr., *In Search of Excellence,* Harper & Row, New York, 1982, pp 157–158.
2. Theodore Levitt, *The Marketing Imagination,* The Free Press, New York, 1983, p. 48.

Index

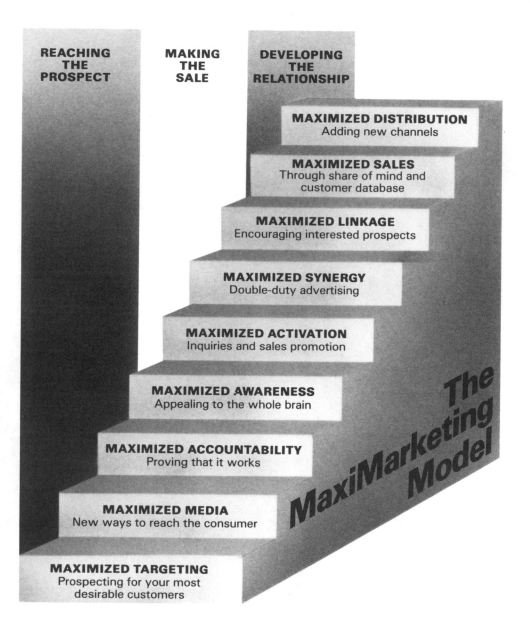

REACHING THE PROSPECT

MAKING THE SALE

DEVELOPING THE RELATIONSHIP

MAXIMIZED DISTRIBUTION
Adding new channels

MAXIMIZED SALES
Through share of mind and customer database

MAXIMIZED LINKAGE
Encouraging interested prospects

MAXIMIZED SYNERGY
Double-duty advertising

MAXIMIZED ACTIVATION
Inquiries and sales promotion

MAXIMIZED AWARENESS
Appealing to the whole brain

MAXIMIZED ACCOUNTABILITY
Proving that it works

MAXIMIZED MEDIA
New ways to reach the consumer

MAXIMIZED TARGETING
Prospecting for your most desirable customers

The MaxiMarketing Model